Pirkei Avot
Ethics of the Fathers
Chapter 1

*with a select treasury of commentaries
compiled by Rabbi Yosef Sebag*

OTHER WORKS BY RABBI YOSEF SEBAG

Ethics of the Fathers - www.dafyomireview.com/489

Duties of the Heart - www.dafyomireview.com/384

Path of the Just - www.dafyomireview.com/447

Gates of Holiness - www.dafyomireview.com/442

Vilna Gaon on Yonah - www.dafyomireview.com/259

Marks of Divine Wisdom - www.dafyomireview.com/427

Torah Authenticity - www.dafyomireview.com/430

yosefsebag@gmail.com

Letter of Approbation (previous book)

Dafyomi **A**dvancement **F**orum
Produced by Kollel Iyun Hadaf • Rosh Kollel: Rabbi Mordecai Kornfeld

'Your Chavrusa in Yerushalayim'

בס"ד

Rosh Kollel:
Rabbi Mordecai Kornfeld

Chairman of the Board:
Rabbi Gedalya Rabinowitz
Manostrishtcher Rebbe

Advisory Board:
Rabbi Berel Eichenstein
Rabbi Aharon Feldman
Rabbi Emanuel Feldman
Rabbi Yaakov I. Homnick
Rabbi Zecharyah Greenwald
Rabbi Elimelech Kornfeld
Rabbi Joseph Pearlman
Rabbi Fabian Schonfeld
Rabbi Berel Wein
Rabbi Chaim Wilschanski
Dr. Moshe Snow
Dr. Eli Turkel
Avi Berger
Samson Krupnick ז"ל
Andrew Neff
Mordechai Rabin, LLM
Kenneth Spetner ז"ל
Uri Wolfson

Talmud-study publications:
In English:
Insights to the Daf
Background to the Daf
Dafyomi Review Q & A
Outlines of the Daf
Halachah Outlines for the Daf
Ask the Kollel (email/fax)
Weekly In-Depth Video Lectures
Daily Quizzes on the Daf
Mishnah Yomis Review Q & A
Revach l'Daf

בעברית:
יוסף דעת (הערות)
יוסף דעת (שאלות לחזרה)
גלי מסכתא (סיכומי סוגיות)
טבלאות לכל דף
חידוני חזרה

Bookmarks & Calendars
Leather-bound 12th-cycle calendar
Yearly Dafyomi-schedule bookmarks
Dafyomi-cycle bookmarks
Rishonim-on-the-Shas bookmarks
Hadran cards

Chovos ha'Levavos, the monumental work of Rabeinu Bachye ben Yosef Ibn Pakuda, a judge in Islamic Spain (circa 1040), is one of the earliest works on Jewish philosophy and beliefs. It remains one of the fundamental works of Musar and Hashkafah. Even the great Rambam (Maimonides) bases a large part of his treatises in these fields on the revered words of the Chovos ha'Levavos. (It has been suggested that Rav Shlomo Ibn Gevirol took ideas from the Chovos ha'Levavos as well.)

Originally written in Arabic, this classic was translated into Hebrew not longer after its original publication, and more recently to many other languages. Among works of Jewish philosophy, its prominence in even the most traditional houses of learning makes it unique. The Chovos ha'Levavos' methodical and systematic analyses or every aspect of the human character makes reading it an experience in growth through introspection.

We owe a debt of gratitude to Rabbi Yosef Sebag for his exceptionally readable English translation of this important work. By adding translations of classic commentaries on the text, he has made the depth of the work available to all. Rabbi Sebag's investment of time and effort is evident in every part of the work, but especially in the Sha'ar ha'Yichud, the somewhat "controversial" section dealing with philosophical proofs of G-d.

I have known Rabbi Sebag for many years, and I have witnessed firsthand his overwhelming dedication to Torah-study and to raising a family on Torah-true ideals. His careful adherence to the instructions of our Torah giants, coupled with his strong will to teach others the timeless lessons of the Torah, has made him a true "Ben Aliyah."

May his investment bear the dividends of allowing him to help many of our brethren improve their faith and strength of character!

With Torah blessings,

Rabbi Mordecai Kornfeld

Rabbi Mordecai Kornfeld

Israel office: P.O.B. 43087, Jerusalem 91430, Israel • US office: 140-32 69 Ave., Flushing, NY 11367
Tel. - Israel: (02) 651-5004 • Fax - Israel: (02) 591-6024 • email: daf@dafyomi.co.il
http://www.dafyomi.co.il • http://dafyomi.shemayisrael.co.il/
U.S. tax ID: 11-3354586   580-28-908-0 עמותה מספר

All Israel

"All Israel has a share in the World to Come. As it reads (Isaiah 60:21): "And Your people are all righteous, for ever shall they inherit the land, the sprout of my plantings, the work of my hands, to glorify Me".

Rabbi Chananya ben Akashia says, The Holy One, Blessed be He, wanted to give Israel merit; therefore He multiplied for them Torah and mitzvot..."

כָּל יִשְׂרָאֵל יֵשׁ לָהֶם חֵלֶק לָעוֹלָם הַבָּא, שֶׁנֶּאֱמַר (ישעיה ס) וְעַמֵּךְ כֻּלָּם צַדִּיקִים לְעוֹלָם יִירְשׁוּ אָרֶץ נֵצֶר מַטָּעַי מַעֲשֵׂה יָדַי לְהִתְפָּאֵר.

רַבִּי חֲנַנְיָא בֶּן עֲקַשְׁיָא אוֹמֵר, רָצָה הַקָּדוֹשׁ בָּרוּךְ הוּא לְזַכּוֹת אֶת יִשְׂרָאֵל, לְפִיכָךְ הִרְבָּה לָהֶם תּוֹרָה וּמִצְוֹת, שֶׁנֶּאֱמַר (ישעיה מב) ה' חָפֵץ לְמַעַן צִדְקוֹ יַגְדִּיל תּוֹרָה וְיַאְדִּיר

🔍 Level 1

Rama M'Pano, Asarah Maamarot, Mamar Chikur Hadin perek 19 - it seems that in the early generations, they would first read this chapter of Mishna ("all Israel has a portion..." Sanhedrin ch.10) in Israel when Isru Chag (8th day of Passover) would fall on Shabbat... (For then there are 7 Sabbaths until Shavuot, in order to finish the 6th chapter of Pirkei Avot before Shavuot). This saying is along the lines of the Haftorah of Chol HaMoed Pesach which speaks of the Resurrection of the Dead and which is destined to occur on Nissan...

🔍 Level 2   Chatam Sofer

Chatam Sofer end of Vayikra - "All Israel has a share in the World to Come" - Rashi there explains: " 'all israel' - even those who incurred the death penalty by Beit Din mentioned earlier." The mishna continues there: "these do not have a portion in the world to come: 'one who says the torah is not from Heaven, the Apikorsim'".

I.e., those who deny the words of the Sages and their received tradition. Therefore, he brings here this mishna: "all Israel (even the wicked) have a portion in the world to come", provided he believes "Moshe received the torah from Sinai..etc.", "Yehoshua received..etc", and "they said three things, etc." So too for the whole tractate. Even though he does not fulfill those things but he believes and transgresses them - he will certainly be punished, but afterwards, he will have a portion in the world to come...

Level 3 — Maharal

Maharal - they set this mishna ("all of Israel...", Sanhedrin ch.10) at the beginning because the sages of the generation saw the long and difficult exile of the Jewish people. Thus, they instituted these words to console their hearts and so they recognize their great and lofty level. Even though the nations are joyous of their material success and prosperity, but the Jewish people should rejoice in their portion and ultimate success.

Thus, they ordered these words one after the other. First "All of Israel has a portion..". This is not at all reward for mitzvah. It is only due to their very being created by G-d (i.e. the main creation and closest to G-d, as explained there), as written "a branch of My planting, the work of My hands in which I will glory". For in their being the work of His hands, they have a lofty level. Therefore, they merit the World to Come. Likewise, the sages said in Chelek (Sanhedrin 110b): "when does a child merit to come to the World to Come? When he is born..." Thus, from the very being created as a Yisrael, who are "a branch of planting" of the Holy One, blessed be He, they are worthy of Olam Haba, and this is not from the aspect of the Mitzvot and deeds.

Afterwards, they also have another quality, namely, good and just character traits. This quality also grows out from their origin of being a good and just creation in essence. Thus, the good character traits follow naturally. Unlike one whose early origin is evil and bitter, of those who do not have good character traits, steeped in lewdness, bloodshed and performing all abominations.. This is the second level.

The third level is the Torah, the crowning level which Yisrael has. Therefore after this comes the saying of Rabbi Chanania ben Akashia "the Holy One, Blessed be He, wanted to give Israel merit; therefore He multiplied for them Torah and mitzvot..." All these levels follow one after the other...

Level 4 — Ruach Chaim

Question: Why does it say "All Israel has a share *TO* the World to Come", instead of "All Israel has a share *IN* the World to

Come"? (literal hebrew reading is "to" not "in")

Ruach Chaim - it is known that when a person thinks to do a mitzva, it has an effect in the higher worlds. An Ohr Makif (surrounding light) is roused (mitorer) on him from the side of holiness and imbues him, surrounding him and helping him to complete the mitzva. It is then as if he is sitting in Gan Eden, quite literally (mamash) in a place of Holiness. The holiness enclothes him (mitlabesh) and through completing the mitzva, this garment (of holy light) strengthens and illuminates within him. Afterwards, the light departs to Gan Eden and this will be his reward in the future.

It is likewise so for the opposite, G-d forbid. Through committing a sin, an evil power clings to him and surrounds him similar to before. And after the sin, everything departs to Gehinom, and the person feels separated from holiness, as written: "But your sins were separating between you and your G-d" (Yeshaya 59:2).

Likewise Chazal said (Eruvin 19): "...Gehinom is made deep for them", which means they themselves deepen Gehinom for themselves. Thus, there is no greater refuge to save oneself from sin than acts of mitzvot. Because through them he becomes covered with this sukkah of holiness and the scent of Gan Eden enters in his life and there is no room for the yetzer hara (evil inclination) to rule over him... This is what our sages said (Avot 4:2): "a mitzva brings another mitzva, a sin brings another sin..the reward of a mitzva is a mitzva".

Because the reward of a mitzva is the mitzva itself that is given to him, namely, the spiritual light that surrounds him, as before. For he sits then in Gan Eden and then it is surely easy to do another mitzva.

Likewise the opposite for sin, G-d forbid. For then he is shackled with ropes of disgrace, and the sin brings more sin.

Thus, the Tanna (sage) did not say "every Jew has a portion IN Olam Haba", but rather "TO Olam Haba". For "in Olam Haba" would have implied it is an independent thing already prepared, and if he merits to do mitzvot, he will be given a portion from there.

Instead, the mishna says: "TO Olam Haba", that he himself makes the Olam Haba through the mitzvot. It is the work of his own hands. For the mitzva itself is the reward. The light is in Gan Eden during man's life, and in the future this is his reward. Understand this.

Translator: in Nefesh HaChaim, he adds *"each person's reward is the holiness he added to Olam Haba"*. If you ask: didn't the Maharal say that each person intrinsically has a portion in the World to Come? Yes, but each person builds this portion according to his deeds, or corrupts it, G-d forbid.

Level 4 — Chida

Chida, Petach Einayim, Sanhedrin ch.10 - "the sprout of my plantings, the work of my hands, to glorify Me" - he gave a reason why all Israel will merit the resurrection of the dead: "the sprout of my plantings", i.e. since G-d's intent in creating Adam HaRishon (the first man) was that he be eternal, like G-d Himself. But, as known, due to his sin, death was decreed on him. Thus, it follows that after rectification of the sin of Adam HaRishon, man will return and become eternal as was G-d's original intent at the time of creation. This is the meaning of "the sprout of my plantings", that he is a "part of G-d" (chelek Eloka memaal) which the Holy One, blessed be He planted in this world, in order "to glorify me", so to speak, in man's creation and service, in the way of: "Give strength to G-d; [over Israel is His pride]" (Tehilim 68:35), and until now, G-d's intent in creating man did not yet materialize from potential to actual. But certainly, he will return to become eternal as G-d's intent.

"the sprout of my plantings" - it is known that a sinner becomes rectified through gilgulim (reincarnations). This is the explanation of "All Israel has a share in the World to Come", i.e. after gilgulim and gehinom, then: "And Your people are all righteous, forever shall they inherit the land".

If you ask: "how is it possible that all Israel are tzadikim (righteous), we see that some are not so proper? And how could he call them all tzadikim and that they will inherit the land? On this he answered: "the sprout of my plantings", to hint on the secret of the gilgulim. Since they are a "nice planting", I replant them again many times. This is why "plantings" is in plural form.

According to the sages of truth (kabala), if there was no rectification at all for three gilgulim (reincarnations), the soul is no longer reincarnated. Thus, when do I say "the sprout of my plantings" in plural? When "the work of My hands, to glorify Me".

Level 4 — Chida
Chida - Maarit HaAryin - "All Israel has a share in the World to Come" - the roshei tevot (first letters of each word) have gematria "Yisrael", to hint that the name "Yisrael" shields and saves one to merit Olam Haba.

Level 4 — Chida
Chida - Zeroa Yamin - "righteous, for ever shall they inherit the land" (tzadikim l'olam yirshu aretz)" - the Roshei Tevot have gematria "anava" (Humility), for this is the ikar (primary matter) of torah and service. Through it one will receive divine light from the Shem Havaya (Yud-Heh-Vav-Heh=gematria 26), hinted in the Roshei Tevot "Your people are all righteous (veamech kulam)" (Vuv-Kaf=26).. thus Moshe, the humblest of all men, received the torah...

Furthermore, the gematria of "anava" (Humility)=131. Thus Tehilim ch.131 begins "my heart was not haughty", to hint that whoever has humility is saved from the Samech-Mem (Samael=Samech-Mem-Aleph-Mem=131). Thus Moshe the humble "received torah", torah=611 to annul "Samael Lilith"=611 from "Sinai" which is also gematria Samael to annul it. Sinai is also Gematria "anava" (humility) as our sages said: "[the small] mount Sinai was chosen for humility".

Level 4 — Ben Ish Chai
Ben Ish Chai - Birkat Avot - "Moshe received..." - one of the reasons the torah was given by a messenger (Moshe) and the Jewish people did not hear the whole torah is as follows. The reward for a mitzva needs to be eternal. For just like a mitzva is eternal, so too its reward needs to be eternal. Thus the Holy One, blessed be He, must necessarily give man reward in Olam Haba which is an eternal world. But in this world which decays and disappears, it is impossible for reward to be eternal. The Holy One, blessed be He, fulfills the whole torah and in the torah

it is written: *"you shall give him his wages that very day"* (Devarim 24:15). Due to this, it is necessary to pay the reward in this world, since the reward of fulfilling mitzvot is as the wages of a worker.

Thus, there is a dilemma either way. If G-d pays in this world to fulfill *"you shall give him his wages that very day"*, it is impossible for the reward to be eternal. And if He gives it in Olam Haba so that it is eternal, it is impossible to fulfill *"you shall give him his wages that very day"*. For this reason the Holy One, blessed be He, gave the torah through a messenger, namely, Moshe Rabeinu, who heard the things from G-d and taught them to the Jewish people.

Thus, the "hiring" on fulfilling the torah occurred by an emissary (shliach), and the halacha (law) is that one who hires a worker through an emissary does not transgress *"you shall give him his wages that very day"*, neither the sender nor the emissary. For the sender did not himself hire the worker and the emissary did not hire the worker for himself. Thus He can now give the reward for torah and mitzvot in Olam Haba for there is no mitzva of *"you shall give him his wages that very day"*..

Likewise for this reason, a man must wait on receiving his reward until Olam Haba and he cannot claim from the Holy One, blessed be He, his reward in this world...

Chapter 1 Mishna 1 - Moshe Received

Moshe received [the] Torah from Sinai and transmitted it to Yehoshua, and Yehoshua to the Elders, and the Elders to the Prophets, and the Prophets transmitted it to the Men of the Great Assembly.

מֹשֶׁה קִבֵּל תּוֹרָה מִסִּינַי, וּמְסָרָהּ לִיהוֹשֻׁעַ, וִיהוֹשֻׁעַ לִזְקֵנִים, וּזְקֵנִים לִנְבִיאִים, וּנְבִיאִים מְסָרוּהָ לְאַנְשֵׁי כְנֶסֶת הַגְּדוֹלָה.

Level 1 — Bartenura

Bartenura - "from Sinai" - since this tractate is not coming to explain a mitzva (commandment) in the torah like the other tractates. Rather, it is all ethics and character traits, and the wise men of the nations also conjured up books of ethics according to their hearts on how a person should live and behave towards others. Therefore, the Tanna (sage) begins this tractate "Moshe received the Torah from Sinai". To teach that the traits and ethics in this tractate were not conjured up by the sages according to their hearts. But rather, even these were said at Sinai.

Level 2 — Chida

Chida - Zeroa Yamin - "Moshe received torah" - we can expand the words of Rabeinu Ovadiah in another aspect. The intent of the tanna is to rouse the hearts of the slumberers, who love to lay down and nap. For they consider in their hearts that it is good for a man to carry the yoke of the ethics of the philosophers, and through this the foolishness of one's heart will be subdued since they are built on the foundations of reason. But on the contrary, their evil inclination deceives them. They think wise the wisdom of the gentiles. For their tongue is quick to speak slick words, appearing right, submitting the evil inclination. Therefore, he opened: "Moshe received torah.."

To teach that these words of mussar are gufei torah (actual torah) and were said at Sinai. i.e. look and see the difference between light and darkness. For all the gentile ethics is useless for annulling the yetzer hara (evil inclination), because it cannot be annulled without torah, as written (Kidushin 30b): "says the Holy One, blessed be He, I have created the Yetzer Hara and I have created the torah as its antidote". Thus, it cannot possibly be annulled without torah and the mussar (ethics) of the gentiles (philosophers, etc.) is as nothing. Why should you err in strange things? But the mussar of the torah sages are completely torah and are capable of annulling the yetzer hara...

Translator: furthermore, one does not receive any torah study reward for learning the secular books and also they are mixed with truth and falsehood in various proportions. Another consideration is that when a person reads something, he receives a hashpaa (spiritual influence) from the soul of the author and tends to become like him.

Level 2

Rabbi Meir Mazuz - notice that the Vilna Gaon's commentary on Pirkei Avot focuses on sourcing every mishna from a verse in scripture. This is because in the talmud Shabbat, it says that something which is called "father" in the mishna is explicitly in the torah. This is why he goes through to source each mishna from a verse.

Level 2 — Tiferet Yisrael

Tiferet Yisrael - a man should not think that it is enough for his soul's perfection if he toils in torah and fulfills it, and even if he does not rectify his character traits he will merit Olam Haba. It is not so, for "the punishment of middot is more severe [than forbidden relations]" (Yevamot 21a, Bava Batra 89b). Likewise, our sages said: "one who toils in torah but does not have faithful business dealings and does not conduct himself pleasantly (b'nachat) with others - woe to him..." (Yomah 26a).

Level 3 — Maharal

Maharal - "fathers" - a father is fitting to give mussar (ethics) to his son. For in his being a father, the frivolousness of youth (yaldut) has left him. Likewise for the mother. They are baalei mussar (exponents of morals), and especially since it is incumbent on a father to guide his son in all matters.

Because this tractate speaks of good and just mussar (ethics), it begins by stating that it is proper to receive mussar from the fathers. And without a doubt, these men are the fathers of the world. For certainly Moshe is a father of the world, and so too Yehoshua who received the torah from Moshe, and likewise the Elders, etc... and so too Antigonus and the other sages mentioned.. They are certainly fathers of the world (i.e. of all humanity). Thus, it is proper for one to accept their mussar just like a son should accept the mussar of his father. And it is proper for them to give mussar to the world, since they are fathers of the world. Therefore this tractate is called Tractate Avot (Fathers). For it contains the mussar teachings of the fathers of the world.

Level 2 — Chida

Chida - Chasdei Avot - the commentaries wrote that this tractate is called "Avot" because the mussar in it is the father of all mussar in the world.. and since the primary good trait is humility, we find the torah mentioned only this trait in Moshe Rabeinu (as written: "and the man Moses was exceedingly humble, more so than any person on the face of the earth" - Bamidbar 12:3). For humility is the main [root] of all good deeds...

Chida - Chedrei Beten, Parsha Shmini - the reason the name of this tractate is "Avot" (Fathers) is because the words are the fathers of all mussars, as the commentaries wrote. We can also say that it is to rouse one's heart to remember the forefathers who were perfect (Shelemim) in all these things, and our sages of blessed memory said: "a man is obligated to tell himself: 'when will my deeds reach the deeds of my forefathers, Avraham, Yitzchak, and Yaakov..'"

Level 3 — Chida

Chida - Maarit HaAyin - in the way of remez (hint) we can say this tractate was called "Avot" to rouse the heart of a Jew that we are obligated to accept their words like the command of a father to his sons. See how much the descendants of Yonadav ben Rachav merited for guarding the command of their father. And do not say "this is mishnat chasidim, (extra piety), and I am not a chasid (extra pious)". Thus it was called "Avot", i.e. these were the deeds of the forefathers and thus think how to resemble your forefathers. Furthermore, if you take this upon yourself, the merit of your forefathers will be a helper and shield to help you fulfill.

Another hint: "avot" is gematria "shafal" (lowly). For he who is truly humble, it will be easy for him to fulfill everything and he will be holy, which is also gematria "shafal" and likewise, "avot".

Level 2 — Tiferet Yisrael

Tiferet Yisrael - "from Sinai" - i.e. through being extremely humble, Moshe received the torah which is compared to water.

For water flows out of high places and collects in low places. Thus, he received the torah from Sinai, [among] the lowest of the mountains (as Megilah 29a). This is to teach that a man can merit torah only through Humility, the source of all just character traits.

Q Level 2 — Raz Chaim

Raz Chaim - "m'sinai" is letters "nissim" (miracles), to hint that only through the humble does the Holy One, blessed be He, perform miracles, as known.

Q Level 2 — Chatam Sofer

Chatam Sofer end of Vayikra - "Moshe received Torah" - he wrote "received torah", not "received the torah". For the latter would imply the torah known and understood by us or at least by Moshe Rabeinu, and not more than this. Therefore, he wrote: "Moshe received torah". For he also did not understand all that is said there. Rather, the book was transmitted thus to Moshe Rabeinu with everything in it, even the fiftieth gate of Binah (understanding) was written there and Moshe did not know it. Therefore "Moshe received torah", and not "the torah".

Q Level 3 — Maharal

Maharal: Why does it not say "received from G-d"?

FIRST ANSWER - EVERYONE RECEIVES FROM G-D

If it had said "Moshe received the torah from G-d", this would imply that only Moshe in particular received from G-d. It is not so. For He is the G-d of all and bestows wisdom to everyone. Therefore, the Mishna did not say "Moshe received from G-d", but rather "Moshe received from Sinai". He inserted here Sinai since certainly Sinai was designated in particular to Moshe's receiving of the torah... But every day we pray "illuminate our eyes with Your torah". Thus, G-d is not designated to Moshe alone in the flow of the torah... Thus, it is not appropriate to designate Moshe alone as receiving from G-d..

SECOND ANSWER - NOT PROPER HONOR

It did not say "received from G-d" because there is no comparison between G-d and Moshe. For it is not proper honor to associate G-d with Moshe, as a teacher to his disciple, to

Chapter 1 Mishna 1 - Moshe Received

equate a human with the Holy One, blessed be He. Thus it says Moshe received "from Sinai" - that the voice of G-d came to Sinai, as if speaking to itself, and Moshe received the Torah from Sinai. If it had said "received at Sinai", then "at Sinai" would have taught only which place he received the Torah. Therefore, it said "from Sinai" [to also teach the above].

Question: Why does it change from the term "received" to the term "transmitted"?
Maharal - "Moshe received the torah from Sinai and transmitted" - it says "received" for the receiver receives according to his ability to receive. And Moshe did not receive the whole torah as brought in the talmud (Shavuot 5a), for it is infinite. Thus it is impossible to say Moshe received the whole torah and understood the whole torah. Rather, he received what he was capable of receiving.

Afterwards, it says he "*transmitted* it to Yehoshua". For it is possible for him to "transmit" all he received to Yehoshua. So too it was possible for Yehoshua to transmit all he received from Moshe to the Elders, and likewise the Elders to the Prophets, and the Prophets to the Men of the Great Assembly. Each was capable of transmitting all he received because their power to receive was strong. But after the Men of the Great Assembly, the generations began to diminish. Therefore, it says "Antigonus *received* from Shimon HaTzadik" and not "Shimon HaTzadik transmitted to Antigonus". For he did not transmit to him all the torah he received. Because the generations began to diminish in wisdom. It says only that Antigonus received. For he received only according to his ability. Similarly in the talmud: "Rabbi Eliezer the Great said: 'I learned much torah from my Rabbis, but received from them only like a dog who licks from the sea.'" (Sanhedrin 68a).

So too for all the pairs of sages mentioned afterwards. Only the term "received" is used. Because after the "Men of the Great Assembly" the torah became diminished. Thus, they needed to exhort the disciples on the torah as will be explained.

Q *Level 3* **Maharal**
Question: Why does it specify Yehoshua? Didn't Moshe teach all of Israel, including Eliezer the high priest?

Maharal - "to Yehoshua" - even though Moshe taught all of Israel, the term "transmit" is used only by one who receives and it remains by him. Therefore, the term "transmitted to Yehoshua" is used instead of "taught to Yehoshua". For "taught" implies learning it even though one may forget it. But the term "transmits" connotes something transmitted and which remains in the person's hands. Likewise, it says in Nedarim 38b: " 'He gave the torah to Moshe..' - at first he learned and forgot, until the torah was given to him as a gift". For "to grasp the torah according to its halacha requires siyata d'Shmaya (divine help)" (Megilah 6b), and this divine help was only by Yehoshua. For he was undoubtedly worthy of this. So too, that which it says "and Yehoshua to the Elders", the Elders were worthy and uniquely capable of receiving the torah from Yehoshua (in being the greatest sages of the generation).

Question: Why does it specify these 5?
Maharal - "Moshe, Yehoshua, Elders, Prophets, Men of the Great Assembly" - these 5 were all special levels. Moshe was like the sun, all light, as if he did not have a physical body. He was completely separate from the physical. But Yehoshua was compared to the moon, which has a [solid] body to receive the light of the sun. Thus, Yehoshua received from Moshe as written "you shall bestow of your splendor on him.." (Bamidbar 27:20). Yehoshua was on a special level. Similar and related to Moshe, like the Sun and the Moon.

The Elders' special level was "wisdom". For an "Elder is only one who has acquired wisdom". They were exceedingly fit for wisdom. Thus, they were more fitting to receive from Yehoshua because [the level of] "wisdom" is closer to Yehoshua than [the level of] "prophecy" as they said "a wise sage is greater than a prophet" (Bava Batra 12a).

But the levels of Moshe and Yehoshua were special in being like the sun and the moon, and certainly their level was above the level of "wisdom" and included it due to their exceedingly high level of prophecy. This is why it says "Yehoshua to the Elders" (and not Yehoshua to the prophets) since they are closer to him.

"The Elders to the Prophets" - for the prophets are close to the

Elders (in level).. and likewise the "Prophets to the Men of the Great Assembly". These latter were a special level by itself. They exceeded in Holiness to such an extent that "Idolatry" was annulled in their times (Yomah 69b). This is a special level not like the level of prophecy. Therefore, it was necessary to designate them a special level to exclude the level of prophecy. For prophets is on one person just like on many. But these had a level of holiness close to G-d, blessed be He... they were 120 members for an amazing reason and this is not the place to elaborate...

Thus, these 5 levels mentioned are all special levels by themselves, and it is proper for the Torah to go from Yehoshua to the Elders. For the level of the Elders is close to Yehoshua, and likewise from the Elders to the Prophets, and the Prophets to the "Men of the Great Assembly". And since the level of Elders is all one level, it was not considered as a special level that which the Elders received from the Elders... and likewise for the other levels.

Level 4 — Chida

Ben Ish Chai - Zechut Avot - that which he said "from Sinai" (m'Sinai) instead of "at Sinai" (b'Sinai), this is to hint with the letter "mem", that Moshe merited to receive the torah through the power of remaining there (fasting) 40 days. The reason for the forty is because a man has 4 physical foundations (which are aligned to the spiritual roots), and they became purified through his fasting 40 days until he became like an angel in the spiritual world. His body became ohr chiyunit (life force light).

Level 4 — Chida

Ben Ish Chai - Chasdei Avot - why did the light of the Shechina descend on the mountain to teach him torah? As we explained, if he went above to learn there, his body would have been purified to be like the angels on high and even more. Then, Yehoshua would have been incapable of receiving the torah from him. For it is impossible to receive from an angel on high.

If Moshe went for himself only, it would have been possible. But since he needed to transmit his learning to the lower creations (humans), they would have been incapable of receiving from him. For the physical of man is totally remote from the "body" (guf) of an angel to the opposite extreme.

Therefore, the lower creations would not be able to stand on his view (l'aamod al daato) and they would not understand what he taught them nor grasp his intent in what he tells them. But since he sat on the mountain, physical ground, and the Holy One, blessed be He, spread His cloud over him, and learned torah in the cloud stationed on the physical mountain, through this, Moshe Rabeinu became included of above and below.

His physical side became purified but not completely like the upper beings. Rather, he was like an intermediate type between the upper and the lower. Due to this, the lower ones were capable of receiving from him torah and wisdom and could understand what he taught them. If he were not an intermediate type, neither Yehoshua nor others could receive from him, since he would have been completely distant from them to the opposite extreme. Through this, you will understand well what the Midrash Rabba says on the verse: "which Moshe the man of G-d blessed" - (Midrash:) "half and below, man. half and above Gd"...

And the first and last letters of Sinai are Samech-Yud, which are the letters of Yesod-Mach (mem-chuf). For Moshe Rabeinu merited that the torah be given through him for two reasons. One, he was the Yesod of Chachmah, and two, he was mach, i.e. humble.

Level 4 — Chida

Chida - Zerua Yamin - Moshe is gematria Pardes plus one. Pardes hints to the four worlds (Atzilut, Beriah, Yetzira, and Asiya), and the four levels of soul (nefesh, ruach, neshama, chaya, and the four levels of torah interpretation (pshat, remez, drosh, and sod). Each part includes the others and there is also the Sod of Sod corresponding to a [sublime] fifth level - Yechida.. It is possible that Moshe also merited a bit of torah at the level of Yechida, as written: "Yet You have made him slightly less than the angels" (Tehilim 8:6). Due to this, his holy name was one more (than Pardes). To hint that he merited to some portion of the level of Yechida. It is known that each world has the Name Havaya (Yud-Heh-Vav-Heh). Therefore "Sinai" is gematria five times Havaya (26x5=130=Samech-Yud-Nun-Yud), corresponding to the four worlds and what is above them which the Name Havaya hints to in the crown of the Yud. This is the meaning of Moshe, gematria Pardes plus one, received the torah in its divisions (Pshat, Remez, Drosh, Sod) from Sinai (five Havayot)...

Chida - Roshei Avot - likewise the Sofei Teivot (last letter of each word) of Moshe Kibel Torah = Heh-Lamed-Heh=40. To hint that he received it in forty days. This corresponds to the four Yuds in the Name Havaya (when letters spelled out), whose gematria is forty.. This is the reason they remained forty years in the desert and after forty years: "Moses commenced [and] explained this Law" (Devarim 1:5). For during those forty years they were receiving the torah which Moshe received in forty days. One year for each day. This is the Oral Torah. They correspond to the four parts of Torah - Pardes (Peh-Reish-Dalet-Samech=Pshat, Remez, Drosh, Sod). And he who does not admit to the Sod (kabalistic meaning) remains a Pered (Peh-Reish-Dalet=mule). On him it is written: "Be not like a horse, like a mule (Pered) that has no understanding" (Tehilim 32:9). These four correspond to the four worlds, four souls, and four receivers of torah from flesh and blood (Yehoshua, Elders, Prophets, Men of great assembly).

Chida - Kiseh David derush dalet - Sinai is gematria 600 thousand, Samech x Yud x Nun x Yud=60x10x50x10=300 thousand, plus the Sinai on high (in the mystical worlds) aligned with Sinai below...

They said three things: be deliberate in judgment, raise up many disciples and make a fence for the Torah

הֵם אָמְרוּ שְׁלֹשָׁה דְבָרִים: הֱווּ מְתוּנִים בַּדִּין, וְהַעֲמִידוּ תַלְמִידִים הַרְבֵּה, וַעֲשׂוּ סְיָג לַתּוֹרָה

Level 2 — Rabeinu Yonah

Rabeinu Yonah - "be deliberate in judgment" - a man who is quick to judge is called "poshea" (negligent). And even though he thought he was saying truth, he is not considered unintentional (shogeg), but rather close to intentional (karov l'mezid). For he did not put to heart to say to himself: "a swift heart will not understand knowledge". For error is common to all men, as they said: "" (4:12). On this Shlomo said: "did you see a man swift in his words? A fool has more hope than him" (Mishlei 29:20), and

Chapter 1 Mishna 1 - Moshe Received

like our sages said: "be careful in ruling, for an error of learning is tantamount to a willful transgression" (Avot 4:7). Therefore, a man who rules needs to deliberate the matter and mull over his thoughts, as they said: "one must delay and let the din (judgment) ferment" (Sanhedrin 35a). For through pondering and waiting, he will find new arguments and deductions until the Din (judgment) will be absolutely true. For on second thought, he will see what he failed to see at first...

Q Level 2 — Tiferet Yisrael

Tiferet Yisrael - "be deliberate in judgment" - be patient before deciding any matter, whether [for a Beit Din] in judging someone if he is righteous or wicked, or when deciding one's own affairs, not being concerned that perhaps one is mistaken. It is also not proper to justify himself and his family in all his matters. But rather he must guide them and others in the ways of righteousness. For his rebuke is more effective... Thus he said, "raise up many disciples", and all the more so does this apply to his own sons (that he must teach them torah).. Every person is also under duty to enact personal fences for himself so as to not go to places where he will easily sin. Thus, every person is a judge, teacher, and law-maker.

Q Level 1

Meorei Ohr - "raise up many disciples" - For in many students wisdom will increase. For the students sharpen the mind of the Rav and ask him questions. Through this he needs to think on what to answer them and will clarify many doubts, and our sages said: " 'it is a tree of life' - why was the torah compared to a tree? To teach you that just like a small tree can ignite a large tree, so too small torah scholars sharpen big ones" (Taanit 7a)...

"make a fence" - from the verse "fenced in with roses" (Shir 7:3). For the torah is as a vineyard. If the stones of the fence have fallen, people and animals will enter and destroy it. The fence is a great guardian for the vineyard. Thus, for every mitzva in the torah - to make a fence around it, such as the Rabbinical prohibitions on forbidden relations...

Q Level 3 — Chida

Chida, Kikar Laeden - you can see that all three things stem from humility. "be deliberate in judgment", this is from the aspect of humility, that one does not consider himself a "Chacham" (wise man), and he suspects himself that perhaps he erred. thus, he deliberates and debates it on all sides until it is totally clear. "raise (stand) up many disciples" - for then they would learn torah while standing, until weakness came to the world afterwards. And through many disciples the study will be clarified. This also stems from the aspect of humility, that one does not rely on his own wisdom and he needs many disciples, and as written: "I learned the most from my students" (Taanit 7a). "make a fence for the Torah" - for one should not trust himself that he will not stumble. Rather, he needs fences. This also stems from the aspect of humility. For he fears that he might come to tread on the Biblical prohibition and he doesn't trust himself that he will be able to guard well.

Level 3 — Maharal

Maharal - Question: Why was tractate Avot placed at the end of Seder Nezikim (laws of damages)? Rambam (intro to zeraim): when the Tanna (author of the mishna) completed what the judge needs to know, he began with tractate Avot. This was for two matters.

One, to make known that the rulings and the Tradition is true and correct, received generation from generation. Therefore, it is proper to honor the [torah] sage and place him in an honorable position. For the Law has reached him, and he in his generation is like them in their generation.. There is in this great mussar to people. They should not say: "why should we accept the ruling of this judge or the enactment of this judge? It is not so. For the ruling is not of this judge, rather, it is the Holy One, blessed be He, who commanded us in it, as written "the mishpat (justice) belongs to G-d". It is all one mishpat (justice), received from one sage to another, generation after generation.

The second matter is that the Tanna wanted to bring the mussar of all these sages in order that we learn from them good middot (character traits). No one needs this more than the judges. For when a common man is not a baal mussar, the damage is not to all the masses. Rather, he damages only himself. But when the judge is not a baal mussar (ethical) and tzanua (refined), he will damage himself and also other people. Therefore, his opening words in tractate Avot were mussar to the judges, as written: "be deliberate in judgment". The judge must reprove himself in all the matters of tractate Avot...

🔍 Level 3 — Maharal

Maharal - Why did the "men of the great assembly" say these three things..? There is no doubt that such wise men could have said many words of wisdom and understanding without limit.

(the Maharal will now give several explanations. In the end he says: "all the explanations we gave follow along the same line if you understand")

> *SUMMARY:*
> 1. To rectify Din (Halacha), torah study, and mitzvah performance.
> 2. To rectify Gedolim, scholars, and unlearned.
> 3. To rectify the 3 branches of intellect: Chachma (wisdom), Binah (understanding), and Daat (knowledge).
> 4. To rectify man's intellect while bound to a physical body.
> 5. To rectify the 3 branches of Torah - Chukim (irrational laws), Mishpatim (rational laws), Mitzvot (in-between laws).

FIRST ANSWER - GENERAL RECTIFICATION OF WISDOM
The men of the great assembly saw that the intellect already started to diminish and mastery of wisdom was lacking. When a doctor sees weakness in a patient's limb, he prescribes a medication which will help complete where the patient's nature falls short. Thus, when the men of the great assembly saw the beginning of diminishing of wisdom, they came to repair this ailment.

The lacking in wisdom causes change in three areas. One, the mishpatim (judging) between man and his fellow. Two, in [understanding] the words of torah, and three in the deeds of mitzvot. There is a need for these three things and each of them is a separate matter by itself.

In the mishpatim (judging), one must understand the root of the law in order to judge correctly, to not obligate the innocent and exempt the guilty. This area depends on the reasoning powers of the mind to delve to the depth of the mishpat (law). It is not included in words of torah. For this is solely reasoning powers of the mind (svara), even for things not explicitly written in the torah. Because the laws in the torah are just main principles. But practical cases between man and his fellow are not written in the torah.

Words of torah are also a separate matter by itself, namely, to understand the torah's words.

Likewise the deeds of the mitzvot are also a separate matter, namely, to not come to transgress a mitzvah. For example, when one sees it is permitted to cook chicken (with milk), he will also cook meat (with milk). Thus, the Rabbis forbade even chicken meat. So too, for the Rabbinically forbidden relations (arayot). If these were permitted people will come to permit those biblically forbidden. Similarly, for the other Rabbinical fences of the torah.

The general principle: these three things rectify everything, namely, the Din (judgment), torah, and the practical mitzvot themselves.

Thus, corresponding to the rectification of Din, he said *"be deliberate in judgment"*. Corresponding to rectification of the words of torah, to clarify their words, he said *"raise up many disciples"*, and corresponding to not coming to transgress the deeds of mitzvot, they said: *"make a fence for the Torah"*. For when there is a fence to the torah, this is the rectification of the deeds of the mitzvot. Thus, through these three things everything will be rectified.

Maharal - SECOND ANSWER - RECTIFICATION OF THREE CATEGORIES OF MEN
Furthermore, these three things correspond to the three categories of men. The first category is the Gedolim (great torah scholars). The second is the Talmidei Chachamim (torah scholars), and the third is the rest of the people. For the Din requires very, very, great wisdom, to the extent that even exceedingly wise torah scholars need rectification, as they said (Sanhedrin 81, Yerushalmi): "in Din, there is no wise man, and as Shimon ben Shetach said: if one requests 'on condition that you judge me a Din torah', I answer: 'I don't know Din torah' ".

But for the words of torah, the Gedolim do not need so much

rectification. For they are already wise in torah and mitzvot. But the disciples (of the Gedolim, i.e. the medium torah scholars) do need rectification here. Corresponding to this he said: *"raise up many students"*. For through many students, the torah will become clarified to them (i.e. to the medium torah scholars).

Corresponding to the lowest category, namely, the people who do not learn, they need a fence to the torah.

When the men of the great assembly saw the diminishing in wisdom, such that it affected all categories of men, namely, the Gedolim, the disciples, and the rest of the men, they rectified the lacking.

By the Gedolim, the great torah scholars who sit to judge, he commanded them to *"be deliberate in judgment"*, to not rule judgment quickly.

For the lacking in the torah scholars: *"raise up many disciples"*. For when they "raise up many disciples", they stand on the torah due to the many disciples, as the sages said: "from my students I learned the most" (Taanit 7a)..

Corresponding to the rest of people who don't know, he said: *"make a fence for the torah"*. For they need a fence and protection. The torah scholars don't need. Only one who is not a torah scholar needs.

These three things are a general rectification. Thus, he said them in a counted manner, *"they said three things"*. For there is nothing at all more than this. These three things rectify everything. Thus, the men of the great assembly chose to say these three mussar teachings. For this was the most relevant for their generation.

THIRD ANSWER - LACKINGS OF THE MIND
Furthermore, these three things are all for lackings of the intellect. For the generation began to diminish in wisdom, and the divisions of wisdom are three: "Chochma (wisdom), Bina (understanding), and Daat (knowledge)", which are mentioned everywhere in Tanach. And when they saw the generation's

lacking in wisdom, the men of the great assembly came and rectified all three. Namely, the lacking in "Chochma", "Binah", and "Daat", as they are written in scripture: "I filled him with wisdom, understanding, and knowledge" (Shemot 31:3), and "G-d founded the earth with wisdom, established the heavens with understanding, with His knowledge the depths were split" (Mishlei 3:19).

You will find some people who err in Chachma (wisdom). Namely, their logical argument (svara) is the opposite of a true logical argument (svara).

There are others whose logical argument (svara) is not crooked and is sound, but when they come to deduce one thing from another through pilpul (deductive reasoning), they have a lacking.

The former is called Chachma, the logical argument (svara) of the mind. The latter is called Binah, the deducing of one thing from another through pilpul (deductive reasoning).

There are also people who lack knowledge, who don't know a thing.

Corresponding to these, he exhorted on these three things. For Din (judging) depends only on logical argument (svara). There is nothing that is more inside the realm of Chachma (wisdom) than Din, as the sages said: "there is no branch of wisdom like monetary laws" (Bava Batra 175b). It is thus necessary to exhort on not erring in the logical argument of the mind. Therefore, he said *"be deliberate in judgment"*.

Corresponding to the lacking that comes in the pilpul (deductive reasoning) of Chochma (logical argument), which is a different level, he said: *"raise up many disciples"*, so that he won't come to err in the pilpul (deductive reasoning) of Chochma.

The thirds depends neither on logical argument (svara) nor on pilpul (deductive reasoning). It is only for one who lacks knowledge such that he has no knowledge. And if you don't fence the torah for those who lack knowledge, they will come to transgress the mitzvot. On this they said: *"make a fence for the Torah"*.

These three things correspond to Chochma, Binah, and Daat mentioned everywhere, and through them is the rectification of everything. Corresponding to Din (judgment), which depends on the logical reasoning (svara) of the mind, he wrote: "be deliberate in judgment".

Corresponding to The rectification of pilpul of the torah, he wrote: "raise up many disciples"...
Corresponding to the error that comes through lack of knowledge, namely, transgressing the torah, he wrote: "make a fence for the Torah".

These three things include everything. Thus he specified them in counted number (minyan). For every counted number implies there is nothing more. So too here, he comes to say that these three things include the total rectification of a man when there is a lacking whether in Chochma, Binah or Daat.

FOURTH ANSWER - INTELLECT WITHOUT BODY
And even though there was no lacking in their generation, and it was proper without lacking. But their generation was not excelling like the Elders and the Prophets. Nevertheless, these instructions are proper for a man in his [inherent limitation in] being a human being. For a human being is not completely intellect. Therefore, it is proper for a man to conduct himself according to his level of human being. Although man has an intellectual soul, but nevertheless, he also has physicality with this.

Therefore they said: *"be deliberate in judgment"*. For a man is not all intellect. If he rushes to judge in Din, without mulling over, it would be as if he were only intellect, without physicality. Because the intellect without any physicality becomes clear, namely, the intellect which is not inside a physical body, it does not need to wait. But when it is in physicality like the intellect of man, it is not completely an actual intellect. Therefore it is proper for a man to conduct himself in the proper way for a man, namely, to *"be deliberate in judgment"*, and not rush as if he were an actual intellect, without physicality.

Likewise regarding *"raise up many disciples"*. For a man does not have a clear intellect for deep matters, because his intellect dwells in physicality. Thus, he needs many students. Through this, it is possible for him to attain a true intellect. Therefore, "raise up many disciples" to not come to error, as the sages said: *"A sword is upon the boasters [baddim] and they shall become fools? A sword is upon the enemies of the disciples of the wise who sit separately [bad'bebad] and study the Torah. What is more, they become stupid. It is written here, 'and they shall become fools', and it is written elsewhere, For that we have done foolishly"...*" (Berachot 63b).

Likewise regarding *"make a fence for the Torah"*. All this applies to a man inherently in his being human, with a physical body, while his soul dwells in a physical body. For if he does not make a fence for the torah, he will come to transgress it..

Therefore the men of the great assembly said three things. But before their time, in the era of the prophets and all the more so, in the era of the Elders, their intellect was on such a high level that it was as if separated completely from their body. For the prophets were not like ordinary men. Therefore, they would not exhort a man just for his being human. For the level of the prophets was above this.

But for the men of the great assembly, since they were not on the level of the prophets, their level did not go out of the realm of other humans. Unlike Moshe, Yehoshua, the Elders, and the Prophets, whose level went outside the realm of "human". For they were designated a special name of "Elders" or "Prophets", and thus their whole generation was on a super-human level. Therefore, it was not necessary to exhort them. But the "men" of the great assembly would exhort on these things. For they are inherently necessary for a man in his being human and his intellect is not completely separated from the physical.

This is the meaning of "they said [three things]..", i.e. they [alone said] but the prophets and all the more so, before them, we do not see at all any words of mussar from the Fathers to the sons exhorting them to go in the path of the just and not in the path of a human who is inherently earthy and physical. For just like it is the way of a father to rebuke his son in his youth when the son's nature is still attached to physicality, and the father exhorts him not to go after these things. But for the prophets who were not like normal humans, there was no words of mussar rebuke at all. Only for the men of the great assembly who did not have a special name designated (for they were called "men" of the great assembly) which would have indicated a special level, and all the more so for the sages who came after the men of the great assembly, that they needed to give mussar to their generation. But before the men of the great assembly, it was not relevant to give mussar rebuke to the generation (for they were like pure intellect).

FIFTH ANSWER - RECTIFICATION OF TORAH

You must know also that these three things stated by the men of the great assembly are a rectification of torah. The men of the great assembly wanted to rectify the generation's lacking in torah, and the torah comprises three categories: statutes (Chukim - laws without reason), laws (mishpatim), and commandments (mitzvot). All the commandments of the torah are included in these three categories.

Mishpatim are those known and which reason (conscience) understands. The opposite of them is Chukim. Their reason is not revealed. There are also mitzvot that are not evident like the mishpatim but are also not revealed like the Chukim, and one can grasp their reason through study. These latter are called mitzvot. These three divisions are mentioned in scripture in many places. The men of the great assembly came to rectify them. They said "be deliberate in judgment" corresponding to the mishpatim. For the primary mishpatim in the torah are the Dinim, as written (Parsha Mishpatim) "these are the Mishpatim that you shall place before them..." (Shemot 21).

Corresponding to the mitzvot they said: "raise up many disciples". For one can grasp the words of torah through many students and through study..

Corresponding to the Chukim which cannot be grasped at all, he said: "make a fence for the Torah". For the Chukim are more in need of a fence and boundary due to their reason being unknown...

All the explanations we gave follow along the same line if you understand...

Know that all these three things stated by the men of the great assembly include most of the mussar of the sages (who came after), which are to perfect a man from all sides, as we will explain. For the number three includes a thing, its opposite and the middle between them. Thus, most of the mussar teachings in this tractate are to make a person whole in one area, its opposite, and the middle between them.

The men of the great assembly said: "be deliberate in judgment", which is completely Din. The opposite of this is: "make a fence for the Torah". This is the opposite of "be deliberate in judgment". For a fence is not Din, since according to the torah, one is not completely obligated. He said "raise up many disciples" - to clarify the torah. This is not like Din. For Din obligates every person who knows that he is thus obligated in Din, and likewise, reason obligates a person on this.

But for the words of torah, even though they themselves are obligatory, and the torah is called "mishpat" (justice) in a few places, nevertheless, it is not obligatory according to man's reason (conscience). For according to man's natural reason, the mitzva is not obligatory, unlike mishpat (justice) which a man's reason obligates him (ex. don't steal). Thus, the men of the great assembly's words include the obligatory Din, its opposite, "make a fence for the torah", which is not at all obligatory, and "raise up many disciples". The latter is not like Din which man's reason obligates, nor is it non-obligatory (like the fences). Rather, it is obligatory according to Daat Torah (torah view) For this is the matter of the students - to clarify what the torah obligates, and this is the tikun (rectification) of the torah itself, and in this they included everything. Understand this well.

So too according to what we said earlier that the men of the great assembly included Chukim, Mishpatim, and Mitzvot - it is also thus. For Chukim are the opposite of Mishpatim, whose reason is known, while mitzvot are in between - they are not so revealed but not completely concealed (like Chukim). All this is because their words are coming to rectify everything, as we said. You should understand this very well.

Level 4 — Ruach Chaim

Ruach Chaim - they said three things: "be deliberate in judgment", corresponding to true in-depth study (iyun), to the utmost possible (daka min hadaka), "raise up many disciples" in order to increase torah and that it not be forgotten from the seed of Jacob.

These latter two traits, raising disciples and true in-depth study assist and bring divine help in grasping the torah...

Furthermore, be exceedingly careful to deliberate in Din, and examine it much and thoroughly. Afterwards, "raise up many disciples" who make their teacher wise by speaking out the questions that came to their minds. For the mouth is like a finger which senses imperfections. Thus when the mouth speaks it out each time, he will feel the imperfections of the intellect, as a fingernail feels the blemishes on a shechita knife. And even after all this, do not think that you have certainly arrived at the truth, after both the intellect and the speaking out have reached a consensus. On this they said nevertheless: "and make a fence for the Torah". And then halevai (would that it were) that you did not step on the ikar din (primary part of the mitzva).

They also said these three corresponding to the three parts of the soul: nefesh, ruach, neshama, which are thought, speech, and deed. For deed is in the realm of the nefesh as written "the souls (nefesh) which do" (Vayikra 18:29), "the soul that will do" (Bamidbar 15:30). Speech is in the realm of the ruach, as written: "ruach Hash-em spoke through me" (Shmuel II 23:2), and "by the ruach of his lips" (Isaiah 11:4). Thought is in the realm of the neshama. A man needs to rectify all these three levels. This is what they said "three things": "be deliberate in judgment", corresponding to thought, to delve deeply in his thoughts into the depths of halacha, to draw out the true Din. Afterwards, to teach it to the students, corresponding to speech, and "make a fence for the Torah" corresponding to deed.

Understand this.

Level 4 — Chida

Ben Ish Chai - Chasdei Avot - "be deliberate in judgment" - to hint that if one sees sufferings and judgments befall him, he should not get angry and say bad things on Above. Rather, he should be patient and silent, and hope to Hash-em till he turns the bad into good...

Level 3 — Chida

Ben Ish Chai - Chasdei Avot - the oral law is called "din". On this, it is written: "min hashamayim hishmata din". As to why it is called "din", in the tikunim, the oral law has 60 tractates, and it is known that each tractate has four parts - pshat, remez, drosh, sod... thus it is called din. din is dalet-yud-nun = 4, 10+50, i.e. to hint that there are 4 parts of pardes in the sixty tractates... and likewise "make a fence (siyag) for the torah" hints to samech, yud-gimmel, i.e. expound the 60 tractates using the 13 attributes with which the torah is expounded. They said "make" to hint the learning needs to bring to action, even when learning, he should "learn on condition to do".

Chapter 1 Mishna 2 - World Stands

Shimon HaTzadik (the Righteous) was from the remnants of the Great Assembly. He would say, "On three things the world stands: on the Torah, on the service (Avodah) and on acts of kindness." שִׁמְעוֹן הַצַּדִּיק הָיָה מִשְׁיָרֵי כְנֶסֶת הַגְּדוֹלָה. הוּא הָיָה אוֹמֵר: עַל שְׁלֹשָׁה דְבָרִים הָעוֹלָם עוֹמֵד, עַל הַתּוֹרָה וְעַל הָעֲבוֹדָה וְעַל גְּמִילוּת חֲסָדִים

Level 1 — Bartenura

Bartenura - remnant after all of them died, the Tradition remained in his hand, and he was the Kohen Gadol (high priest) after Ezra.

He would say - i.e. this was an expression on his tongue always. So too for all the times in this tractate when it says Rabbi so and so would say. The explanation is that he was used to saying this always.

the world stands - it was created for these three things.

Level 2 — Rabeinu Yonah

Rabeinu Yonah - For these three things the world stands. The explanation of "stands" is that the world was created for these things because they are the will of the Holy One, blessed be He. That is to say, He created the world because His creations would in the future find favor before Him through doing these things... For them the world was created, in order to do them.

Level 2 — Tiferet Yisrael

Tiferet Yisrael - i.e. one who is careful in these three things will have his world stand. His life will endure in this world and in the next.

Level 2

Mili D'Avot: "on three things the world stands" - the kiyum (continuance) and Shelemut (perfection) of man who is called a "miniature world", depends on three things: "torah, Avodah, and Acts of Kindness".

Torah - aren't the Avodah and acts of kindness a part of torah? Rather, torah here refers to torah study (not torah commandments). Likewise in the Talmud: "torah is greater than deeds for it leads to deeds" (Kidushin 40b). This is the first and foremost Shelemut (perfection) of man.

Avodah (service) - what is between man and G-d such as the korbanot, prayer, tefilin, sabbath, holidays, etc. It is called Avodah for G-d does not receive any benefit from this. Nor is it a kindness to G-d. It is only "avodah". To teach that G-d's intent is only that man subjugate himself (sheyishtabed) (the word "subjugate" has the same root as "avodah"), and fufill His will.

This is as our sages taught: "what does G-d care if an animal is slaughtered from the throat or the back of the neck? Rather, the mitzvot were given only to purify human beings" (Ber. Rabba 44). Namely, to remove from them wickedness (zadon) and arrogance. These are like the impurities in silver. This is so that man will serve his Creator and subjugate himself to Him.

Level 2 — Chatam Sofer

Daat Sofer, Lech Lecha - "on three things... acts of kindness" - all of them need to be joined with "kindness". In "torah", one needs to do kindness to also teach others, as our sages expounded: *"Torah studied in order to teach it to others that is a 'Torah of kindness'"* (Sukkah 49b). A person should not hold torah for himself alone.. Rather, let him learn with others and grant them merit also with his torah. Likewise for Avodah, one needs to do kindness. For example, to pray for his fellow and join together (ex. in prayer) with the troubles of the public. All Yisrael is like one man and one body. Each person needs to feel the pain of his fellow, as our sages said: *" 'Israel are scattered sheep' (Jeremiah 50:17) - why are Israel likened to a sheep? Just as a sheep, when hurt on its head or some other body part, all of its body parts feel it. So it is with Israel when one of them sins, everyone feels it..." (Vayikra Rabba 4)*. Thus, we see Torah and Avodah (prayer) need to be intertwined with the trait of kindness.

Level 3 — Chatam Sofer

Ketav Sofer Avot - the [Jewish] people of the world are divided ino three levels: those who sit and toil in torah always, day and night. These are the pillars of torah and their great merit shields on the rest of the world. The second level is those who are not bnei torah but they are found in the synagogues always, two or three times a day, at the prayer times. They are the pillars of

Chapter 1 Mishna 2 - World Stands

service, in the way of "let us render [for] bulls [the offering of] our lips" (Hoshea 14:3). The third group are the businessmen who travel always around the world. Most of the year, they travel to the marketplaces to profit and amass much money. Due to this they have great ability to bestow kindness to the pillars of torah and service. This is the pillar of kindness...

Level 3 — Ruach Chaim

Ruach Chaim - "three things" - this hints to three levels of soul. Torah is the level of speech. Avodah which is the Korbanot (temple offerings) is thought. For it depends on the thoughts of the Kohen. He can invalidate it with the wrong thought (pigul). His main thought needs to be to elevate the Nefesh Behemit (animal soul) above. So too in our times, the service of prayer is in place of the Korbanot as our sages expounded on "to serve Him with all your heart" (Shema). "What is the service of the heart? Prayer."

For the matter of prayer is giving one's life (Mesirut Nefesh) to HaKadosh Baruch Hu (G-d) similar to a korban (temple offering). Since in every word one utters out of his mouth, there is a part of his soul [that comes out]. And as our sages taught: "moving one's lips is considered an act" (Keritut 4a).

Prayer needs to be primarily with heart and soul, not body alone, as written: "praise G-d, my soul" (Tehilim 146). For the soul also praises.

"Acts of kindness" - is with one's body and money. The reason he preceded speech (torah) before thought (Avodah) is in order to precede Torah. For Torah is the primary thing and on it depends the shefa (divine flow) of life to all the worlds. If the whole world were to be idle from torah study for one second (no one learning torah on our planet), then all the worlds would literally collapse to utter emptiness. Their continuance of existence is from the torah.

Level 4

Rabbi Avraham Azoulai - Ahava b'Taanugim - (kabalistic)
Torah - because through toil in torah one pulls down shefa (divine flow) from above, the Source of blessings, to imbue life in this world. On this it is written: "you shall contemplate it day and

night" (Yehoshua 1:8). For this bottom world is the world of the klipot (shells, i.e. forces of evil), far from holiness, the life-force of the worlds. It has no life or kiyum (continued existence) except through continual toil in the spiritual torah. Through toil in torah, shefa descends from above to the person toiling in it and then all the worlds receive life and shefa through him. This is why uninterrupted toil in torah is necessary always. For if the toil in torah is intterupted, the shefa which is mekayim (sustains) the world also interrupts (and all the worlds collapse).

Avodah - this is the work of the temple offerings when the temple existed. Today, it is the "avodah of the heart", namely, prayer. For the kavana (in them) was to stir up a rousing from below to above (lehaalot hitorerut mimata lemaala) in the Sod (secret) of mayim nukvim as explained in the Zohar. Through this, the shefa descends to all the worlds to sustain and bestow life to them.

Acts of Kindness - i.e. the yichud elyon shemashpia tzadik b'tzedek, and they bestow kindness to each other. This occurs through the power of acts of kindness, as known to the kabalists. We may also say that through word, thought, and deed, the divisions of the creation endure. For through toil and words in the toil in torah, the world of yetzira endures. Through the avodah of the heart, namely, thought in prayer, the world of Beriah endures.. and through action, namely, acts of kindness, the world of Asiyah endures. This is the meaning of "on three things the world stands.." (see the book Shaarei Kedusha for an intro to the mystical worlds).

Level 4 Chida

Chida - Roshei Avot - he chose torah first because torah includes all three. For when one toils in torah, it is as if he brings an offering (menachot 110a). And it is said: "torah of kindness was on his tongue", for he bestows kindness to the whole world.. (as before since he pulls down shefa to all the worlds).

Chida - Marit Haayin - "the world stands" - it is referring to man who is a miniature world. There is no kiyum (existence) for man to annul the evil inclination except through torah, as the talmud brings: "I created the evil inclination and I created the torah as its antidote". From there he will ascend to fulfill the mitzvot. This is the meaning of "on three things the world (i.e. the miniature world, i.e. man) stands. On torah (to nullify the yetzer hara, and after nullifying him,) on avodah (positive mitzvot between man and G-d) and acts of kindness (mitzvot between man and his fellow).

Perhaps also, these three hint to (the sefirot) chesed (kindness), gevurah (might), and tiferet (splendor). The avodah hints to gevurah, that one mitgaber (strengthen himself) to do the service of G-d against the yetzer hara which wages war with him always. Torah corresponds to tiferet (as known) and acts of kindness corresponds to chesed.

Level 4 — Maharal

Maharal - It is proper to ask: why was it necessary to say he was *"a remnant of the men of the great assembly"*, and not just that he was *"of the men of the great assembly"*?

This demonstrates the explanation we said (last mishna), that the mussar rebuke is according to the generation. Thus, we do not find mussar before the men of the great assembly, as we said (last mishna). Only from after the men of the great assembly. For they were all together a holy assembly. And certainly the generation was on a higher level before these men departed to their eternal abode and then only Shimon Hatzadik was left as a remnant.

When he alone remained alive, the state of the generation was already like the next generation, for there was no longer all the men of the great assembly except for this single sage. Thus, the generation was similar to the next one, whereby only singular sages were found who were fathers of the generation. Hence, next mishna it continues "Antigonus.. who was after Shimon Hatzadik", and likewise the pairs of sages after Antigonus..

"He would say on three things the world stands" - such an exhortation is before everything. For one must first build the foundation. Therefore, Shimon Hatzadik who was the remnant of the men of the great assembly would exhort them to be careful on the things which are the foundation and pillars of the world upon which everything is built.

According to our explanation, the words of the men of the great assembly come even before this. They said: "be deliberate in judgment, raise up many disciples and make a fence for the Torah".

Those things stated by the men of the great assembly are the rectifications and inherent lackings in a man in his being human. It is human nature to err in these things, namely, the torah, and wholeness (shelemut) is necessary there. And since it is the rectification of torah and torah is first and foremost over everything, the men of the great assembly rectified that first.

Afterwards, Shimon Hatzadik exhorted on that which is the foundation of the world. This is after torah..

It is proper to ask on what he said: *"Torah, Service (Avodah), and acts of kindness"*. Why on these things and not on others? On the Brit Mila (covenant of the circumcision), for examples, it says: "If you break My covenant (Brit)..." (Yirmiya 33). Similarly for other things that are fitting for being what the world stands on.

(the Maharal will now bring several explanations. The following first explanation will also answer why it says "on three things the world stands" instead of "on three things man stands", as they seem to be things to rectify man, not the world.)

FIRST EXPLANATION - man must be whole in three areas

Summary of First Explanation
- Only that which has good is worthy of being created and enduring

- The world was created for man.

- Man has 3 relations which he needs to be whole in: between man and himself (Torah), between man and G-d (Service), between man and his fellow (Kindness). When man corrupts these three and turns to their opposite, the world has no longer any foundation and destruction comes, as indeed happened during the generation of the flood.

The background for explaining this mishna is as follows. The creations were created because they have good. If they did not

Chapter 1 Mishna 2 - World Stands

have good, they would not have been created. For a thing which is not itself good, it is not proper for it to be granted existence. It is more proper for it to not exist than to exist. Thus, existence of something is because of the good it contains. And just like its creation is because of the good it has, so too, and how much more so, that the whole world and all its creatures are granted existence and continuance because they contain good. If the creations did not have any good, it would not be proper for them to exist. Each creation's existence is only due to the particular good it contains.

It is because of this that G-d sealed each stage of creation with *"and G-d saw that it was good"* (Genesis ch.1). This was stated for each and every detail by itself, and likewise for the totality of the whole creation: *"and G-d saw all that He had made, and behold it was very good"* (Gen.1:31). For when a thing is good, it is worthy of being created and of existing, and likewise a thing only has continuance (kiyum) due to its good aspect.

In all the six days of creation, the torah says: "it is good" except for the second day. Our sages said: *"because dispute (machloket) was created"* (Midrash Gen.Rabba 1). This is what our sages said: *"any dispute which is not for the sake of Heaven will not endure"* (Avot 5:17). For "it is good" was not said on this. And even though the dispute which broke out on the second day was for the sake of Heaven and it was needed for the world, but nevertheless, since in and of itself dispute has no continuance, only from G-d's side it endures when it is for the sake of Heaven, therefore, it was not proper to say there "it is good". For that is only for something which endures in and of itself.

We have clarified that a thing has continuance only due to the good it contains. Thus, when a created thing has a lacking (evil), thereby becoming not good, it draws nearer to total non-existence. But that which is good, without evil and lacking, is far from non-existence and it is proper for it to be created and have continuance of existence.

G-d testified on the general things that they contain good, even though there may exist lackings in their individual particulars (one particular individual), and thus, those particular individuals are certainly subject to non-existence (destruction). But the general things stand, and on them G-d testified that the creation is good. For each species created has good. Likewise for the totality of creation as a whole, the torah also testified on it saying *"and G-d saw all that He had made, and behold it was very good"* (Gen 1:31).

There is no need to elaborate further on this. For they are clear matters which everything testifies on, namely, the non-existence (destruction) a created being is subject to is due to the lacking it has, that is to say, the evil which attaches to it subjects it to non-existence (destruction).

When this has become clear to you, you should know that all the creations depend on man. For they were created for man. Thus, if man is not as he should be, everything becomes useless. This is as written regarding the generation of the flood: *"for all flesh had corrupted its way on the earth"* (Gen:6), and in the Midrash:

> "An analogy to this is of one who made a wedding for his son. He built a canopy with elaborate decorations, etc. for his son. But afterwards, he became furious on his son and smashed what he built. The king explained: "Did I not build all this only for my son. Now that he is gone what need have I for all this?" Thus, "behold I am bringing the flood.. to destroy all flesh with spirit of life.. all that is upon the earth will perish".

Thus, all the creations were created for man. Hence, when man is no longer worthy of existence, everything becomes useless and the world ceases to have a reason to exist. Our sages have expressed this concept in many places - that everything was created for man.

When it is clear to you that the world exists for man, it follows that man must contain good. For then it is proper for him to be granted existence. And when it is proper to grant him existence, then it is also proper to grant existence to the whole world. For everything depends on man.

The torah does not explicitly say "good" by [the creation] of man. It hints only "[and G-d saw all that He had made, and behold] it was very good", and the Midrash (Gen.Rabba ch.9) teaches

Chapter 1 Mishna 2 - World Stands

"very" (meod - mem-aleph-dalet) - these letters spell "Adam" (aleph-dalet-mem). This is tangibly visible because human [nature] is lacking and a "man is born as wild donkey" (Iyov 11:12).

Afterwards, man ascends to the level of good. Thus, man needs to acquire for himself the level of "good". This "good" is on three levels:

One, when he is good in and of himself, from his own intrinsic aspect.. (between man and himself)

Two, it is proper for him to be good towards G-d who created him. Namely, that he serves G-d and does His will.

Three, it is proper for him to be good towards other human beings around him. For a man does not exist by himself. Rather, he exists alongside other people.

A man needs to be good in all these three aspects with which he is tested.

(1) He needs to be good in and of himself. For after the creation of the world, the torah immediately says regarding the world that it is good. Thus, we see from this that the world needs to be good in and of itself.

(2) Likewise, man needs to be good with respect to the Cause whom he owes his existence.

(3) Thirdly, he needs to be good with respect to other human beings.

The general principle: he needs to be good in all these three aspects, and each one is not like the other two as we explained in the introduction to this book.

In the talmud (Kidushin 40a):

> "'A good Tzadik (righteous man)... will eat the fruits (dividends) of his deeds' (Isaiah 3:10) - are there Tzadikim who are not good?! Rather, a Tzadik who is good to G-d and

people is a good Tzadik. A Tzadik who is good to G-d but bad to people is not a good Tzadik" (Kidushin 40a).

And certainly, and all the more so, that a man needs to be shalem (whole) with himself (the first of the three levels). Since otherwise he is not a tzadik at all. For it would have been superfluous to say on him ("a good tzadik"), since every creature itself has good (at creation as explained earlier).

Thus, the tzadik needs to be good from all sides. Therefore, this Tanna (sage) opened his words saying: *"on three things the world stands, on torah..."*. For when a man has torah, in and of himself he is considered good in his having the torah intellect (hatorah hasichlit).

But if he does not have torah, he is not considered good in and of himself. For he lacks the torah which is the completion (hashlama) of man's being, and he is like an animal. Such a man is not considered a proper creature and is not worthy of existence. On this, our sages said:

> "there was evening and there was morning, the sixth day" (Gen.1:31) - What is the purpose of the additional word 'the'? This teaches that the Holy One, blessed be He, stipulated with the Works of Creation and said: 'If Israel accepts the Torah, you shall exist; but if not, I will turn you back into emptiness and formlessness.'" (Shabbat 88b).

Why man must have torah

The explanation of this is as follows. All the creatures that were created do not have the supernal divine wisdom (chachma Elokit elyona). Even though man possesses an intellect, but this is merely human intellect which is associated with physicality. The world is not worthy of existence just for this [small] good. For mere human intellect is lowly and deficient. Rather, only for the torah which is the divine, transcendent intellect. It is the complete good.

Then the world has a virtue, for it contains the divine torah intellect, and this is not human knowledge and human intellect. Therefore, the shelemut (completion) of man himself, such that he is considered the important creature which has the good, this is through torah. Namely, when one can say on the man that he is a baal torah (possessor of torah).

This matter does not need a proof. For without a doubt, the creation of man is lowly when he turns to become like an animal. Rather, man's loftiness is when he is separate from the animals. This is only through the torah intellect. Through possessing this transcendent intellect, he is considered a good, whole creature, possessing virtue in and of himself. There is nothing else in the world besides torah through which a man can be considered possessing virtue (baal maala) in and of himself. This is explicit. For the torah is called good, as written "For I gave you good teaching" (Mishlei 4:2). And in the Talmud (Menachot 53b):

> " 'Let the good come and receive the good from the Good for the good' - 'Let the good come' — that refers to, Moses, as it is written, 'And she saw that he was good' (Shemot 2:2); 'And receive the good' — that is the Torah, as it is written, 'For I give you good doctrine' (Mishlei 4:2)..."

Thus torah is called "good". This is entirely because it is completely [transcendent] intellect, not human intellect, like other wisdoms.

This is as we explained at length elsewhere, that [in general] a thing which is intellect (sichli) is separate from the physical completely, and is complete good. Therefore, the torah is the complete good in particular. Conversely, a thing which is physical is complete evil. We have already explained this in several places already. Here is not the place to elaborate. For it is clear that evil attaches to the physical, as we explained in the introduction. Thus, that which is far from the physical, like the torah, which is clear divine intellect (sechel Elokei habarur) - it is complete good.

Therefore, the torah intellect is what elevates man beyond the animalistic and above the status of lowly creature. Through the torah, man attains transcendent intellect (sichli), separated from the physical, and then he becomes a whole creature, worthy of existence. Therefore, the wholeness (shelemut) of man in and of himself is only through the torah and nothing else. Thus, the holy Tanna (sage) said that the torah is one pillar upon which the world stands. For the torah is what completes man such that he is a whole creature in and of himself.

Man Between G-d - Avodah (service of G-d)

Afterwards, he said "Avodah". For the Avodah (service of G-d) which is Avodah (service) foremost and in essence is the service of the Korbanot (temple offerings). There is nothing more "foremost" than this. But all the other things whereby one performs mitzvot (commandments) to fulfill the will of G-d are all included in the term "Avodah".

Thus, the Avodah is a pillar of the world. For from this, a man will be considered shalem (whole) and good to He who created him. This is when man serves G-d. For man needs to be whole and good towards his Creator.

THIRD LEVEL - Man with other people
Corresponding to man's need to be good towards other human beings, this is through "acts of kindness". When a man does kindness to his fellow for free, there is no doubt that in this he is good towards his fellow. [In this area,] there is nothing more good than this, namely, doing good to his fellow for free. For then, he is completely good.

We have clarified that it is proper for these three things to be pillars of the world. For they complete a man so that he is good in all three levels we mentioned.

For nothing exists besides G-d, blessed be He, since He is the mechuyiv hametziot (Necessary Existence, First Cause) and also the existing beings which He brought into existence. Thus, certainly a man has a relationship with his Creator in that G-d created man and man is created by G-d. Hence, it is proper for man to guard this relationship. For if he does not guard this relationship, his creation is for nothing.

Furthermore, a man was created by himself. And if he himself is corrupt and unimportant, then he is a shallow, insignificant creature.

Thirdly, this man is not alone in the world. Rather, G-d created

Chapter 1 Mishna 2 - World Stands 43

him with other human beings. Therefore, he needs to guard this relationship he has with other people. Thus, he said: *"acts of kindness"*.

To summarize: through the *"torah"*, a man himself is not an empty insignificant creature. But rather, an important creature. And through the *Avodah* (serving G-d), he guards his relationship towards his Creator who granted him existence. And through *"acts of kindness"* the man has a connection to other people. For a man was not at all created by himself, but rather, with other people. And when a man does kindness to his fellow, he has a connection to his fellow. Through this a man is [just] as G-d created him. For man was not created to be alone in the world. This becomes apparent when he does acts of kindness to others. Man should not tell himself: "I have no business with other people". These things are evident.

With this explanation, we have already clarified why the mishna used the expression "the world stands" instead of "a man stands". For man is the foundation and pillar of the whole world, as we explained...

In the generation of the flood, the world was not destroyed until they sinned in all three things the world stands upon and came to their opposite. When they turned to the opposite, the world, from man to beast, was destroyed. They sinned in idolatry, which is the opposite of the pillar of Avodah, as our sages said:

" 'And the earth was corrupt before G-d' (Genesis 6:11)' - anywhere that the term 'corrupt' is stated, it is referring to licentiousness and idol worship " (Sanhedrin 57a).

These two things are the opposite of the two pillars the world stands on, namely, Avodah and Torah. They also had theft as written "and the earth became full of robbery" (Gen.6:11). Theft is the opposite of "acts of kindness". For it is stealing of his instead of giving him. These three things are the complete opposite of the three things upon which the world stands. Thus, when they uprooted the three pillars and they tended to the complete opposite, that generation did not have a foundation and pillar to support them and destruction came to the world.

From this, you will understand what our sages said: "if a man is commanded: 'transgress and you won't die' he may transgress and not suffer death, except for idolatry, forbidden relations (ex.adultery) and murder" (Sanhedrin 74a). Although they gave a logical explanation for murder, namely, "who knows that your blood is more red? Perhaps his blood is more red". But for "lewd relations",they did not give a reason. We only learn it from the verse, as explained there. Nevertheless there is a logical reason. For those three cardinal sins are the opposite of these three things upon which the world stands.

For example, without a doubt, idolatry is the opposite of Avodah which is to G-d. Murder is the opposite of acts of kindness. For the latter is bestowing good to another and doing to him something he is not obligated to do, while murder destroys him completely.

"Forbidden relations" is the opposite of torah. For we already explained above that the quality of torah is that it is transcendent intellect, completely separated from the physical, and that only through torah can a person become separated from physicality.. The opposite of this is "forbidden relations" which is going after zenut (lewdness). In this he is going after the physical until he is considered completely like an animal and a donkey.

Likewise, our sages taught that the act of zenut (lewd relations) is an animal act. And in tractate Sotah (15a) "just as her actions were the actions of an animal, so too, her offering is animal food".

No proof is needed for this. An act of zenut (lewd relations) is an animal act of base physicality. They also said there:

" 'if a man's wife go astray (lit.folly)' (Bamidbar 5:12) - this teaches the adulterer does not commit the transgression unless a spirit of folly enters into him " (Sotah 3a).

We learned from here that a man goes after zenut only after a ruach shtut (spirit of folly) enters him. He becomes like a base physical animal, and then there is adultery. Therefore, the zenut (lewdness) of forbidden relations is the opposite of the level of torah. The latter is torah intellect, while the former is an act of physicality.

Thus, for these it is proper to give up one's life rather than transgress them, since the continued existence (kiyum) of man depends on these three things taught here, which the world stands on. And if he wants to transgress and not give up his life, then nevertheless it is as if he has no existence whatsoever. Better that he die meritorious (zakai) than live guilty (chayiv). For when he is the opposite of good, it is as if he has no existence at all. And even in the case where he is forced (to transgress), but nevertheless, since these things turn away from existence completely, it is not relevant to say "you shall live by them [and not die]". For in these sins is the essence of death and non-existence. They don't have any existence at all, and existence is life.

SECOND EXPLANATION - three ways the world receives standing from G-d
Summary of Second Explanation
•In three ways the world receives continued existence from G-d

•Torah - without torah, the world is petty and not worth creating.

Avodah - without service of G-d, the world would not be worthy of creation, since it is outside G-d.

•Acts of Kindness - through acts of kindness between human being, G-d sustains the world in kindness, measure for measure.

You must understand another explanation of this mishna. One who understands the root and truth of the matter will grasp that it is all one matter.

Just so that the language [of the mishna] should be clearer, that which he said: "On three things the world stands: on the Torah, on the service (Avodah) and on acts of kindness". You should know that this world G-d created cannot possibly stand on its own. Rather, [it stands] only through G-d. For everything is from

Him.

Three things are needed for the world for it to receive existence (kiyum) and standing from G-d.

(1) (acts of kindness) - (after creation) the world still needs His goodness and kindness, namely, His influence (hashpa). For after it was created, the world still needs its maintenance and continued existence from Him.

(2) (Avodah) - Furthermore, it is a continuance of existence (kiyum) to the world when it is created for serving G-d. For if it were not created for the honor of G-d, and it were not entirely dedicated to G-d, then it would not have been worthy of being created... But in this that it was created to serve G-d, it is all entirely dedicated to G-d. Through this, it has existence. For through this, it does not go outside of G-d, since it was created to serve Him.

(3) (Torah) - Another thing which is a continuance of existence (kiyum) to the world is the wholeness (shelemut) of the world. Namely, that it not be a tohu (formless, insignificant) existence and one deficient. For then, it would not at all have been worthy of existence.

Through these three things the world stands. Namely, it was created to serve G-d (Avodah). It is a whole creation and not deficient (Torah). And when G-d bestows His kindness and goodness (which happens measure for measure when humans do kindness to each other)...

Torah: the wholeness (shelemut/perfection) of the world is for the torah. This was hinted in the verse "Yom HaShishi.." ("the sixth day..." Gen.1:). Our sages said:

"there was evening and there was morning, the sixth day" (Gen.1:31) - What is the purpose of the additional word 'the'? This teaches that the Holy One, blessed be He, stipulated with the Works of Creation and said: 'If Israel accepts the Torah, you shall exist; but if not, I will turn you back into emptiness and formlessness'" (Shab.88b).

This is because if the world did not have the torah, it would not have any significance whatsoever due to its pettiness. For why would G-d busy Himself with such a petty world? Without torah, the world would have been "emptiness and formlessness", without any substance. Therefore, the world would have completely gone back to "emptiness and formlessness", if not for the torah which is the importance and supernal virtue in the world. Through this, the world is worthy of creation. Thus, the torah is a pillar of the world as we explained.

Avodah: also for this the world was created - to serve G-d. This is what they said: "without the ma'amadoth (part of the temple service), the heaven and earth could not have endured" (Megilah 31b).

The explanation is that Avraham knew that the world was created only for G-d, as written: "the L-ord made everything for His praise" (Mishlei 16:4). For nothing is worthy of existence unless it is for G-d. Thus, everything is for G-d. This was explained by the sages:

"Everything that the Holy One, Blessed be He, created in this world, He created only for His honor, as it says (Isaiah 43:7): 'Every one that is called by My name, and whom I have created for My honor, I have formed him, I have made him'" (Avot 6:11).

For if it is for itself, then ch"v, there is something besides G-d. But if it exists for G-d's glory, i.e., to serve Him, in this it is *"for His praise"*.

Thus they said "Avodah". For in this serving of G-d, the world is not something by itself, whereby we would say there is something else besides G-d. For a servant has no existence by himself. The servant's existence is entirely for his master. When one is a servant to someone, he has no name of his own. Therefore, Avodah is the second pillar. Thus, automatically when people do not serve G-d and they veer from Him, they are deserving of destruction and annihilation from the world. For they were created only for His honor, to serve Him.

When G-d answered Avraham that He will not destroy them. Avraham replied: "with what will I know" (Gen.15:8). For it is not at all conceivable that they should sin and not be destroyed, since from the beginning, the world was created only to serve Him. On this G-d answered that He enacted for them the Korbanot (temple offerings) through which they will receive atonement for their sins and which are also service of G-d that the world was created for.

He also stated "acts of kindness". Because besides all this, without the kindness of G-d, the world could not endure at all. For they need His kindness and all the more so for their livelihood. In His kindness, G-d provides for all and bestows to all. Therefore, the mishna says: "acts of kindess". For when human beings do acts of kindness in this world, G-d also directs the world with kindness and bestows kindness to them. Thus, if there is no kindness in the world, it cannot endure...

THIRD EXPLANATION - the three forefathers

Summary of Third Explanation
- The three forefathers are fathers of the world, thus they are pillars for each of these three things

- Kindness - Avraham, Avodah - Yitzchak, Torah - Yaakov

Know that for these three things, torah, Avodah, and acts of kindness, just like they are pillars of the world, so too, they were granted to the three forefathers, Avraham, Yitzchak, and Yaakov, who are also foundations and fathers of the world. Thus, it is proper for them to have these three things which are foundations and pillars of the world.

You will find "acts of kindness" was the trait of Avraham, as written in the torah. He would perform all acts of kindness with great zeal, namely, receiving guests...

Yitzchak merited the trait of Avodah. For he offered himself up on the altar. And in the midrash:

"the day Avraham placed his son on the altar, G-d enacted the two daily offerings in the temple. Why all this? When the Jewish people offer the daily tamid offerings on the altar and read the verses, G-d recalls the binding of Yitzchak, son of Avraham.." (Vayikra Rabba 2). We learn from here that the temple service to G-d was due to the binding of Yitzchak...

Yaakov had the trait of torah as written: "an innocent man who sits in tents" (Gen.25:27), and as our sages said "I dwelled with (the wicked) Lavan and nevertheless guarded the 613 commandments". Thus, Yaakov had the trait of torah.

If you ask: "Avraham also guarded the torah as written: 'because Abraham hearkened to My voice, and kept My charge, My commandments, My statutes, and My torahs' (Gen.26:5), and our sages expounded this (Yoma 28b): 'that Avraham fulfilled even the (small) mitzvah of eiruv tavshilin'".

Answer: there is a difference. For Avraham guarded the torah in deed. But torah study was specially to Yaakov. For specifically regarding him, it was written: "sits in tents", which refers to torah study. Furthermore, although Avraham guarded the torah, we don't find it was given to the Jewish people in his merit, as we find by Yaakov, as written: "And He established testimony in Jacob, and He set down a Torah in Israel" (Tehilim 78:5) - for Yaakov and Yisrael the torah was given. You can understand this also from: "give truth to Yaakov, kindness to Avraham" (Micha 7:20), and "torah of truth was on his mouth" (Malachi 2:6). Thus, the torah was specifically to Yaakov...

FOURTH EXPLANATION - the three foundations stand on these three things

> *Translator:* note that in Midrashic literature, the world is viewed as being constructed of four basic elements: earth, water, air and fire (Bamidbar Raba end of 14:12; Zohar 1:27a, 2:23b-24b; Tikunei Zohar intro; Sefer Yetzirah Ch. 3; Ramban Bereishit 1:1; Etz Chaim kitzur aby'a ch.10.
>
> Modern science has combined everything with $E=mc^2$ but this is because the scientists focus only on physical phenomena they can measure with physical instruments. But the earth, water, air, fire system incorporates the spiritual

roots as well. This is why there are four types of creations in our world (inanimate, plant, animal, human), four dimensions 3D+time, four levels of soul in humans, and many other interesting things. Ultimately, they are aligned with the four mystical worlds and ultimately rooted in the four letter Name of G-d. Back to the Maharal...

These explanations we presented go out and branch out from the true explanation in this mishna from the depths of wisdom. You already know that the foundations of the world are three. They are called "Emesh" (aleph-mem-shin) in the Sefer Yetzira, namely, water, air, and fire.

The foundations are always three. The fourth one, earth, is not mentioned, for a reason known to the understanding person. These three foundations mentioned by the Sefer Yetzira are the supernal foundations, called "Emesh", which are the foundations of everything. From them, everything was created as explained there.

These three foundations connect to G-d through these three things in the mishna. He is the foundation of all, and through this, the world stands on its existence through G-d.

For the torah is a ruach chachma u'binah (a spirit/wind of wisdom and understanding). The Avodah is fire. Thus it is called everywhere, such as "My offerings, My bread for My fires" (Bamidbar 28:2), and "a fire offering, a pleasing fragrance to the L-ord" (Vayikra 1:9). This is well known. The shechita (slaughtering) of the animals is specifically in the north. For from there is the trait of fire (in kabala).

Acts of kindness is the trait of water, as written: "Send forth your bread upon the surface of the water" (Kohelet 11:1), and "Fortunate are you who sow by all waters" (Isaiah 32:20), which our sages taught refers to acts of kindness (Bava Kama 17a).. and it is known that a kind man bestows to another like water bestows (to the soil).

Therefore, they said: "on three things the world stands". For this world which is founded on the three foundations we mentioned connects to Him, blessed be He, through these three things.

The foundation of ruach (wind) is connected to torah, which is a ruach (spirit). The foundation of water is connected to acts of kindness, the trait of water. The foundation of fire is connected to the Avodah which is fire. Through these three things [in the mishna] each of which connects to one foundation, together, they connect to G-d, blessed be He. For the torah, Avodah, and acts of kindness have a connection to G-d, so that everything is connected to G-d. Thus, without a doubt, these three things are the pillars of the world.

The verse hints at this: *"G-d (E-l), G-d (Elokim) the L-ord (Hash-em), spoke and called to the earth"* (Tehilim 50:1), i.e. He called the earth to stand before Him, as written: *"Even My hand laid the foundation of the earth, and My right hand measured the heavens with handbreadths; I call them, they stand together"* (Isaiah 48:13). For this world which has the 3 foundations is connected to these three holy Names through these three things mentioned in the mishna, namely, torah, avodah, and acts of kindness. The verse stated two holy Names (E-l, Elokim) before the special Name (Ha-Shem, the Yud-Heh-Vav-Heh). The reason being in order to put it next to the [word] earth. For this Name stands up the earth first.

The verse stated the Name E-l, which is the attribute of kindness, as our sages said "E-l, this is the attribute of kindness, as written: *'E-li, E-li why did you abandon me'* (Tehilim 22:1), i.e. to the attribute of justice".

The foundation of water connects to this Name through acts of kindness. We already said that kindness is the trait of water.

The verse stated the Name Elokim. The foundation of fire connects to this Name through the Avodah. For the Avodah is from the side of Din (justice), which is the Name Elokim. The Korbanot (offerings) are called "Ishai" (My fires) in the torah..

The verse stated the Name of Ha-Shem (Yud-Heh-Vav-Heh). For the foundation of Ruach (wind/spirit) connects to this Name through Torah, which was given through this Name. It was made known to Moshe the receiver of the torah.

Thus it has been explained what the mishna stated that the world stands on three things.. Understand these things very well. For everything we stated is the explanation of the mishna. It all goes to one place and comes from the same root.

FINAL WORDS
You should understand that the words of Shimon Hatzadik, who was the remnant of the men of the great assemby, are connected with the words of the men of the great assembly (previous mishna). For they came to rectify the torah (study/clarity), mishpatim (laws), and mitzvot, all of which are relevant to the torah, so that it won't fall, as we explained earlier. On the other hand, Shimon Hatzadik came to rectify the world so it won't fall, as he said 'on three things the world stands..'. And the level of torah is above and precedes the level of the world.

When you understand the words of Shimon Hatzadik, you will know and understand that these things he said are similar to the words of the men of the great assembly. For he was also a remnant of them. They said three things: *"be deliberate in judgment, raise up many disciples and make a fence for the Torah"*. Corresponding to "be deliberate in judgment", Shimon Hatzadik said "on the Avodah". Because Avodah and Din are connected to each other. This is what they said: "to teach that the Sanhedrin must be placed next to the Altar [of the temple in Jerusalem]" (Sanhedrin 7b).

Shimon Hatzadik said "torah" corresponding to "raise up many disciples", and "acts of kindness" corresponding to "make a fence for the torah". For the fence one accepts on himself to do is beyond what the letter of the law obligates. Likewise they said:

"The ministering angels said before the Holy One, Blessed be He: Master of the Universe, in Your Torah it is written: "The great, mighty and awesome G-d who favors no one and takes no bribe" (Deuteronomy 10:17), yet You, nevertheless, show favor to Israel, as it is written: "The L-ord shall show favor to you and give you peace" (Numbers 6:26). He replied to them: And how can I not show favor to Israel, as I wrote for them in the Torah: "And you shall eat and be satisfied, and bless the L-ord your G-d"

(Devarim 8:10), meaning that there is no obligation to bless the L-ord until one is satiated; yet they are exacting with themselves to recite Grace after Meals even if they have eaten as much as an olive-bulk or an egg-bulk. Since they go beyond the requirements of the law, they are worthy of favor" (Berachot 20a).

That is to say: because they enter and go beyond what the letter of the law obligates, therefore I too will enter and go with them beyond what justice obligates. For a person should make a fence for the torah even though he is not obligated according to the letter of the law.

We explained earlier that the men of the great assembly included in their mussar teaching a thing, namely, Din ("be deliberate in judgment"), and the thing which is its opposite, namely, "make a fence for the Torah", and a thing which is intermediate between them, namely, "raise up many disciples".

Everything was to rectify man in all, whether from the side of Din or its opposite, or the intermediate between them. Thus are most of the mussar in this tractate. So too for the words of Shimon HaTzadik when you understand the explanation above. For these things Shimon HaTzadik stated correspond to the foundations Alef-Mem-Shin, whereby water is opposite to fire and air is intermediate between them, and there is very great wisdom in this. So too for the other explanations we brought... Understand this very well for it is the true explanation of the words of the men of the great assembly and of Shimon HaTzadik.

Chapter 1 Mishna 3 - Be Like Servants

Antigonos of Sokho received [the Tradition] from Shimon HaTzadik (the Righteous). He would say, "Do not be as servants who serve their master in order to receive reward; rather, be as servants who serve their master not in order to receive reward; and may the fear of Heaven be upon you."

אַנְטִיגְנוֹס אִישׁ סוֹכוֹ קִבֵּל מִשִּׁמְעוֹן הַצַּדִּיק. הוּא הָיָה אוֹמֵר, אַל תִּהְיוּ כַעֲבָדִים הַמְשַׁמְּשִׁין אֶת הָרַב עַל מְנָת לְקַבֵּל פְּרָס, אֶלָּא הֱווּ כַעֲבָדִים הַמְשַׁמְּשִׁין אֶת הָרַב שֶׁלֹּא עַל מְנָת לְקַבֵּל פְּרָס, וִיהִי מוֹרָא שָׁמַיִם עֲלֵיכֶם.

Level 1 — Bartenura

Bartenura - "reward (Peras)" - "peras" this refers to what a person gives to someone who served him but he is not legally obligated to pay him anything. For example what a person gives to his young son or his servant due to being pleased with something he did for him. Thus, do not serve G-d even for hope of such a gift. Rather, solely out of love.

"fear of Heaven upon you" - even though you serve out of love, also serve out of fear. For one who serves out of love is quick in the positive commandments, while one who serves out of fear is careful in the negative commandments. Thus, his service will be whole. Likewise our sages said: "serve out of love, serve out of fear. For if you verge on hating, know that you [must] love and one who loves does not hate. Serve out of fear for if you verge on rebelling, know that you [must] fear and one who fears does not rebel."

Level 2 — Rabeinu Yonah

Rabeinu Yonah - one should not do the mitzvot for the reward even though he should think that there will be reward for his service... but man should serve G-d due to the kindness G-d bestowed on him already and because of the exaltedness of the Master, that it is befitting to serve Him... This is to serve G-d out of love and fear. As a servant who serves his master due to his greatness and also considers that the master is capable of punishing him. Thus he serves him with fear, not fear of punishment but fear of the greatness of the master who has the ability to punish.

Chapter 1 Mishna 3 - Be Like Servants

Q Level 2 — Tiferet Yisrael

Tiferet Yisrael - i.e. do not observe your three duties mentioned previously (torah, service, and acts of kindness) like a servant of lowly character traits who seeks reward for every little act of service he does for his master. For then, his intent is only for himself. Rather, consider yourself like a pierced servant (eved nirtza, see Exodus 21:6) whose body is acquired by his master (gufo kanui l'rabo). How then could he be so brazen to seek reward? Also consider as if all your service is just a small service and is not worthy of any reward.

Q Level 3 — Zerah Yitzchak

Zerah Yitzchak - "fear of Heaven upon you" - as written (Ketubot 111a):

" 'but you who cleave to the L-ord are all alive this day' (Devarim 4:4) - but is it possible to cling to the Shechina (Divine Presence)? Is it not written 'the L-ord your G-d is a consuming fire' (Devarim 4:24)..."

For this fear should befall a person. This is why one recites before every mitzva the "l'shem Kudsha Berich Hu, u'Shechintei b'Dechilu u'Rechimu.." (for the unification of the Holy One.. and the Shechina.. with fear and love...)

For when performing a mitzva, one is clinging to the Shechina (Divine presence), and it is proper for fear and awe to befall him, lest he transgress a bit and the great fire consumes him, as the zohar writes on the verse: "ve hachayot ratzo vshav (the Chayot angels would run and return, like the appearance of lightning)" (Yechezkel 1:14) - Zohar: "they yearn to look above and go out of their place. But they are unable to bear the intense light. Thus they run (ratzo) above and immediately return (shav) due to fear of the great fire."

So too, a man should have intent when doing a mitzva that it be with fear and love (b'rechimu ub'dechilu). And the reason he used the term "Heaven" for G-d's Name. This is because the fear here is not fear of punishment, but rather, fear from the aspect of G-d's greatness. The term Heaven teaches this. For the heaven teaches on His greatness and power in creating the heavens and vast celestial spheres, moving them without pause..

It is said of this fear: *"the fear of G-d is pure enduring forever"* (Tehilim 19:9). For the fear of punishment, suffering, poverty, death, etc., is destined to be annulled in the future. For there will be liberation from death, governments, etc. There will be no Satan nor bad mishaps. But the inner fear due to G-d's greatness will exist in the future and more, when one beholds His greatness and Almighty power.

Level 4 — Ben Ish Chai

Ben Ish Chai - Chasdei Avot - "and may the fear of Heaven be upon you" - the term "Peras" was used and not "reward" or "good", since "Peras" connotes "half", such as "your kingdom has been split and given to Madai and Persia" (Daniel 5:28)..

Some conduct themselves in fear of Heaven in the manner of a man with his wallet of money. It is hidden away in his pocket and he does not see it every second. Only when he needs to purchase an object or purchase food from the shop. But after purchasing the thing he becomes obligated to pay and the seller claims from him the money, he then takes out the wallet from his pocket and uses it to pay his debt.

So too here. The man does not remember his fear of Heaven always and he does not place it before his eyes. Only after he transgressed and stumbled in a sin, the fear rouses in his heart. For he is worried perhaps he will be punished. Then he does teshuva (repentance) on his sin. This is not the way "to the abode of light" (Job 38:19). Rather, the fear needs to be placed upon him, like a garment that he wears on his body. Every second he sees it and does not forget it momentarily (mesiach daat).

On this [fear] Rebbi Meir says in the Beraitha of Avot regarding learning torah lishma: "it clothes him with humility and fear", through this: "it makes him fit to be righteous, pious, correct and faithful". On this it is written: "I put on righteousness and it clothed me" (Job 29:14). For fear is termed with the name "tzedek" (righteousness) as known. This is what he said here specifically: "and may the fear of Heaven be upon you". That it be visible to your eyes like a garment over you. Not like a wallet of money hidden in your pocket which you do not see, except when you need to pay to your debtors.

Chida

Q Level 3

Ben Ish Chai - Chasdei Avot - there are some people with fear [of Heaven] who refrain from a forbidden thing and are careful to do mitzvot, but do this only when the refraining from the forbidden or the doing of the mitzva does not run counter to their temperament and nature. But if the thing runs against their nature, they will not fulfill them and will transgress the forbidden or not fulfill the positive commandments.

Certainly, there is not fear of Heaven in this. For fear of Heaven needs to be whole, without difference whether or not things run against one's nature. This kind of whole fear you will find in the Heaven as our sages said on the verse "who makes peace on high (oseh shalom b'imromav)" regarding the fire and water which comprise the Heaven which make peace against their nature to fulfill the decree of the Creator... (note that this refers to deep spiritual matters of kindness versus justice, i.e. chesed and din)

Maharal

Q Level 3

Maharal - we have already explained that since these men were fathers of the world and the greatest [torah sages] of their times, they would teach mussar (ethics) to the world. And the level of their mussar teaching was according to their level of greatness. For the mussar said by Shimon HaTzadik encompassed the whole world, as he taught: "on three things the world stands.." Thus too is the mussar of Antignos Ish Socho. For his words are on the service of G-d and without a doubt, the service of G-d encompasses all of man's actions. Because all of a man's actions should be directed towards the service of G-d. Therefore, he said: "Do not be as servants who serve their master in order to receive reward.. and may the fear of Heaven be upon you". We will also explain the order of Antignos after Shimon HaTzadik.

It is often asked on this:
how could he possibly say: "Do not be as servants who serve their master in order to receive reward". Isn't the whole torah full of this? - "in order that it be good for you" (Devarim 22:7), "in order that your days be lengthened" (Shemot 20:12), and many other places. Furthermore, we learned:

Chapter 1 Mishna 3 - Be Like Servants

"One who says: 'I hereby give this money to Tzedakah in order that my son may live' or 'in order that I merit a share in the World-to-Come', is considered a complete Tzadik" (Rosh Hashana 4). How then can he say: "rather, be as servants who serve their master not in order to receive reward.."?

Another difficulty: he said "rather, be as servants..." Who are these servants who do not serve on condition to receive reward? He should have just said: "do not serve to receive reward.."

Another difficulty: why did he say: "fear of Heaven upon you", and not "fear of HaMakom (the Place) upon you" or "fear of the Holy One, blessed be He, upon you".

The explanation of this teaching is that certainly the primary service is for one to serve G-d out of love. And if he does serve for the reward, this is not the primary service of G-d.

But nevertheless, even if he serves for the future reward, he is a complete tzadik. For the good of the Jewish people is G-d's will, blessed be He. Thus, that which he said "to be in the World-to-Come" - this is G-d's will.

The explanation [of "he is a complete tzadik"] is not that he is a big tzadik. But rather, that he is a tzadik without deficiency and without added piety (bli Tosefet Chasidut).

But the higher trait is for one to be called: he who serves completely out of love, i.e. one who is completely devoid of this [trait] of: "serving on condition of receiving reward".

They said thus explicitly in the first chapter of tractate Avodah Zara (19a):

> "'He delights greatly in His mitzvot' (Tehilim 112:1) Rabbi Elazar says: The person delights in His mitzvot themselves and not in the reward for performing His mitzvot. And this is the as we learned in a mishna (Avot 1:3): 'Antigonus of Sokho would say: Do not be like servants who serve their master in order to receive reward; rather, be like servants who serve their master not in order to receive reward'"

Thus, it is clear that the primary mitzva is for one to yearn for His

Chapter 1 Mishna 3 - Be Like Servants

mitzvot. On this David said: "fortunate is the man..." (Tehilim 1:1). That is to say, he is the most fortunate when he desires G-d's mitzvot and not their reward. But nevertheless, he is a tzadik even if he serves in order to be in the world to come. The torah spoke of such a tzadik and therefore said: "in order that it be good for you" (Devarim 22:7).

Alternatively, one can also explain that the verse is not saying to make the good, i.e. the reward, as one's goal. Rather, the verse means that thus it will be, that the good will come from G-d. But not that one should serve the Holy One, blessed be He, for this good. Rather, the main service is for one to serve G-d out of love and to not have any objective for receiving reward. Only that the reward comes from G-d by itself. Thus, the intent of "in order that it be good for you" (Devarim 22:7), is not that you should do the mitzvot for this... but rather that this follows from Him. This is a clear explanation - that it is not proper for the primary service to be in order to receive reward.

Regarding that which he did not say: "serve out of love", this is because it would not have implied that one should love G-d due to His own intrinsic aspect instead of [loving G-d] from the aspect of the good He bestowed to him or will bestow to him.

It would only have implied that whoever G-d has bestowed good to, he should love Him and serve Him. For that is also a form of love, namely that he loves G-d because of the good He bestowed to him.

Therefore Antignos said that one should serve G-d not on condition of receiving reward. For this is not the primary service. Although he is certainly and clearly a complete Tzadik when he serves G-d for the good He bestowed on him or will bestow on him. But the primary service is for one to love G-d and desire to do His commandments. In this, one clings to G-d from His own aspect.. For the primary love [of G-d] is when one loves G-d from G-d's own aspect, namely, when he recognizes G-d's greatness and exaltedness, and that He is Truth and His commandments are Truth.

Therefore, one loves to do His commandments. This is certainly greater than one who serves G-d [only out of gratitude] for good He bestowed to him or will bestow to him...

"may the fear of Heaven be upon you" - after he exhorted on love, he also exhorted on fear. This is because it is the way that when one loves another, his heart cleaves to him and this causes an annulment of fear. For it is proper for a man to be fearful and moved upon hearing the Name of G-d uttered, due to fear [of G-d].

Therefore, Antignos said that even though I have exhorted you on love of G-d, do not consider G-d to be your beloved which you are casual with. Rather, consider it as if G-d is in the heavens while you are on the land. Thus you should regard it - the Holy One, blessed be He, is in the heaven and you are on the earth. Through this fear of heaven will be upon you and the love will not annul the fear. Thus, he said "fear of Heaven" and not "fear of HaMakom (the Place)".

Thus, regarding fear it says "fear of Heaven", but regarding love it does not say "love of Heaven". For regarding fear, one needs to consider that the Holy One, blessed be He, is completely remote from Him. But regarding love, one needs to consider that he is clinging to Him, blessed be He, as written: "to love the L-rd, your G-d.. and to cleave to Him" (Devarim 11:22)..

We already said that this teaching is proper for Antignos since it encompasses all of the service of G-d, [establishing it] with proper love and fear. This teaching comes after Shimon Hatzadik who gave pillars to the whole world. Now the mishna comes to give a man, who exists in the world, how he should conduct himself towards his Creator, through love and fear. For the world was created for man, so that he may serve his Creator, and the service is through love and fear.

This teaching is certainly proper to be given by Antignos. For he is one person in place of two (subsequent mishnas are taught by pairs of sages). Because the primary love and fear stem from the same root (recognizing G-d's greatness and exaltedness as before). For a man needs to love G-d and fear Him. This is proper for man. It is not proper for him to fear without love or love

Chapter 1 Mishna 3 - Be Like Servants

without fear. For some acts have love alone while others have fear alone. But the man himself should have both love and fear simultaneously. Thus, for Antignos who comes to exhort on both love and fear, it is proper for him to be alone, without a pair. But for the pairs of sages who came afterwards, one comes to exhort on an act which has love alone, while the other exhorts on an act which has fear alone, as will be explained. Always one exhorts on an act which has love while the other exhorts on an act which has fear.

Q Level 4 — Chida

Chida - Roshei Avot - in the Likutei Rabeinu Chaim Vital he writes: the other sages were pairs. Yehoshua ben Perachya was the Nassi in the Sod of Chasadim (side of kindness [right line in the Sefirot]). Therefore, he said a positive commandment: "make yourself a Rav, acquire for yourself a friend and judge every person as meritorious". All positive commands from the Chasadim (kindness).

Nitai HaArbeli was the Av Beit Din (head judge) in the Sod HaGevurot (secret of justice, left line of the Sefirot). Therefore, he said a negative command: "Distance yourself from a bad neighbor, do not join a wicked person and do not despair from retribution", in the Sod HaGevurot.

But Shimon HaTzadik was in the Sod of Yesod, which is by itself (middle line of Sefirot, which is why he was called "tzadik" which corresponds to Yesod). Thus he was the remnant who collected all the Chasadim which collect there in the Sefira of Yesod. He continued there to explain the whole mishna kabalistically. That which he said they are pairs afterwards, the intent is after Antignos who received from Shimon HaTzadik. and that which he said regarding the Nassi and Av Beit Din, you will see that almost all of the pairs afterwards are in this same way.

Q Level 4 — Ben Ish Chai

Ben Ish Chai - Chasdei Avot - (Kabalistic) "in order to receive reward (Peras)" - the term "Peras" was used and not "reward" or "good", since "Peras" connotes "half", such as "your kingdom has been split (Peras) and given to Madai and Persia" (Daniel 5:28)..

For the three worlds Beriah, Yetzira, and Asiya contain a mixture of evil. Thus, the good in them is not whole since they have a mixture of impurity. Thus it is "Peras" (half), and man needs to serve Hash-em, blessed be He, in order to receive Shefa (divine flow) from the Atzilut (fourth world), of which it is written: "evil does not abide with You" (Tehilim 5:4, a reference to Atzilut). For it is the complete good.

Level 4 — Chida
Chida - Chasdei Avot - (Kabalistic) "and may the fear of Heaven be upon you" (vihi morah shamayim) - the Sofei Tevot (final letter of each word) is gematria 91, same as Havaya-Ado'nai, to hint that everything should be l'shem Kudsha beruch Hu u'Shechintei (the Holy One, blessed be He and His Shechina).

Level 4 — Ahava b'Taanugim
Rabbi Avraham Azoulai - Ahava b'Taanugim - (kabalistic) - Since Shimon Hatzadik said above that one needs to toil in torah, Avodah, and acts of kindness for these are the kiyum (existence/maintenance) of the world, as mentioned. Now Antignos comes to teach the manner of toiling in torah and mitzvot and the kavana (intent) in doing them. He said: "do not be as servants..." The explanation is as follows.

We already mentioned briefly earlier that there is no yichud (unification) above (in the mystical worlds) except through the actions of the righteous Jews (below), through toil in torah and mitzvot, and in Tefila (prayer).

Even if all the angels above and all the hosts of the heavens and all existing beings were to join together in a combined effort, nevertheless, they would not have the ability to do anything whatsoever except through the deeds of those below (humans), through their divine service, as mentioned in the Zohar (Teruma 155a, Acharei Mot 66, see also what Rabeinu wrote in Chesed l'Avraham Meain Rishon, Nahar 6).

And according to the amount of hitorerut (rousing) and hechsher (correctness) of the deed and kavana (intent) will be the

Chapter 1 Mishna 3 - Be Like Servants

corresponding widening of the tzinor (spiritual channel) and the shining of the shefa elyon (divine flow). For one who has intent for the pshat (plain meaning) of the words in his prayer is not like one who has intent for the Sod (mystical meaning).

Now, those who toil in torah, tefila, and mitzvot are of two types. Those whose service and toil in torah and mitzvot is in the way of "pshat" (plain meaning) of the words. These people are called "serving in order to receive reward". For one who did not study in the way of Sod (Kabalistic), even if he is perfect in his service, serving out of love and without any outside motive whatsoever, serving out of great love of G-d's lofty greatness, and his motive is not for any reward whatsoever. Rather his intent is absolutely perfect.

But nevertheless, he will always be referred to: "one who serves in order to receive reward". For when he prays to his Master or takes a lulav or brings an offering in the temple, etc. likewise, when he says "refaenu Hash-em veNerafe" ("heal us and we will be healed" in the Amida), or the like, all his intent is according to the meaning of the words he is uttering.

If he says "bless for us this year" ("barech aleinu.."), or "heal us..", etc., all his intent is for his own benefit, to mashpia (bring down) great good to the world. The more he increases and exerts himself in intent of his prayer, the more he is asking for a bigger reward from his Master, blessings, life, peace, etc., as it says "remember us for life" (zachrenu l'chaim..) Likewise, for his intent when shaking the Lulav to "stop bad dew" (l'atzor telalim ra-im) (Sukkah 37b), or the like. Thus, he is always taking a reward from his Master, since he did not learn the Sod of the matter.

But one who serves not in order to receive reward, he is the one whom has been graced by his Master to enter inside the inner chambers of the hidden wisdom. He knows and understands that when he says "barech aleinu" or "refaeinu", the intent in them is to draw down beracha and shefa to a certain Sefira. each blessing for a particular Sefira, as known by us. Behold, such a man serves HaKadosh Baruch Hu u'Shechintei (the Holy One, blessed be He, and His Shechina), like a son or servant who

Chapter 1 Mishna 3 - Be Like Servants

serves his master perfectly, out of love, without hoping for any benefit from him.

"and may the fear of Heaven be upon you" We may say that there is a big difference between the act of one who possesses wisdom of Sod versus the act of an Am Haaretz (ignorant person). For when the wise man has [kabalistic] intent in his prayer, his soul ascends through his rousing (hitoreruto) from level to level and from cause to cause until it reaches favorably and appears before its Master and clings to its Source, the Source of life.

Then G-d will (mashpia) send on him great shefa (divine flow) and he will be a vessel and receptacle for the flow and from there to all the worlds, as brought in the Zohar (Teruma 133, Reyah Mehemna 177), until he cleaves to the Shechina. This is the meaning of "and may the fear of Heaven be upon you". Namely, the light of the Shechina itself, it is called "fear of Heaven", it will rest on you and you will be a throne (Kiseh) for it, and the Shefa will flow to you as mentioned. For you are in place of the great tzinor (spiritual channel), in the place of the tzadik yesod olam.

But it is not so for one who has intent for the pshat (plain meaning) of the words and does not have intent in the way of Sod, as mentioned in the Zohar (Chukat 183b). He will not enter to see the face of the Shechina, and if he will be answered, it will be through an outside messenger for he is in hester panim (concealment).

Level 4 — Chida

Chida - Marit HaAyin - if you will truly merit to serve not in order to receive reward, you will merit to the resting of the Shechina and the fear of Heaven will be upon you, and you will be a merkava (chariot) to the Shechina. Some explain this to mean be careful to serve not in order to receive reward. Perhaps you will say, chas v'shalom, that He needs our service. To this he answered: "may the fear of Heaven be upon you" - everything is for man's benefit. For if he merits to serve wholy and cleanly, not in order to receive reward, his reward will be multiplied over many times. Understand this well.

Level 4 — Ruach Chaim

Chapter 1 Mishna 3 - Be Like Servants

Ruach Chaim - in the zohar (I-11:2): "there are various forms of fear, but the primary fear is to fear G-d because He is great and sovereign (shalit), and He is the source and root of all worlds".

The explanation is as follows:
"fear G-d because He is great" - i.e. due to His greatness and glory.

"and sovereign" - due to his having dominion and power to punish and exact retribution to all.

"and He is the root and source of all the worlds" - the state of all the worlds depends on His will. He grants life to everything every second... Thus it is fitting to serve Him even without reward.

To illustrate, consider if a great king would pass through the town and the king asked those standing on the street: "give me a bit of water". Certainly, all the townsmen would run to fulfill his will. The man who merited to bring the water first would undoubtedly pride himself in this always, even though the king does not recognize him and the king is from another kingdom and has nothing to do with him...

But if the visitor were from his own country then even if he was not the king and was merely a general or minor ruler, then every person would hurry to serve him due to fear of him. And if the commander were his benefactor who provides his sustenance and livelihood, he would run even if the command was for the pettiest matter. And if the visitor combined all three matters, a great king, from his own kingdom, and provider of his sustenance, how much more so, is it proper for him to be watchful and energetic, fearful and careful, to fulfill his will..

This is the intent of the Zohar. The "primary fear is to fear G-d because He is great and sovereign, the root and source of all the worlds." (all 3 conditions)

Furthermore, consider that in a kingdom, whoever is closer to the king receives greater reward. The lowly slave receives far less wages than the officer in the king's inner circle who sits with the king and can look at his face. But this high pay is only if he were an important and honorable official before this.

Namely, that due to his exceptional wisdom or talents, he merited to be in the king's inner circle. But if previously he were a mere peasant farmer working the ground and suddenly he found favor in the eyes of the king, and the king elevated him above all his officers and appointed him to be among those who sit in his innermost circle, then there is no room whatsoever to be so brazen as to ask for more reward from the king for his work..

For this privilige is already the greatest possible... so too we thank and praise on every mitzva "who sanctified us with His commandments and commanded us", and as the Zohar writes that he is among those in the King's palace, and especially for those who toil in the torah to guard it and fulfill it, whereby from every word is made a crown and garment to the Eternal King, so to speak, and he merits to be among the "sons of the King's palace"...

Thus one who seeks reward is like a peasant farmer invited to sit at the king's table and instead of basking in the king's presence, he focuses on the food on the table...

SERVING FOR REWARD IS ACTUALLY THE HIGHEST LEVEL
Nevertheless, on a deeper level, since G-d's primary intent in creation is to bestow good to his creations, then it follows that the highest and most accepted level of service is "on condition of receiving reward". For he is serving so that G-d will bestow good to him thereby granting gratification (nachat ruach) to G-d. In truth, if one has only this intent in his service, this is the lofty form of service. But if his intent is for his own benefit, then it is the lower form which we are exhorted against.

The test is if one were to tell him "serve so that your fellow will receive reward". For in the good of his fellow, G-d will also receive gratification. If he does not want this, but instead wants that the good be to specifically to himself, then his true desire is for his own benefit, not to fulfill G-d's will. But if he truly wants to serve in order that his fellow will receive good thereby granting gratification to G-d, then this Chasid (pious person) is performing the higher form of service which ascends above. For this was

G-d's purpose in creation, to bestow good...

Chapter 1 Mishna 4 - Dust Of Feet

Yossei ben Yoezer of Tzreidah, and Yossei ben Yochanan of Jerusalem, received the tradition from them. Yossei ben Yoezer of Tzreidah would say: "May your house be a meeting place for the wise; become dusty in the dust of their feet, and drink thirstily their words". יוֹסֵי בֶּן יוֹעֶזֶר אִישׁ צְרֵדָה וְיוֹסֵי בֶּן יוֹחָנָן אִישׁ יְרוּשָׁלַיִם קִבְּלוּ מֵהֶם. יוֹסֵי בֶּן יוֹעֶזֶר אִישׁ צְרֵדָה אוֹמֵר: יְהִי בֵיתְךָ בֵית וַעַד לַחֲכָמִים, וֶהֱוֵי מִתְאַבֵּק בַּעֲפַר רַגְלֵיהֶם, וֶהֱוֵי שׁוֹתֶה בַצָּמָא אֶת דִּבְרֵיהֶם

Q Level 1 — Tiferet Yisrael

Tiferet Yisrael - "received the tradition from them" - from Shimon Hatzadik and Antignos. At first they learned from Shimon Hatzadik, and when he died they completed receiving the tradition from Antignos.

Q Level 1 — Rashi

Rashi - "may your house be a meeting place for the wise" - to study [torah].

Q Level 2 — Bartenura

Bartenura - when the sages want to get together, let your house be ready for this. So that they are used to saying: "let us get together in the house of ploni". For it is impossible for you to not learn some wise thing from them. The analogy is to one who enters a perfume store. Even though he buys nothing, it is impossible for him to not absorb some of the good fragrance.

Q Level 1

Vilna Gaon - "become dusty in the dust of their feet" - i.e. go always after them as written: "He who goes with the wise will become wise.." (Mishlei 13:20). The analogy where the dust remains on him. And in Avot d'Rebbi Natan: "sit before them on the ground and receive their words with awe, fear, trembling, and sweating, in the way our forefathers received the torah at Sinai, as written in Berachot (21b).

Q Level 2 — Chida

Chida - Kikar laeden - "your house", i.e. your best and most important house give it to the sages to meet.. if you say, yes I want my house to be a meeting place for the torah sages. But nevertheless, I want them to honor me too. On this he wrote:

"become dusty in the dust of their feet", it should not be for your honor. Rather, "become dusty in the dust of their feet", to serve them like a slave.. if you honor them thus, you will merit to learn from them and: "drink thirstily their words". For they are the words of the living G-d. From this you will realize that which you did to provide your house, it was for your own benefit. For the torah is your life.

Sforno
Level 2

Sforno - "your home" - i.e. let your home be in a neighborhood where there is a meeting place of sages (i.e. a torah community). "become dusty in the dust of their feet" - even outside the batei midrash, as written by Elisha: "he got up and went after Eliyahu" (Melachim-I 19:21) (one who walks behind others becomes dusty from the dust raised by their feet).
"drink thirstily their words" - even their mundane words, as our sages said: "even the mundane words of torah scholars needs study" (Avodah Zara 19b).

Rabeinu Yonah
Level 2

Rabeinu Yonah - "drink thirstily their words" - this is as written: "A sated soul tramples honeycomb, but to a hungry soul all bitter is sweet" (Mishlei 27:7). He who is satiated from words of torah and his desire is not in them, even if he is told pearls of torah, his soul will trample it. But one who is hungry for them and lusts to hear them, even if he is told something [dry] without a reason, it will be sweet to his palate and he will rejoice in it because he knows it is truth after his Rav said it.

Ruach Chaim
Level 2

Ruach Chaim - "become dusty (wrestle) in the dust of their feet" - in the 48 ways through which the torah is acquired (chapter 6, mishna 6), one of them is: "making wise one's teacher", i.e. through his sharp questions which expand the matter. It is known that torah study is called war (milchama), as written: "milchamta shel torah (war of torah)" (Kidushin 30b). If so, the students are called warriors, and as our sages said:

"'they shall not be shamed when they speak with their enemies in the gate' (Tehilim 127:5), even a father and son or a rabbi and his student, who are engaged in Torah together in one gate become enemies with each other due to the intensity of their studies.." (Kidushin 30b)

And it is forbidden for a student to accept the words of his Rabbi when he has questions on them. Sometimes, the truth will be with the student, and "as a small piece of wood kindles a big piece" (so too students ignite the wisdom of their Rabbi).

This is the meaning of: *"become dusty (hitavek, wrestle) in the dust of their feet"*, from the word: "Jacob was left alone, and a man wrestled (became dusty) with him until daybreak" (Gen.32:24), which is a matter of battling in war. For it is a war of mitzva. So too are we against our holy teachers (buried) in the land, whose souls are on high, the famous commentaries. Their books are with us. Behold, through the books in our homes, our homes are a "meeting place" to these sages. We have been exhorted and granted permission to wrestle and battle their words and answer their questions, not to favor any man, only to love the truth. But even so, one must be careful to not speak with arrogance when finding room to disagree.. Rather it needs to be with great humility. This is the meaning of "become dusty", as before. But on condition of "in the dust of their feet", i.e. with humility and submission, to judge before them on the ground.

Alternatively explanation, "dust yourself", even if you yourself don't understand and you are just dusting yourself with the dust of their feet, nevertheless, drink thirstily their words with great desire. For it is as one who enters a perfume store and absorbs the scent (even if he buys nothing).

Q Level 3 — Maharal

Maharal - We already explained why there was no pair with Antignos of Socho as there is from here onwards. Without a doubt, this is no coincidence. The explanation is that when the Tradition passed from Moshe to Yehoshua and from Yehoshua to the Elders, etc., the latter was always on a lower level (of wisdom) than the former.

AFTER ANTIGNOS, THE TRADITION IS NO LONGER IN EACH SAGE SEPARATELY

It was not proper for the Tradition (Oral Law) to go from the "men of the great assembly" to the pairs because they are so far apart from each other. For during the pairs [of sages], the Tradition was not entirely in the hands of each one. Rather, it was in both of them together. This was unlike the Elders and Prophets. Even though they were many, the Tradition was entirely in the hands of each individual. For it does not mention how many elders or prophets so that you could deduce that the Tradition was in all of them together, as it mentions the pairs by name. This teaches that [for the pairs] the Tradition was combined in both of them together (not in each individual separately as was the case for Antignos and before him).

But the Elders, Prophets, and "men of the great assembly" were not mentioned by name. This is because the Torah Tradition was in the hands of each and every individual sage. This is why the mussar given by the "men of the great assembly" was stated in plural tense: "be deliberate in judgment" ("be" is in plural tense in hebrew). Likewise for the mussar of Antignos: "do not be like servants.." (plural tense in hebrew). But the mussar of the pairs is given in singular tense "let your house.." (singular tense in hebrew).

The reason for the plural tense (of Antignos, Shimon Hatzadik, etc.) is because there is no one with him (for he has the entire tradition in his hands). Therefore, he speaks in plural tense just like he is considered (important) as many.

But for the pairs whereby each one was not by himself and he did not have everything (i.e. the entire Oral Law), thus, the plural tense was not used, only the singular tense, just like he was a single person (i.e. not important enough to be in plural tense since he did not have the whole Oral Law).

RECTIFICATION OF ONE'S HOME

We already mentioned that the mussar is according to the greatness of the sage. Yossi ben Yoezer comes to exhort on a man's home, where he lives, that there should be wisdom there. Without a doubt, it is of great primary importance that the place where one lives should be a holy place of G-d. For a man is always there, and when his home is on a high level, it is considered that he has a great and high level. We will explain later that he is coming to rectify man's home in the service of

G-d, especially in love and fear of G-d.

We already said that Antignos rectified man himself. But man is not alone. For he needs a home, wife, and children. This pair (of sages) are coming to rectify the home he needs with love and fear. Thus, he said: "May your house be a meeting place for the wise". Namely, that there be Chachamim (torah scholars) inside his home. This is a great Shelemut (perfection), to have one's home in use by Chachamim.

He said: "become dusty in the dust of their feet". That is to say, he should not consider them as (equal) friends. For in this, he would be diminishing the virtue of wisdom since he is not yet a Chacham like them. Rather, he should connect with them, namely, lower himself under their feet. This is the meaning of "become dusty in the dust of their feet", which is their lowness (shiflutam) until he connects to their lowest part. Thus, he should mitavek (dust himself) with them to lower himself completely until he connects to their lowness (shiflutam).

This is proper because the intellect (sechel) is also separate (nivdal), and if he connects to the wise man like two friends, the chacham will not be by him at the level of Intellect which is separate (nivdal). [So too] he should not be totally separate from the Talmid Chacham, for then the talmid chacham would not be to him as the level of intellect is inside man.

Because the intellect in man is as a human being inside a house. The human is the intellect whereas the physical body is as the house. The intellect is separate (nivdal) from man. Only that man has a connection with the intellect, and through this, man is mitavek (dusts himself) with the intellect.

Thus he should relate with the talmid chacham in his house. Namely, that the talmid chacham be inside his house but that he not have a full connection to them, only "become dusty in the dust of their feet". It is proper to conduct oneself thus, just like for one's own intellect, where it is separate from man and he does not have a full connection with it. It is only found inside him. Understand this.

Chapter 1 Mishna 4 - Dust Of Feet

"drink thirstily their words" - the explanation is that just like the intellect completes (mashlim) a man, and when there is no intellect inside man, he is lacking. Hence, through the intellect man becomes complete.

Therefore so too, "drink thirstily their words". For the man who does not drink will be lacking, and if he drinks he will be complete. Therefore, (if his body lacks water) he drinks thirstily. He is very eager to fill his lacking, and all the time he is lacking, he is not in a good state. Therefore, drink thirstily their words also. For in the talmid chacham is the completion (hashlama) of men, just like the intellect is the completion of man, and when he does not have intellect, he is lacking.

Yossi ben Yoezer taught and exhorted a man on rectifying his home, that it be a house of wisdom, and that there be wise men there.

This is proper for one's home. Since, it is proper for one's home to resemble the "home" of the body. For man's body also receives the intellect. The intellect dwells in man and resides within him. Therefore, if a man wants to rectify his home so that it be proper, let his home be a "meeting place for the wise".

For all these things are also found in the intellect. The intellect is separate from man, but it has an existence within him. Corresponding to this: "may your house be a meeting place for the wise; become dusty in the dust of their feet". For this teaches on the talmid chacham, the intellect, being separate, only that he has an "existence connection" (kesher metziut) since the talmid chacham is in his home. This is only an "existence connection" (kesher metziut). For the talmid chacham is with him. But it is not a complete mixing and joining. All this follows from the way the intellect exists inside man as we explained. And because the intellect completes a man, therefore, he should also drink their words thirstily. For this shows he receives completion (hashlama) from the talmid chacham. It is proper to understand this.

Chapter 1 Mishna 5 - Home Open Wide

Yossei ben Yochanan of Jerusalem would say: "Let your home be open wide, and let the poor be members of your household. And do not converse excessively with a woman." This was said regarding one's own wife; all the more so regarding the wife of another. From here the sages said: "whoever converses excessively with a woman causes evil to himself, neglects the study of Torah, and in the end inherits Gehinom".

יוֹסֵי בֶּן יוֹחָנָן אִישׁ יְרוּשָׁלַיִם אוֹמֵר, יְהִי בֵיתְךָ פָתוּחַ לִרְוָחָה, וְיִהְיוּ עֲנִיִּים בְּנֵי בֵיתֶךָ, וְאַל תַּרְבֶּה שִׂיחָה עִם הָאִשָּׁה. בְּאִשְׁתּוֹ אָמְרוּ, קַל וָחֹמֶר בְּאֵשֶׁת חֲבֵרוֹ. מִכָּאן אָמְרוּ חֲכָמִים, כָּל זְמַן שֶׁאָדָם מַרְבֶּה שִׂיחָה עִם הָאִשָּׁה, גּוֹרֵם רָעָה לְעַצְמוֹ, וּבוֹטֵל מִדִּבְרֵי תוֹרָה, וְסוֹפוֹ יוֹרֵשׁ גֵּיהִנֹּם

Tiferet Yisrael
Level 1

Tiferet Yisrael - *"let your home be open wide"* - as much as you can to the poor and to the rich. So that whoever seeks help whether physical, financial, advice, will find it in your home.

"do not converse excessively.." - do not speak to her too much regarding the guests for "a woman is more stingy with guests than a man" (Bava Metzia 87a).

Bartenura
Level 1

Bartenura - *"let your home be open wide"* - like the house of Avraham, peace be unto him, which was open from all four directions so that guests would not need to go around it to find the entrance.

"let the poor be members of your household" - instead of buying servants to serve you. Better that Jews benefit from your property than the cursed seed of Canaan.

"do not converse excessively.." - as our sages expounded on the verse: "Who declares to man his speech" (Amos 4:13) - even casual talk between a man and his wife is related to a man at the time of judgment" (Chagiga 5b).. Another explanation, when a man tells his wife his happenings, such and such happened with so and so, she incites him to start an argument. For example by Korah, when he told her what Moshe did in lifting and waving the

Chapter 1 Mishna 5 - Home Open Wide

Leviim, and through her words, she brought him to start a dispute with Moshe. Alternatively, when her husband tells her how so and so disrespected him and embarrassed him, she will also scorn her husband in her heart. Thus he brought evil unto himself.

"neglects the study of Torah" - he is drawn after idle talk and does not study torah.

Q Level 1 — Rambam
Rambam - "whoever converses excessively with a woman causes evil to himself" - he will acquire lowly traits, namely great lust.

Q Level 1 — Ahava b'Taanugim
Ahava b'Taanugim - one who is drawn after physical pleasures becomes idle from torah. For torah and physical pleasures are like two competing wives. When one rises the other falls.

Q Level 1 — Rabeinu Yonah
Rabeinu Yonah - "all the more so for the wife of your fellow" - for the yetzer (lust) is very strong. For he thinks perhaps she will be permitted to me in the future. And even more so for the wife of a gentile (who is forbidden) since "stolen waters become sweet" (Mishlei 9:17).. And thoughts of torah cannot exist in one's mind while his heart turns to a woman and her talk. For they are two [opposite] types of thoughts which the heart cannot hold at the same time.

Q Level 2
Midrash Shmuel - "all the more so for the wife of your fellow" - why did he not say a single woman? It seems the answer is that the greater the sin, the greater the yetzer hara (evil inclination) to sin. Thus, there is a very powerful pull towards sinning with a married woman. For this he warned specifically against this.

Q Level 2 — Ruach Chaim
Ruach Chaim - "let your home be open wide" - do not be enticed by your yetzer (evil inclination), and especially in these difficult times, when he tells you: "is it not enough that you just barely provide for yourself and your household? Why should you squander your money on others?".

On this the Tanna said "let your home be open wide". On the

contrary, from this you will have a "widening" (harvacha). As before, the nature of tzedaka is that it makes wealthy. And as our sages said: "the salt (preservation) of money is to diminish it" (Ketuvot 66b).. and "the poor man does more for the host (baal habayit) than what the host does for the poor man" (Midrash Ruth).

One must also appease the poor man with words and speak to him with a pleasant facial expression, as he does with the members of his household.. and on this: *"do not converse excessively with a woman"* - even for a poor woman.

Level 3 — Maharal

Maharal - Both are together as one pair, for one was Nassi (chief rabbi) and the other was Av Beit Din (chief judge); and both together were fathers of the generation, thus, they both spoke on one matter, namely, rectifying a man's home. This is a major matter and is necessary for one to be completely rectified.

It is proper to ask on the words of Yossi ben Yochanan, who said: *"let your home be open wide, and let the poor be members of your household"*. What is the connection between these two things and *"do not converse excessively with a woman"*? It seems they are not connected to each other.

Furthermore, he said: *"this was said regarding one's own wife"*. From where is it implied that their words refer to one's own wife? He should have just said: "do not speak excessively with your wife, and all the more so, with your fellow's wife".

Furthermore, what is the matter of this evil he causes himself in speaking excessively to a woman?

Another question: he says that he becomes idle from torah study. It is superfluous to say this. For anyone who speaks much useless speech is automatically idle from torah. Furthermore, "he descends to Gehinom" - what is this great fury that he descends to Gehinom?!

The explanation is as follows. Yossi ben Yochanan of Jerusalem comes to rectify man's home to make it holy. Thus, these three things apply to a man's home. For when a man has a home,

Chapter 1 Mishna 5 - Home Open Wide

people come there to borrow things or the like. Guests also come to him when he has a home. Secondly, there are necessarily members of his household living with him in the home. Thirdly, there is his wife who takes care of the home..

Therefore, he said: *"Let your home be open wide"*, that there should be people coming there to ask their needs.

Secondly, he should not lock his door to the travellers. Rather, let them come in and receive sustenance. Corresponding to this, he said: *"let poor people be members of your household"*. That there be always poor people in his home until the poor are members of his household, thereby receiving their sustenance with honor.

Corresponding to the third tikun (rectification), namely, the wife, he said: *"do not converse excessively with a woman"*. For if he wants his home to be a holy home, as is proper, he should not *"converse excessively with a woman..all the more so regarding the wife of another"*.

For certainly, that which they said: "do not converse excessively, etc.". This is because he is coming to rectify man's home. And since his wife is the housekeeper (akeret bayit), for all matters of the house depend on her, therefore, it was necessary to rectify and say: "do not converse excessively with a woman", even for matters of the home, do not converse excessively without need. And all the more so, for the wife of your fellow which is not relevant to rectifying your home. Thus *"this was said regarding one's own wife - all the more so regarding the wife of another"*..

"From here, the sages said: "One who excessively converses with a woman causes evil to himself" - i.e. once they exhorted that even for one's wife, he should not converse excessively, then from here they said that "whoever excessively converses with a woman causes evil to himself". For if this were not so, why would they forbid [excessive] speech with one's wife?

The explanation of this is as follows. One who talks excessively with his wife tends and is drawn towards a state of existence which is lacking and clings to "inexistence" (he'ader) which is evil (i.e. since he fails to fulfill his role in the world).

And as we said earlier in the introduction, that once the woman was created, the Satan was created with her. For from "in the beginning.." (Genesis 1:1) until the creation of the woman (Genesis 2:21), the letter "Samech" is absent. But when the woman was created, the letter "Samech" appears to teach you that "once the woman was created, the Satan was created with her" (Ber.Rabba ch.17).

The explanation of this matter is as we said. For a woman is more physical than a man. Man is on the level of Tzura (form) relative to woman. And since the woman is more physical, the Satan was created with her. The Satan is the angel of death. He is a power from which "inexistence" comes to the creations. For inexistence follows from physicality, as known of the physicality that clinged to him (Adam) and drew him to inexistence.

This is the meaning of "once the woman was created, the Satan was created with her" (Ber.Rabba ch.17), i.e. relative to the (higher, more abstract) level of man, lacking and inexistence clings to the woman. This is the meaning of: *"whoever converses excessively with a woman causes evil to himself"*, i.e. when man is drawn after a woman on which clings the inexistence, and there is no greater evil than inexistence.

(translator - whereby he fails to full his purpose of bringing down torah to the world. The women's role is to build a home, raise children and other stage settings. Her role is not torah study and illumination of wisdom.)

This matter is known. However this is not at all a debasement of the woman herself. Only that this matter that a man descends from his level to be drawn after the woman by excessive talk, in this, he turns from existence towards inexistence. For him, this is a lacking and an evil. For he turns from his level of man to a level which is lacking relative to his level.

Because of this, the Tanna (sage) is not coming to diminish love between man and woman. For certainly one should "love his wife like his body". He is not at all speaking on this. Only that excessive talk with the woman lowers him fom his level of male and draws him towards the physicality which inexistence clings to. Due to this, he causes evil to himself.

This is also what they said: "neglects the study of Torah". For the woman is [more] physical. "Her wisdom is only in the spindle" (Yomah 66b). Therefore, whoever speaks excessively to the woman "neglects the study of torah".

Thus, when he turns to the speech of a woman who is physical, this is the opposite of words of torah. This is not similar to a case where he turns to mundane speech or the like (with a man). For that does not annul him from words of torah and immediately when he stops, he can return to torah.

But for speech with the woman, through this, he turns to the physical woman and clings to her. For a man clings to his wife. Such a thing is a total turning away from the torah. For he separates to increase speech with the physical woman. Through this is drawn the bitul (annulment) from words of torah.

"in the end inherits Gehinom" - this is the same matter we spoke. For "inexistence" clings to the woman, and when he increases speech with her, he turns from his level and turns towards inexistence (i.e. he goes down from the higher existence he has to illuminate himself and the world with the wisdom of torah - Translator). Therefore, he inherits Gehinom. For Gehinom is but absence of existence, as we will clarify.

(Gehinom is the state of "non-existence." It is the consequence of a person failing to fulfill his role in this world, since he then lacks any connection to an eternal existence - Rabbi Shaya Karlinsky)

This is not the same as the woman herself on whom clings inexistence. For due to that she cannot be called a "baalat Gehinom" (designated for Gehinom). The woman's portion is in Gan Eden just like the man.

But this that the man turns from his level to increase speech with the woman upon whom inexistence clings to relative to his level, on him it says "in the end inherits Gehinom". For in Gehinom, there is the Avadon (destruction) of man, and absence of his existence. For Gehinom is called "Avadon" (destruction). It is also called "tzia" and "neshia". All the names of Gehinom teach on he who comes there, that he is a "possessor of inexistence" (baal he'eder).. Thus they said: "in the end inherits Gehinom"..

Without a doubt, this is the correct explanation of the words of our sages, unlike those who explain this with imagination and their own logic. These things we said are words of wisdom which are also brought in other places by our sages. In the talmud (Bava Metzia 59a):

"Rav says: whoever follows the counsel of his wife falls into Gehinom, as it is stated: 'But there was none like Ahab, [who did give himself over to do that which was evil in the sight of G-d, whom Jezebel his wife incited]' (I Kings 21:25). Rav Pappa said to Abaye: But don't people say a popular saying: 'If your wife is short, stoop and whisper to her and consult with her?' The Gemara answers: This is not difficult, as this statement of Rav instructs that one not follow her counsel in general matters; and that saying instructs that one follow her counsel in household matters. The Gemara presents another version of this distinction: This statement of Rav maintains that one should not follow her counsel in matters of Heaven; and that saying maintains that one should follow her counsel in worldly matters."

There they explained all the things mentioned here:

In the first statement of Rav: *"whoever follows the counsel of his wife falls into Gehinom"* - for the man who is tzura (form), if he is drawn after the woman, who is of physicality and the physical is of inexistence, and he listens to her and goes after her advice, without a doubt it is proper for him to fall into Gehinom. For the matter of Gehinom is nothing but complete inexistence. Thus the names of Gehinom teach, such as she'ol (pit), avadon (destruction), tzelmavet (shadow of death). And since the tzura (form) turns from its level to be drawn after the physical in which clings inexistence, he falls in Gehinom, just like [by him] the Tzura (form) was drawn after the physical.

They asked: "But don't people say a popular saying: 'If your wife is short, stoop and whisper to her and consult with her?' The Gemara answers: This is not difficult, as this statement of Rav instructs that one not follow her counsel in general matters; and that saying instructs that one follow her counsel in household matters".

The explanation is that for "household matters", it is not called that the man is turning after the woman. Because the woman is the Akeret Bayit (housekeeper) of a man. This is the normal order of the world. Thus, if he goes after her advice in this, we don't say that the man who is the Tzura (form) turns and is drawn after the physical and turns away from his level. For in the woman's being the Akeret Habayit (housekeeper), in this aspect, inexistence does not cling to her. On the contrary, she is the foundation of the existence of the house, and it is proper to follow her advice there. But for other things in which the woman is not primary, if the man follows her advice, he is then drawn after inexistence and falls to Gehinom.

"Another version of this distinction: This statement of Rav maintains that one should not follow her counsel in matters of Heaven; and that saying maintains that one should follow her counsel in worldly matters."

According to the "second version" whereby in "worldly matters" one should follow his wife's advice.. and it is not considered then that he is drawn after inexistence. The explanation is that this world, which is physical, it's level is the level of the woman who is of physicality. Therefore from this aspect he does not have a fall in Gehinom. On the contrary, it is proper for him to follow his wife's advice for matters of this world. For they are physical matters and the woman is primary in this. But in matters of Heaven whereby certainly the man is Tzura (form) and the woman is of physicality, inexistence clings to her. Then it is relevant to say that the man is drawn after the inexistence, and if he goes after her advice, he falls in Gehinom, namely, he will come to inexistence and lacking. (he will fail to fulfill his role).

We wrote these things to clarify to you that our explanation is a clear matter.

Furthermore in Berachot (61a): "after a lion but not after a woman", i.e. although a lion can kill a man, but nevertheless it is not as dangerous as one who goes after a woman. For the lion's power over "inexistence" is not like the woman's power. Thus, after a man is drawn after a woman, in this, the man who is Tzura (form) is drawn after the physical. It is total destruction for the Tzura when it is drawn after the physical. Without a doubt, it is a greater evil for him than to go after a lion. Even though the lion can inflict damage, but this is not in essence of the lion. It's intent is only to kill and eat. But the inexistence that clings to the physical, this matter is in its essence. Thus, the lion sometimes damages and sometimes does not like all incidental matters, But it is not so for one who goes after the woman. We will explain more later with G-d's help.

We have clarified that these two sages, Yossi ben Yoezer and Yossi ben Yochanan, both came to rectify man's home in the service of G-d.

You will find that Antignos of Socho (previous mishna) exhorted man on the service of G-d itself, that it be with love and with fear. For he was only one receiver (of the torah). He was in place of a pair (of sages).

After him, the receivers of the torah were in pairs. Therefore, Antignos gave mussar like two sages of the pairs. For in the pairs, one exhorted on the service of G-d out of love while the second exhorted on the service of G-d out of fear, so that together, they would perfect (mashlim) a man in love and fear of some matter which is proper to perfect.

But Antignos who was first, he exhorted a man on the love and fear itself. Since he was first and earlier, it was proper for him to exhort on the first matter in the service of G-d, namely, love and fear itself. For love and fear are the primary beginning of the service of G-d.

Afterwards, Yossi ben Yoezer and Yossi ben Yochanan came to rectify man's home which is a great primary matter. It is close to man himself, for that is where he resides. They came to rectify it will love and fear.

Thus, Yossi ben Yoezer exhorted that there should be sages in his home and that he become dusty with the dust of their feet.

Our sages said (Sifri Devarim): " 'to love the L-ord your G-d and to cling to Him' (Devarim 11:22) - but is it possible for man to cling to the Shechina (Divine presence), is it not written 'the L-ord your G-d is a consuming fire' (Devarim 4:24)? Rather, cling to the Sages and their disciples, and I will consider it as if you had clinged to the Divine presence".

Thus, clinging to the sages is love of G-d, or at least, a branch of love of G-d. Therefore, Yossi ben Yoezer, disciple of Antignos who exhorted on love, came to rectify man's home. Namely, that there exist there love of G-d through love of the sages which is the trait of love of G-d, or at least a branch or lower level of love of G-d.

Yossi ben Yochanan rectified man's home with fear of G-d. This is what he said: "Let your home be open wide", i.e. there should be people entering to ask their needs (ex.to borrow things), or "Let your home be open wide" to guests coming in and out. Likewise for "let the poor be members of your household", all this so that one not be stingy with his money. For one who is stingy towards people and all the more so towards the poor, he diminishes fear of Heaven. Thus, he does not pay attention (mashgiach) to people that need him. For one who fears Heaven is submitted (nichna, humble) not having haughtiness of spirit. Therefore, he does not send away the poor who are submitted (humble, due to their poverty). Likewise for the guest who is wandering (from place to place). Rather, one who fears Heaven draws close the poor who are submitted. But one whose eye is stingy towards others and does not pity the poor, he is a sinner and is removing from himself the yoke of fear of Heaven.

All the more so, "do not converse excessively with a woman", for this is lightheadedness (kalut rosh) and removal of the yoke of fear of Heaven. Thus Yossi ben Yochanan came with these three things to rectify man's home.

Chapter 1 Mishna 5 - Home Open Wide

We already explained that Yossi ben Yoezer rectified man's home so that it be in the likeness of the man himself. For the Intellect stands in man's body and man's body is like a meeting house. Thus, Yossi ben Yoezer exhorted that one's house be similar to how G-d created man, as we explained earlier.

For the soul (nefesh) inside man sits in his body and is the master of the house. This soul which sits in his house is "open wide" to provide for inside, namely, the inner organs, who receive their life force and maintenance from the soul. This soul, the master of the home, does not have a complete connection with the physical. Rather the soul (nefesh) is separated (nivdal). It is not fixed in it.

On this Yossi ben Yochanan said: "Let your home be open wide", to provide for those who come from outside. Through this he is like the soul who sits in the house (body) which provides [life force] for the organs who are from the outside.

He said "and let the poor be members of your household", that you provide for the poor inside. For the soul which provides for the inner organs which are considered "members of his household" (bnei beto), so that he provides for all, whether the inner and outer organs, and all the inner powers and the powers which receive their life force from the soul.

(Translator: note that what scientists study about the body is only the outermost physical shell of what's happening. For living things are a composite of physical and spiritual powers. Go and see how scientists are totally incapable of fully understanding even the "simplest" bacteria. The more they go in the more baffled they become at all that's happening in that little universe of bottomless complexity. And that is but the outermost physical shell.)

And just like the soul is separated, it does not at all have a full connection to the physical, so too it is not proper for the master of the house (baal habayit) to have too much connection to the woman with idle speech.

Understand according to this what he said: "whoever converses excessively with a woman causes evil to himself, neglects the study of Torah, and in the end inherits Gehinom". For when the soul is attaching to the physical it is certainly idle from torah. Thus, he certainly causes evil to himself. For he clings to the evil physical and certainly descends to Gehinom which is inexistence.

Understand these things very much and you will understand the theme of the words of the sages. For Yossi ben Yoezer rectified the intellect, and the intellect is the Nassi (leader, chief) just like he was the Nassi. While Yossi ben Yochanan of Jerusalem rectified the soul (nefesh). For the nefesh (soul) is the Av Beit Din (chief judge).

This is known from the words of our sages. In the Midrash Rabba (Vayikra ch.4):
" 'when a nefesh sins' (Vayikra 4:27), the nefesh is set at a place of mishpat (judgment). Since it went out of its place of mishpat, therefore it must bring an offering".

Here is not the place to elaborate on this. For it is a matter of wondrous wisdom.

Now you will understand how the first pair of sages rectified a man with mussar totally like the mussar of Antignos. For Antignos rectified the man himself with love and fear. While his disciples, the first pair (of sages) rectified what is similar to man with love and fear, namely, man's home.

With this you will understand the whole order of things. For the "men of the great assembly" began with three matters of mussar related to the torah which is above everything. For all three things from the "men of the great assembly" were to rectify the torah and the intellect (sechel) whether in judgment (mishpat), or [understanding] words of torah, or mitzvot of the torah.

These things encompass everything that applies to the torah and the torah is above all existence and above the whole world. Afterwards, Shimon Hatzadik came to rectify the pillars of the world which are below the torah. Afterwards, his disciple Antignos came to rectify man himself who is primary in the world.

Man is like a miniature world, a world by himself. Afterwards, the first pair came to rectify man's home. Namely, that it be analogous to man himself in everything, as we wrote. Without a doubt, this is the true and clear order of things [in this mishna]...

Level 4 — Chida

Chida - Zeroah Yamin - "inherits Gehinom - he used the term "inheritance" (yerusha) because our sages said (as brought in Yearot Devash pg.74): the Serpent flees from fire. For it is from the foundation of earth, as written: "the serpent - earth is his bread" (Isaiah 65:25), and the foundation of earth is completely distant from the foundation of fire. In Kidushin (30b): "says the Holy One, blessed be He, 'I have created the evil inclination, and I have created the Torah as its antidote'". For the torah is holy fire and the yetzer hara is earth which flees away from fire. This is why the wicked are sentenced to Gehinom, to burn off the filth of the serpent. For he can only be rectified with fire. This is also why they said: "The removal of chametz (leavened bread) is to be accomplished only through burning" (Pesachim 21a).

This is the meaning of: *"whoever converses excessively with a woman"*. For she is a mishkan (Sanctuary) of the Sitra Achra (i.e. man brings tumah on himself by speaking too much with a woman due to natural animalistic lust - translator). All the more so when she is a Nidda, for her Tuma is strong.

"causes evil to himself" - the black garment (gunda) of the serpent, "to himself", for it clings to him and his flesh. This leads to being drawn to idleness from torah which is the antidote to the Yetzer Hara. When it strengths more and he stops to learn (torah), there is no medicine to remove the filth and chase away the serpent except for Gehinom.

He used the term "inheritance" which implies it is prepared and comes by itself to a man. So too from the time he came to excessive talk with the woman, one evil after another comes to him. For both the Sitra Achra and Gehinom are called "evil", and it is prepared for him like an inheritance.

Level 4 — Chida

Chida - Kikar l'Eden - This person brought himself to excessive speech with the woman, bringing sin upon his shoulders. For kol b'isha erva (the voice of a woman is nakedness/incitement to lust), v'histaklut b'nashim zima v'avon plili (staring at women is lewdness and a great sin). Thus, he allowed and prepared himself for the ruling over him of the Sitra Achra, which is called "evil". This is the meaning of "causes evil to himself". The Sitra Achra strengthens over him and does not allow him to learn torah. It wraps around him and he has many beteilim (distractions) preventing him from learning. One evil after another befalls him. For Gehinom is called "evil". He inherits his fellow's portion in Gehinom for he did not merit (Gan Eden), leaving him with his portion and his fellow's in Gehinom, as our sages said:

"Every person has two portions, one in Gan Eden and one in Gehinom. If he merits, by becoming righteous, he takes his portion and the portion of his wicked colleague in the Gan Eden; if he is found culpable by becoming wicked, he takes his portion and the portion of his colleague in Gehinom" (Chagigah 15a).

This is the meaning of "and in the end inherits Gehinom", like an inheritance which comes by itself.

Level 4 — Chida

Chida - Petach Einayim Eruvin 53b - Another explanation, through much talk he will come to lashon hara (slander), whereby he exchanges his merits with the sins of the person he spoke on. Thus he "inherits" Gehinom coming from another place.

Just how far is this fence of "do not converse excessively with a woman", we can learn from the Talmud: "Rabbi Yosei HaGelili was walking along the way, and met Berurya (the wife of Rabbi Meir). He said to her: 'On which path should I walk in order to get to Lod?' She said to him: 'Foolish Galilean, didn't the Sages say: Do not talk much with women? You should have said your question more succinctly: Which way to Lod?'" (Eruvin 53b).

We learn from here just how far is the fence of "do not converse excessively with a woman". He should have said: "Which way to Lod". All the rest is "excessive talk". Woe to us from the Day of Judgment, Woe to us from the Day of Rebuke.

Chapter 1 Mishna 6 - Make A Rav

Yehoshua ben Perachiah and Nitai of Arbeli received from them. Yehoshua ben Perachia would say: "Make for yourself a Rabbi, acquire for yourself a friend and judge every person to the side of merit"

יְהוֹשֻׁעַ בֶּן פְּרַחְיָה וְנִתַּאי הָאַרְבֵּלִי קִבְּלוּ מֵהֶם. יְהוֹשֻׁעַ בֶּן פְּרַחְיָה אוֹמֵר, עֲשֵׂה לְךָ רַב, וּקְנֵה לְךָ חָבֵר, וֶהֱוֵי דָן אֶת כָּל הָאָדָם לְכַף זְכוּת

Level 1 — Rashi

Rashi - "Make for yourself a Rabbi" - do not learn on your own from your own logic. Rather, from a Rav and from the Tradition (Mesorah).

"acquire for yourself a friend" - some say books and others say an actual (human) friend , since "two are better than one" (Kohelet 4:9). Likewise they said: "A sword on those who hate the students of the Sages, who sit and busy themselves with Torah alone. Not only that but they become more foolish.." (Taanit 7a).

"judge every person to the side of merit" - on whatever you hear about him, say that he had good intentions, until you are certain that it is not so. If you judge thus, you will be judged meritoriously in Heaven, as explained by our sages (Shab.127b).

Level 1 — Sforno

Sforno - "judge every person to the side of merit" - for without this trait no friendship can endure. For in most words the listener can find a way to judge the speaker unfavorably. Thus, any friendship will be destroyed without a doubt.

Level 1

Meorei Ohr in name of Rabeinu Yedaya hapnini - "acquire for yourself a friend" - they exhorted that one even spend money and give a house full of gold and silver. For the friend will be more beneficial and will grant you more wisdom than the Rav. This is because one is embarrassed from the Rav to ask him all his questions, and "a bayshan (shy and self-conscious person) cannot learn properly" (Avot 2:5). But he will not be embarrassed from his friend and both will ask each other and clarify the

Halacha and sharpen each other, arriving at the truth of the matter.. as they taught: "I learned much from my Rabbis, and even more from my friends" (Taanit 7a). For a man will learn more with his friend than from the Rav as we explained.

🔍 Level 2 — Rabeinu Yonah

Rabeinu Yonah - "make for yourself a Rabbi" - even if your level of knowledge is equal to his, nevertheless make him a Rav on yourself. For a person remembers better what he learned from his Rav than what he learned by himself. Furthermore, even if both of you are equal in wisdom, sometimes you will understand better than him and wind up teaching him.

"acquire for yourself a friend" - for three things one needs a good friend. One, for torah, as they said: "I learned much torah from my Rabbis but more so with my friends and most of all from my students" (Taanit 7a).

Two, for mitzvot. For even if one's friend is less pious than him. Nevertheless, sometimes one also acts improperly due to lusting for something [bad]. But one will not desire that his friend do that [bad] thing since one does not stand to gain any benefit from his friend's sin, as our sages said: "a man does not sin unless he gains benefit" (Kidushin 63b).
Thus, when he rebukes his friend for sinning, his friend will do the same to him and both will do teshuva (repentance) do to each other.

Three, for advice. To take him as an advisor for help in all his matters and to obtain good advice and be a trustworthy keeper of secrets... on this Shlomo said: "Plans are foiled for lack of counsel, but they are established through many advisers" (Mishlei 15:22).

He used the term "acquire [for yourself a friend]". For if you cannot find him for free, acquire him using your money. Spend money abundantly to acquire a good friend, or befriend him with nice words and a gentle tongue. Do not become insulted (makpid) by his words and bear his mouth. Even if he says something (bad) against you do not answer him. For otherwise the love will not remain and the friendship will split. Sometimes you will ask for something and your beloved friend will answer:

"that is not right!" If you don't tolerate him and let it pass, the cord of friendship will unwind.

This is what Shlomo said: "He who covers an offense seeks love, but he who harps on a matter separates close friends" (Mishlei 17:9), i.e. one who covers over when his friend wrongs him - seeks love. For by bearing his misdeeds, their love will endure. But "he who harps on a matter" - if one's friend says something against him and one gets upset saying: "see what he said against me!", will nevertheless "separates close friends", i.e. his friend.

"judge every person to the side of merit" - and in a tzadik, even if his act was certainly bad without a doubt, nevertheless judge him favorably as our sages said: "if you saw a torah scholar commit a sin at night, do not suspect him at day for certainly he repented" (Berachot 19a)...

Ruach Chaim
Ruach Chaim - *"acquire for yourself a friend"* - even with money, in order to obtain advice from him even on religious matters. For if you are wise in your own eyes, the yetzer hara can blind your eyes and make the crooked appear straight. Therefore seek counsel with your friend. For your yetzer hara is not so close to him to deceive him (i.e. your friend is more objective in your matters, thus he can see more clearly than you in them).

Rambam
Rambam - *"Make for yourself a Rabbi"* - even if he is not fit to be a Rav to you. Nevertheless, make him a Rav to you and consider him a teacher. Through this you will gain wisdom. For learning by oneself is not the same as learning through another. Learning by oneself is good, but learning from another will endure more and be clearer, even if the person is equal to you in wisdom or below you.

"acquire for yourself a friend" - he used the term "acquire", not "make for yourself a friend" or "join others". The intent in this is that one needs to acquire a friend for himself so that he will rectify his deeds and matters through him, as they said: "or a friend or death" (Taanit 23a).
If he does not find one, he needs to strive with all his heart, even if he needs to spend money in order to draw his love until he

becomes a close friend.

Do not sway from being drawn after his will always until the love strengthens. And as the mussar masters said: "when you love, do not love according to your trait but rather according to the trait of your beloved". (explained below)

When both friends intend on this command, the intent of each of the two will be to find favor with the other (lehafik ratzon chavero), and undoubtedly both will have a unified intent (i.e. there will be peace and harmony).

And how good is the saying of Aristotle:

The beloved is one but the lover is of three types: "love of benefit", "love of tranquility", and "love of virtue".

"love of benefit": such as the love of two (business) partners, or the love of a king and his army.

"love of tranquility (menucha)": this subdivides into two types. One, love of pleasure and two, love of trust (bitachon).

Love of pleasure: such as the love of men to women, or the like.

Love of trust: is when a man has a friend whom his soul trusts. He will not guard from him in deed or speech. He will tell him of all his matters, whether good or bad, without fear of incurring a loss to himself or others. When a person reaches this level of trust in his friend, he will find great tranquility in his matters and abundant love.

"Love of virtue" is when both friends desire and have the same intent, namely, good. Each wants to help the other, so that both reach the good together. (end quote)

This is the type of friend we were commanded to acquire. It is like the love of a Rav to the Talmid (disciple), and the Talmid to the Rav.

Q *Level 3* **Maharal**

Maharal - It is proper to ask here: Why did he say "make for yourself a Rabbi" and not "take for yourself a Rabbi?". Another question: why the change of terms to say "make for yourself" regarding a Rav and "acquire [for yourself]" regarding a friend. Another question: how are these three things connected? Another question: why did he not also say "make for yourself a student". For our sages said: "I learned the most from my students" (Taanit 7a).

The explanation of this is as follows. The previous pair rectified a man's conduct in his home, which is close to him. We also clarified (last mishna) that man's conduct in his home is similar and related to his own conduct (with himself).

This pair, who were their disciples, now come after them to rectify how a man should relate to the public.

The first two (Rabbi and friend) are outside his home. But nevertheless they are also very close to him. The third is regarding other people. For a man is with his Rabbi then afterwards with his friend and afterwards with other people.

"make for yourself a Rabbi" - the intent is not for his main Rabbi (Rav Muvhak). On that he would not have said: "make for yourself". Rather, the explanation is to make for oneself a Rabbi even though the person is not (completely) on the level of being one's Rabbi. This is the meaning of "make for yourself". For it is impossible for you to not learn at least something from him. And for that something it is enough to "make" him a Rabbi [on yourself].

"acquire a friend for yourself" - by a friend it is relevant to say "acquire". For a friend is your acquisition (kinyano). Unlike the Rabbi who is not the acquisition of the student. Thus there he said "make for yourself a Rabbi".

But it is the way of friends to do favors for each other, taking care of each other's needs. Thus they are like acquisitions (assets) to each other.

Regarding both, even if the Rabbi is not completely on the level to be his Rabbi and likewise the friend is not on the level to be his friend, but nevertheless two are better than one, and acquire him anyways as a friend.

"judge every person to the side of merit" - if he sees something (bad) in someone, he should judge him favorably and not distance him thinking he is a wicked man.

These three things concern man's conduct with people outside his home. Namely, make for yoursef a Rabbi even if he is not completely fit to be your Rabbi. Acquire a friend even if he is not completely fit. While for other people who are not on your level, do not distance them at least all the time it is possible to judge them favorably.

He did not say "acquire for yourself a student". For it is not proper for a man to make himself into a Rabbi and take for himself an important title telling others to learn from him..

These three things correspond to three types of people. The first is those who are considered above him like the Rabbi. The second is those who are similar to himself like a friend. The third is the rest of people, even those of lower level than oneself. Thus, "judge every person to the side of merit". Even if he is lower than you do not judge him badly...

Regarding the connection between these three things we can also explain as follows. That which he said "make for yourself a friend", the intent is that the making of the Rabbi be complete and enduring. Llikewise for the acquiring of a friend, that the friendship not depart at all for all the days of one's life, as written: "Do not abandon your friend and your father's friend" (Mishlei 27). For since he is your friend and was also your father's friend, do not abandon him. For this is a faithful friend, not one who comes anew. Therefore, he said: "judge every person favorably". For since he is habitually with the Rabbi or the friend, it is impossible for there to not arouse times when you think he wronged you. For you spend much time with him and thus you will come to break off and separate Therefore he said on this: "judge every person to the side of merit".

When you judge him favorably, there will not be separation

between you and the Rabbi or you and the friend. For you will judge him favorably when you suspect he wronged you. This is clear.

Level 3 — Alei Shur

Alei Shur II 6:10 - "judge every person to the scale of merit" - every deed of every person can be weighed on scales - meritorious or guilty? This is because there are two driving forces in man: the good inclination and the evil inclination. In every deed it is possible that its source is from this or from that. But since man can only see what appears to his eye, he cannot examine the heart and thoughts [of others], therefore we have been commanded to *"judge every person to the scale of merit"*. Our sages learn this from the verse: *"you shall judge your fellow with righteousness"* (Vayikra 19:15).

Divrei Binah (Admorei Biala)

Divrei Binah (Admor Biala) - this needs understanding. Why did he say: "make yourself a Rav" and not: "accept on yourself a Rav". What relevance (shaychut) is the term "make" on the matter of accepting a Rav?

(Answer:) the primary Shlemut (perfection) of a man is that he strives to sanctify and purify (lekadesh u'letaher) his 248 limbs (evarim) and 365 sinews (gidim) until they are elevated to the level where the limbs and sinews themselves pull him to fulfill Hash-em's commandments, blessed be He. And from his own self he will be capable to learn and understand the ways of G-d and His will, blessed be He. As we find by our holy forefathers, that on their own they fulfilled the whole torah before it was given.

For through the holiness of their bodies and limbs, on their own, they could understand and sense His will, blessed be He, in all their deeds. Through this, they would fulfill all the 613 commandments which correspond to the 248 limbs and 365 sinews. This is the meaning of "make yourself a Rav". Namely, see to it to make yourself and your body a Rav and mentor, so that through the holiness of your body, you will be able to sense His will, blessed be He, on your own.

Acquire for yourself a friend (chaver) - through this, you will merit to be connected and attached to Hash-em, blessed be He. For the word "mitzva" is from the word "communion" (tzavta) and attachment (chibur). It is an aspect of "acquiring" (kinyan), as our sages said on the verse: "Who acquired Heaven and Earth" (Lech lecha) - Rashi: "through making them, He acquired them and they are His".

This is the meaning of: "acquire for yourself a friend (chaver)", see to it to acquire (make) yourself to be on the aspect of "chaver" to Him, blessed be He.

And then "remove yourself from doubt" (later in Avot 1:16), your deeds will no longer have any suspicion and any doubt of sin, ch'v, and all your deeds will be l'Shem Shamayim in truth, without any doubts...

Q Level 4 — Chida

Chida - Zeroa Yamin - perhaps the words are referring to the yetzer tov and yetzer hara (good and evil inclination). Thus, "make for yourself a Rabbi" on the yetzer tov. Namely, recognize his wisdom and accept him as a Rav to do all that he commands. While the yetzer hara is the "chaver" (friend), as they said in Chagiga (16) on the verse: "believe not a friend" (Micha 7:5). There it learns out that the Creator called him "evil from youth". All agree that he is an "evil friend".. the main job is to sweeten and change the yetzer hara into good. This is the meaning of "acquire for yourself a friend", i.e. the known "friend" who is your "friend" from the day of your birth. Acquire him to make him good. Acquire him to sweeten his bitterness.

Q Level 4 — Chida

Chida - Marit Haayin - perhaps too, these three correspond to the three Sefirot Chagat (Chesed, Gevurah, Tiferet). "make for yourself a Rabbi" corresponds to Tiferet (Torah). "acquire for yourself a friend" corresponds to Gevurah, to strengthen oneself (lehitgaber) to not be makpid (upset) at all and love him like yourself, "judge every person to the side of merit" corresponds to Chesed, abundant Chesed to judge favorably.

Chapter 1 Mishna 7 - Bad Neighbor

Nitai of Arbeli would say: Distance yourself from a bad neighbor, do not join a wicked person, and do not abandon belief in retribution.

נִתַּאי הָאַרְבֵּלִי אוֹמֵר, הַרְחֵק מִשָּׁכֵן רָע, וְאַל תִּתְחַבֵּר לָרָשָׁע, וְאַל תִּתְיָאֵשׁ מִן הַפֻּרְעָנוּת

Q Level 1 — Tiferet Yisrael

Tiferet Yisrael - a bad neighbor - an angry person, an arrogant person, a jealous person, or the like. Not only should you not join him lest you learn from his deeds and damage your soul, but even distance from him lest he damage even your body.

Q Level 1 — Rashi

Rashi - "do not abandon belief in retribution" - if you are rich, do not trust in your wealth. For troubles can come quickly, as written: "Fortunate is the man who is always afraid, [but he who hardens his heart will fall into evil]" (Mishlei 28:14). So too, if troubles befall you, do not give up hope for salvation is near to come, as written: "Behold, the hand of the L-ord is not too short to save" (Isaiah 59:1).

Q Level 2 — Rabeinu Yonah

Rabeinu Yonah - "Distance yourself from a bad neighbor" - to one who looks to rent or buy a house, just like one inquires whether the house is nice and in a good location, so too, he should inquire on the neighbors. If they are bad, distance. If they are good, approach.

"do not join a wicked person" - it is a great punishment without equal. For if one committed a serious sin, it is one sin. But this person has a portion in all the sins the wicked man committed as a reward for joining his company. Thus he commits many great and severe sins even though he did nothing and did not derive any benefit. "Woe to the wicked, woe to his neighbor". Thus it is explained in Avot D'Rebbi Natan (30:3): "whoever joins the wicked receives punishment like them even though he does not do like them; whoever joins the righteous receives reward like them even if he did not do like them". On this it is written: "When you joined Ahaziah, the L-ord has broken your work" (Divrei

Hayamim II 20:37).

"do not abandon belief in retribution" - do not tell yourself: "I will join the wicked now while he is in prosperity and success and when his good situation changes, I will distance from him!" You will not be able to. For you cannot know what today will bring. In an instant his calamity can come and you will be struck with him.. it is a great sin to flatter the wicked in this world... his calamity will come suddenly and you will not be able to save yourself.

Level 2 — Ahava b'Taanugim
Rabbi Avraham Azoulai - Ahava b'Taanugim - "do not join a wicked person" - i.e. if he joins you, namely, you are primary (ikar) while he is subordinate (tafel) then it is good. For there is hope he will listen to your words since you are primary. But if he will be primary (ikar) and you will be subordinate. He will certainly not listen to your words. On this "do not join" him, i.e. when you are subordinate to him.

Level 3 — Maharal
Maharal - like Yehoshua ben Perachya, Nitai HaArbeli comes to rectify one's conduct with others outside the home. Only that Nitai HaArbeli rectifies this with mussar of Yirat Shamayim (fear of Heaven).

It is proper to ask on his words. Why bring these three things together?

The explanation is that Nitai HaArbeli came to rectify man's conduct with other people outside his home. He said to distance oneself from a bad neighbor so as not to be burned by the hot coal of a bad neighbor, as written: "woe to a wicked person, woe to his neighbor" (Negaim ch.12). Therefore "distance yourself from a bad neighbor", as written: "when you joined Ahaziah, the L-ord broke your work" (Divrei HaYamim II 20).

That which he did not use the same term throughout, such as "do not draw close to a bad neighbor, do not join with a wicked man", or "distance from a bad neighbor and from joining a wicked man". (But instead he changed terms "distance from a bad neighbor", "do not join a wicked man").

The reason is that the two are different matters. For even if he does not draw close to a bad neighbor and the bad neighbor comes to him, he needs to distance from him. This is not relevant to say by a friend "distance from a bad friend". For it is enough to not join him. For when he does not join him, he is already distant from him.

"do not abandon belief in retribution" - do not think you are distant from evil and therefore you can come close to potentially evil things and no harm will befall you. On this he said: "do not abandon belief in retribution", thus do not draw near evil.

A deeper look
"distance yourself from a bad neighbor, do not join a wicked person, and do not abandon belief in retribution" - that which he said "do not abandon belief in retribution" is also similar to "distance from a bad neighbor, etc." For evil is also like a neighbor to people. As known of the matter of evil. It dwells and is joined to existing things. Thus he said: "do not abandon belief in retribution". For evil is the neighbor of people. Therefore do not not join or go near evil for you will be harmed, and "do not abandon belief in retribution" who is close by and a neighbor of people.

This refers to inexistence (he'eder) which clings to people. It is more of a neighbor than one's (human) neighbor nearby, and nearer than your closest friend. For it sits opposite a man to destroy him. Thus, he said these three things together.

Understand their order "distance yourself from a bad neighbor, do not join a wicked person, and do not abandon belief in retribution", which is opposite man.

The latter is a warning to man to not think it is not possible for him to be struck with retribution. He did not say to worry about sufferings. For worrying about sufferings is a bad trait, as we wrote on the Netiv Habitachon with G-d's help. Rather he said "do not abandon belief in retribution", as happened to Haman.

He trusted in his great wealth and in the blink of an eye all his success flipped on him. This is the meaning of "do not abandon belief in retribution".

Some explain "do not abandon belief in retribution" as a reason for "distance yourself from a bad neighbor, do not join a wicked person". Namely, do not tell yourself: "even if I don't distance from a bad neighbor and from the wicked man, I will still be at peace. For what could possibly happen to me?"

On this he said: "do not abandon belief in retribution". For it is possible for calamity to strike suddenly. Therefore, don't say that, and because of this "Distance yourself from a bad neighbor, do not join a wicked person".

All this is coming to exhort on fear of Heaven (yirat shamayim) so that he does not come to sin. For without a doubt, a bad neighbor and a wicked friend bring a person to sin.

Thus, Yehoshua ben Perachya (previous mishna) came to rectify man's conduct with those who are outside his home but relevant to him, such as the Rabbi, friend, and other people. This was a rectification and branch from the side of love of G-d.

Here Nitai HaArbeli came to rectify man in fear of G-d in things opposite to this, namely, the wicked. Thus, "distance yourself from a bad neighbor, etc."

Hence, both of their teaching is on one matter...

Level 4 — Chida

Chida - Zeroah Yamin - perhaps he is exhorting on the yetzer hara, whom the Creator called "evil" (Chagiga 16). He is within you lying in ambush. Thus, "distance yourself from an evil neighbor", i.e. that neighbor who is called "evil".. For if you don't distance, you will become a sanctuary of the Sitra Achra (forces of evil).

If you say: "since he is the angel of death and is appointed over all suffering and damage (tzaar v'nezek), if I join him, he will protect me. Just like a criminal is protected when he joins the rebels against the king". On this he answered: "do not abandon belief in retribution". For it is the way of the Sitra Achra to slaughter those who listen to him, as written in the holy Zohar.

Level 4 — Chida

Chida - Roshei Avot - "distance yourself from an evil neighbor" - from the yetzer hara as we explained earlier, and "do not abandon belief in retribution". i.e. even though you greatly distanced from the yetzer hara don't think you already reached perfection (Shelemut). For who knows what you damaged in previous Gilgulim (lives)..

Chapter 1 Mishna 8 - Legal Advisors

Yehuda ben Tabai and Shimon ben Shetach received [the Tradition] from them. Yehuda ben Tabai would say: "Do not make yourself like a 'legal advisor'; and when the litigants stand before you, they should both be as wicked in your eyes; and when they depart from before you, they should both be as meritorious in your eyes, when they have accepted the judgment." יְהוּדָה בֶּן טַבַּאי וְשִׁמְעוֹן בֶּן שָׁטָח קִבְּלוּ מֵהֶם. יְהוּדָה בֶּן טַבַּאי אוֹמֵר, אַל תַּעַשׂ עַצְמְךָ כְּעוֹרְכֵי הַדַּיָּנִין. וּכְשֶׁיִּהְיוּ בַּעֲלֵי דִינִין עוֹמְדִים לְפָנֶיךָ, יִהְיוּ בְעֵינֶיךָ כִּרְשָׁעִים. וּכְשֶׁנִּפְטָרִים מִלְּפָנֶיךָ, יִהְיוּ בְעֵינֶיךָ כְּזַכָּאִין, כְּשֶׁקִּבְּלוּ עֲלֵיהֶם אֶת הַדִּין

Q Level 1   Tiferet Yisrael
Tiferet Yisrael - "they should both be as wicked in your eyes" - suspect that their claims are false and perhaps you will catch them in their words.

Q Level 1   Bartenura
Bartenura - "they should both be as wicked in your eyes" - do not turn your heart towards one of them thinking "he is an important person and would not claim falsely". For if you do this, you cannot see in him fault.

Q Level 2   Ruach Chaim
Ruach Chaim - for in examining the witnesses, sometimes one needs to employ strategies and deceptions to trick the witnesses in order to extract the full truth from their mouths. But one must do this with great wisdom so that the witness does not notice this and so he won't tell himself: "the judge is trying to trick me, thus it is permitted and I will do the same". For he does not realize that this is permitted only for the judge but not for him, and he sins.

Q Level 1   Tiferet Yisrael
Tiferet Yisrael - "and when they depart from before you, they should both be as meritorious in your eyes" - do not suspect the claimant was a thief or the defendant swore falsely. For how great is the punishment for "suspecting a kosher person" (choshed b'kesharim) (Shab.97a), and how great is the reward for judging your fellow to the side of merit (Shab.127b).

Q Level 1   Rashi

Chapter 1 Mishna 8 - Legal Advisors

Rashi - "when they have accepted the judgment" - since they accepted the judgment, and one was obligated to swear and he swore and left. Don't suspect him in your heart thinking he swore falsely.

Level 1 — Sforno
Sforno - even if you found out they both lied or one of them lied, they should not be suspect in your eyes to sin. For sometimes a person claims a lie not in order to steal from his fellow but rather to buy some time, as they said: "he is trying to delay thinking when I have money, I will pay him" (Bava Metzia 2b).

Level 2 — Rambam
Rambam - "legal advisor" - these teach people the legal claims and laws until a person is proficient (baki) in his court case. They compose questions and answers. "When the judge says this, answer this", "when the claimant says this, answer this". As if they are arranging the court case and the two sides are before them. Thus, they are called "legal advisors" (archei dayanim) as if they arrange the court case before them. The sages exhorted us not to resemble them, i.e. not to teach one of the two litigants a claim which will help him saying: "say thus", or "deny in such and such a way". Even though you know he is wronged and the other person is lying.. Nevertheless, it is not at all permitted to teach him a claim which will save him and help him.

Level 2 — Rabeinu Yonah
Rabeinu Yonah - "legal advisor" - this is not referring to a case where one instructs his friend to blatantly lie. Because that would make him a completely wicked person and it is not necessary to say that one should not do this for it is a great sin. Rather, the explanation is that even if one does not teach him to lie, and he merely organizes his claims and arranges the laws before him and explains to him his judgment, nevertheless, it is not proper to do this. For people will suspect him and speak bad of him. This is as the case of Rabbi Yochanan (Ketuvot 52b) who initially thought to help his relative citing the verse: "from your flesh (relative), you shall not hide" (Isaiah 58:7) but then abstained saying "an important person is different" (for it causes a desecration of G-d's Name).

Level 3 — Maharal
Maharal - we already said that the mussar of these sages is on things which are necessary and of primary importance. Yehuda

Chapter 1 Mishna 8 - Legal Advisors

ben Tavai saw that it was a great stumbling block for the public that which the judges were doing and even many great sages and tzadikim as brought in the talmud (Ketuvot 52b):

"Rabbi Yochanan said: 'we made ourselves like legal advisors (orchei dayanim)'", and likewise later there: "Rabbi Nachman said 'we made ourselves like legal advisors (orchei dayanim)'" (Ketuvot 86b).

Thus, Rav Nachman said on himself: "we made ourselves like legal advisors (orchei dayanim)". Due to this, a great exhortation is necessary. For with merely a few words one becomes "a legal advisor". And this is forbidden in mishpat (judgment) and din (justice), for it is a very serious matter to distort mishpat and din. And because this sin very much needs exhorting so that one does not stumble therein, therefore Rabbi Yehuda ben Tabai comes on this...

Thus, this pair of sages came to rectify judgment which is extremely necessary, to not be like the "legal advisors (orchei dayanim)". For this needs exceedingly great guarding. Since it is of great importance in judgment. Therefore, they exhorted to not cause the judgment to come out distorted.

Likewise it is very common for a judge to stumble thinking one of the two litigants to be more righteous than the other (thus he said "when the litigants stand before you, they should both be as wicked in your eyes").

Similarly, for the words of Shimon ben Shatach, to "examine the witnesses extensively". For their testimony can vary in many ways. This matter is a great foundation. For sometimes the witness adds something in his testimony or leaves out one word in which everything depends [thereby changing the whole testimony].

So too, the judge needs to be careful in his words when interrogating the witness. For through the question, the witness can deduce the intent of the questioner and correct his words to strengthen his lie. This matter does not need explanation. Thus, these two sages came to rectify justice with something which is an extremely great and primary matter...

FULFILLING JUSTICE IS LOVE AND FEAR OF G-D

Fulfilling justice is a close branch of love of G-d. For he who loves G-d, loves His judgments. For "Judgment belongs to G-d" (Devarim 1:17).

(Rashi there: "Whatever you unjustly take from someone, you will oblige Me to return to him. Consequently you have perverted a judgment against Me, San. 8a").

Therefore, due to love of G-d, he does G-d's justice truthfully . For this is very much G-d's will. Likewise G-d hates wrongdoing and falsehood in judgments, and it is an abomination in His eyes. Therefore, the G-d fearing person fears from G-d to distort the word of justice. The mussar of this pair of sages is also a further branch of love and fear of G-d...

ORDER OF THE MISHNAS

We already explained earlier how the flow of mussar from these sages follows one after the other until they are all connected to each other. The words of this pair of sages is likewise connected to that of the previous pair. For the previous pair rectified a man's relation with the public near to him. Thus he said: "Make for yourself a Rabbi, acquire for yourself a friend and judge every person to the side of merit". All this is relevant (shayich) to a man. Likewise, the previous pair before rectified one's home properly.

For one needs to first rectify himself. This was the tikun of Antignos of Socho. Afterwards, he needs to rectify his home. This was the tikun of the first pair (after Antignos). And afterwards, the rectification with the public outside his home but which is relevant (shayich, i.e. near) to him like the Rav (teacher), the friend, and other people. This was the tikun of the second pair. For the Rav and friend are very important to a man. Afterwards, the third pair rectified how a person's conduct, such as the judge should be towards the public. For the judge judges and establishes judgment on the public.

Chapter 1 Mishna 8 - Legal Advisors

The earlier ones rectified a man regarding his conduct with the public greater than him, as explained. This pair, and also the next one, comes to rectify how the Gadol (great man) should conduct himself towards the public which is below his level.

A Gadol (great man) is on two ways. One is the judge. This pair rectified him.

Two, the baal serara (person of authority, ex. community Rabbi). The next pair came to rectify him that so that everything relevant to a man is rectified...

Q Level 4 — Chida

Chida - Zeroa Yamin - "do not make yourself like a 'legal advisor'" - besides the plain meaning, there is possibly also a hint of mussar rebuke to a man. Namely, do not seek arguments to diminish your sin and make it smaller with empty and patched up claims, hanging it with cobwebs like the "legal advisors" do. For even though the defendant's obligation is clear, they seek ways to justify him with various claims and fine distinctions. For this is the primary wisdom of the yetzer hara (evil inclination), to diminish man's sin and seek merits for him. And as the early ones explained on the verse: *"And the L-ord saw that the evil of man was great in the earth, and every imagination of his heart was **only** evil all the time"* (Gen.6:5). "only" is a mi-ut (coming to exclude), i.e. to diminish the evil (try to make it smaller than it really is).

This is not the way of a baaal nefesh (upright person). On the contrary, if he committed a small sin, it will be very big in his eyes. For he transgressed the word of Hash-em, G-d of the world, and in a hair's breadth, there is already no medicine for his illness. It is a kal v'chomer (logical inference) from flesh and blood kings of the land who strike down, punish, and execute for the slightest transgression of their word.

This is what king David said: "For I relate my iniquity; I worry about my sin" (Tehilim 38:19), the word "agid" (worry) is like "devarim kashim k'gidim" (things hard as sinews). Namely, "my sin agid", in my eyes it is very severe. Even on a [minor] sin I am very worried. For every day I worry anew in that the sin was to the King of kings. The holy Tanna hinted this in his mussar "do not make *yourself* like a 'legal advisor'" - *yourself* specifically, in something which touches on yourself, "do not be a legal advisor", to seek justifications.

I am teaching you that when the litigants are standing before you, they should be in your eyes as wicked. If so, you yourself are always a baal din (litigant) standing always before G-d, as written: "a man is judged every day". If so, you are like a Rasha (wicked man). And even if you repented and received sufferings, don't trust in this. For "they are *like* meritorious", implying "like" but not really meritorious (zakaim mamash), even though they accepted the judgment. So too, you should always suspect that you are not meritorious (zakai, i.e. always try to improve)...

Chapter 1 Mishna 9 - Check Witnesses

Shimon ben Shatach would say: שִׁמְעוֹן בֶּן שָׁטַח אוֹמֵר, הֱוֵי "interrogate the witnesses extensively, מַרְבֶּה לַחְקֹר אֶת הָעֵדִים, and be cautious with your words, lest שֶׁמָּא וֶהֱוֵי זָהִיר בִּדְבָרֶיךָ, through them they learn to lie." מִתּוֹכָם יִלְמְדוּ לְשַׁקֵּר

Q Level 1 — Tiferet Yisrael
Tiferet Yisrael - "interrogate the witnesses extensively" - perhaps through this they will contradict themselves.

Q Level 1 — Rabeinu Yonah
Rabeinu Yonah - investigate and question them much. Through this, you will uncover the secret. For "When words are many, sin is not absent" (Mishlei 10:19). And from their words you will learn whether or not they are lying.

Q Level 2 — Chida
Chida - Roshei Avot - "investigate much" (marbe lachkor) - possibly included in his words is that the examination of witnesses he does now should be different from previous examinations of witnesses. This is the meaning of "investigate much". That the examination be different for all witnesses. For if they are all in one standard way, they may learn to lie. Since they know of previous examinations and prepared themselves.

Q Level 1 — Bartenura
Bartenura - "and be cautious with your words, lest through them they learn to lie" - the judge should not say: "perhaps it happened in such and such a way", or "if it happened like this, he would not be guilty". For from those words, the plaintiff, defendant, or witnesses may learn to say something that did not happen (lie).

Q Level 1 — Rashi
Rashi - be careful when you examine the witnesses, perhaps through your words, they will sense what is in your mind and will understand how to lie saying what did not happen.

Q Level 1 — Rabeinu Yonah
Rabeinu Yonah - when you question them on the matter, you might speak in a way that they will understand from what angle

their beloved friend will be found guilty. Thus, from your words, they will learn how to lie to absolve him.

Level 3 — Ben Ish Chai

Ben Ish Chai - Chasdei Avot (on Mishna 1: "be deliberate in judgment") - The Tanna (Sage) came to teach the proper way for the judges of Israel on how to conduct themselves properly so that a calamity of corruption of justice will not occur through them, namely, to take out money from one person wrongly, due to frauds. Such as, when one claims a fraudulent claim to steal the money of his fellow.

Even more, one needs to be careful that a false oath is not uttered in his court, whereby a swindler swears falsely and wins his case, thus causing a desecration of the honor of torah.. All these mishaps can occur if the judge does not put to heart to contemplate the claims the litigants place before him. For if he does not examine properly with the eyes of his intellect and to think of tricks to bring out the trickery to light, so that they will not need to swear a torah oath.

In truth, one needs to be a Chacham (wise man) and Navon (understanding). For when he detects one of the litigants is a fraud, he needs to find a way to speak with him.

For example, there was a true story where one person was walking on the street and he saw a gold coin on the ground. The street was very long. He took it and put it in his pocket. Another person was on the other end of the street and saw him from far picking up the gold coin. He approached him and said:

"That gold coin you picked up from the ground is mine. It fell from me a few minutes ago when I was walking here and I had just sensed it and came back to search for it on this street and I saw that you picked it up. Give it to me. It is mine."

The other claimed: "you are lying. The gold coin did not fall from you. This coin fell from someone else and I acquired it as a lost object".

They both came to the Rav for a judgment and spoke their words. The swindler said he was willing to swear with a sefer

Chapter 1 Mishna 9 - Check Witnesses

torah that three minutes before he was walking on that street and the gold coin fell from him and no one else walked there for four minutes. Therefore, without a doubt that gold coin is mine.

In his wisdom, the Rav detected that this claimant is a fraud and that he wants to swear falsely with a sefer torah. The Rav thought how to bring out this fraudery to light so that the sinner will not profit to steal the gold coin from he who rightly acquired it and will not swear a false oath.

What did he do? He told the fraud: "go and stand outside and close the door. I would like to question the defendant privately to clarify the matter." He went out immediately and shut the door. The fraud stood outside next to the door in order to listen to what the Rav speaks to the defendant. The Rav spoke with a slightly louder than normal voice, not whispering, so that the fraud will hear. For he understood that certainly the fraud is lending his ear to listen behind the door.

He told the defendant: "let me see the gold coin". He gave it to him. After the Rav took it, he told the defendant: "look, this gold coin has a siman muvhak (distinguishing sign). It has a small hole on the right side. If so, why should this person take an oath? Let's ask him to give a siman (sign) and if he says this siman of the hole on the right side, certainly it is his. And we can give it to him without an oath. And if he does not give a sign, it is yours and I will give it to you."

He smiled as he said this in order that he understand that he is speaking in order to trick the trickster. For the defendant can see that there is no hole on the coin.

Afterwards, he yelled and called out the swindler standing outside and told him to enter. He told him: "the gold coin is in my hand and it has a siman (distinguishing sign). now, if it is yours, tell me the siman and you can take it without an oath."

The fraud said: "good thing. I will tell you the siman it has. It has a small hole on the right side!"

The Rav asked: "this is the sign and there is none other?". He replied: "yes, it has no sign other than the hole on the right side".

The Rav laughed and opened his hand to reveal the coin. He told the fraud: "see. this gold coin which you claim from this man does not have any hole. If so, it is not yours. For according to your words, your coin has a hole and this one does not. Thus, it must have fallen from someone else and this man acquired it."

The fraud was humiliated and left.

Chapter 1 Mishna 10 - Love Work

Shemayah and Avtalyon received from them. Shemayah says, "Love work, hate Rabbanut (positions of authority) and do not become known (intimate) with the ruling power (government)." שְׁמַעְיָה וְאַבְטַלְיוֹן קִבְּלוּ מֵהֶם. שְׁמַעְיָה אוֹמֵר, אֱהֹב אֶת הַמְּלָאכָה, וּשְׂנָא אֶת הָרַבָּנוּת, וְאַל תִּתְוַדַּע לָרָשׁוּת:

Q Level 1 — Bartenura
Bartenura - love work - even if one has money to live on, he is obligated to toil in work, for "idleness brings to shiamum (mental instability)" (Ketuvot 59b)

Q Level 1 — Tiferet Yisrael
Tiferet Yisrael - if nevertheless you were appointed a Rav, at least hate to be lording over your flock. Lead them with mercy as a father to his sons, not like a master rules over his slaves. For you were not appointed for that, and like Rabban Gamliel said:

"Do you imagine that I am granting you authority? I am granting you servitude, as it is stated: 'And they spoke to him saying: If you will be a servant to this people today' (I Kings 12:7)" (Horayot 10a).

Whoever becomes haughty is as one who worships idols (Sotah 4), and for a leader who becomes haughty over his congregation, his sin is very great before G-d (Rosh Hashana 17a). And all the troubles and anger he causes is guarded for him. This is what our sages said: "Rabbanut buries its possessor" (Yomah 86b), i.e. lording of the Rav will bury him despite his physical health, his honor, his intellect, his righteousness - all of them will melt away with him.

Q Level 1 — Rabeinu Yonah
Rabeinu Yonah - "do not become known (intimate) with the ruling power (government)" - for the work of the shiltonut (ruling power) is very hard. And if he accepts on himself the yoke of the shiltonut, eventually he will remove the yoke of the kingdom of Heaven. For he fears the shilton (ruler) and his extensive work. Thus he will cut corners in the work of G-d due to this work.

Furthermore, in the end, they will take away all his property for nothing. For they draw him close only for their benefit..

Rambam
Level 2

Rambam - *"hate Rabbanut"* - he will have trials and evils in this world. For since people will be jealous of him and will argue against him, he will lose his emunah (faith) as they said: "one who is appointed as a leader of the public becomes wicked (power corrupts)".

Likewise for knowing the rulers and being close to them in ancient times. It is very difficult to save oneself in this world. It causes one to lose his emuna (faith). For he will be concerned with nothing other than what will draw him close to this. You know the story of Doeg (who lost everything) despite that the ruler he drew near to was the "anointed of G-d", a prophet, and chosen by G-d (king Saul).

Chatam Sofer
Level 2

Chatam Sofer end of Vayikra - *"ruling power (reshut)"* - "reshut" i.e. ruling power (malchut). He used the term "reshut" (literally "permission") to say that they have the ability to do as they wish and no one can stop them. In truth, it is impossible to join a man who has no ruler or authority over him. For who can know which path he will choose next? In an instant he can transform to trample and kill. Thus if not for the fear of the justice of the king, one could not join anyone. If so, the king himself who has reshut (permission) in his hand, it is proper to distance from him. So too for people who think themselves hefker (free), and there is no G-d nor human king below watching them (atheists). All is included in "do not become involved with the ruling power".

Maharal
Level 3

Maharal - see next mishna.

Level 4

Rabbi Avraham Azoulai - Ahava b'Taanugim human society is generally divided into three divisions. This is besides the special "solitary ones" (mitbodedim) who toil in wisdom and are above everyone and who have no occupation with other people.

The first division comprises all the various workers and businessmen in the world, whose intent is to work to earn money.

Chapter 1 Mishna 10 - Love Work

The second division is the leaders and judges of the people, each generation and its leaders, judges, etc.

The third division is those who have power to be in the palace of the king and the officials who are close to the government.

Regarding the first division, he said it is the choicest of the three and it is proper to love this [path] for it is the best one for man to toil in.

Regarding the second division, he said it is proper to hate it. But it is not proper to distance from it totally. For sometimes necessity brings one to become a judge or a leader, namely, when there is no one there more fit than himself. Then it is not proper to distance from it. All [important] positions and leadership (minui v'hanhaga) is included in the term "Rabanut". (as written in Avodah Zara 17b: "rabbi (master) of weavers".

This is the meaning of "hate Rabbanut".

Regarding the third division, he said: "do not become known (intimate) with the ruling power". Avoid it completely. For there is no benefit. Only evil all day.

He said "love work", and not "engage in work", i.e. habituate yourself until the work becomes second nature and it is not a heavy yoke on you.

He did not say "love the earnings of work", but rather "love work", even if you have money and don't need the earnings. For as the talmud says: "idleness brings to shiamum (mental instability) and immorality" (Ketuvot 59b).

Also hate Rabanut for in this, man becomes haughty and haughtinesss brings to sin and perhaps he will sin. All the more so "do not become known (intimate) with the ruling power". For with the "ruling power" certainly he will sin. Because the reshut wants only someone who flatters it and brings it benefits and he will sometimes take other people's money wrongly.

Chapter 1 Mishna 11 - Watch Your Words

Avtalyon would say: "Chachamim (scholars), be careful with your words; lest you be liable for (the punishment of) exile, and are exiled to a place of evil waters, from which the disciples who come after may drink and die, and thus the Name of Heaven will be desecrated." אַבְטַלְיוֹן אוֹמֵר, חֲכָמִים, הִזָּהֲרוּ בְדִבְרֵיכֶם, שֶׁמָּא תָחוּבוּ חוֹבַת גָּלוּת וְתִגְלוּ לִמְקוֹם מַיִם הָרָעִים, וְיִשְׁתּוּ הַתַּלְמִידִים הַבָּאִים אַחֲרֵיכֶם וְיָמוּתוּ, וְנִמְצָא שֵׁם שָׁמַיִם מִתְחַלֵּל

Level 1 — Rashi

Rashi - "be careful with your word" - do not leave room for the heretics to err.

"lest you be liable for exile" - even though there are no heretics in your place, you shoud nevertheless be concerned that perhaps it will cause sin and you will incur [the punishment of] exile winding up in a place where people expound torah not in line with halacha (called metaphoricaly "bad water"), and they will understand improper things from your words, and the students after them will drink from those heretical things and die in sin.

"and thus the Name of Heaven will be desecrated" - those improper views will remain in the world, as happened to Antignos of Socho with Tzadok and Beitus his disciples. He told them: "Do not be as servants who serve their master in order to receive reward...", and they told themselves: "how could a worker work strenuously all day and receive no wages at the end of the day?". They went out and became heretics along with their students. They are called Tzadukim and Beitusim until today. (translator: last remnants today are the Karaites)

Level 1 — Sforno

Sforno - they will think this is your view only that you don't want to publicize it openly. This will cause a desecration of G-d's Name for the masses will think that bad view is yours.

Level 2 — Tiferet Yisrael

Tiferet Yisrael - "be careful with your words" - he exhorted the rabbis to be careful not to say something which can be

Chapter 1 Mishna 11 - Watch Your Words

interpreted in two ways. For perhaps you will be in a place where heresy strengthens and they will interpret your words in line with their heretical views and the students afterwards will turn to the heretical views and die, and the world will blame you thinking they learned that from you, thereby desecrating the Name of G-d.

Level 2

Vilna Gaon - as the torah was careful in its words, as written: "R. Yohanan said: In all the verses which the heretics have taken [as grounds] for their heresy, their refutation is found near at hand. For example: 'Let us make man in our image' (implying multiple gods), next verse: 'And G-d (singular tense) created man in His image'..." (Sanhedrin 38b).

Level 3 — Maharal

Maharal - this pair of sages, Shemaya and Avtalyon are also coming to exhort on something which is a very primary matter. Namely, man's conduct with the public..

It is proper that the Name of Heaven be beloved [to others] through the torah sages, as the Talmud says (Yomah 86a):

" 'And you shall love the L-ord your G-d' (Deuteronomy 6:5), which means that you shall make the Name of Heaven beloved. How should one do so? One should do so in that he should read Torah, and learn Mishna, and serve Torah scholars, and he should be pleasant with people in his business transactions. What do people say about such a person? Fortunate is his father who taught him Torah, fortunate is his teacher who taught him Torah, woe to the people who have not studied Torah. So-and-so who taught him Torah, see how pleasant are his ways, how proper are his deeds. The verse states about him and others like him: 'You are My servant, Israel, in whom I will be glorified' (Isaiah 49:3)" end quote.

That which is honor of torah and honor of G-d causes love of Hash-em, blessed be He. Namely, when the torah scholar does not need others.. For this causes annulment of the honor of torah.. When they need others, every Rav acquires a master over himself. Therefore Shmaya said: "hate Rabbanut", for it distances work.

Do not think that work is not honorable. On the contrary it brings honor to a man.. and he will not receive disgrace until he needs the [charity] of others.. Therefore he said: "love work". For if one says work is a dishonor, it is not so. Above all, it saves one from many sins and also grants one honor...

Understand the sages' emphasis on love of work, namely, to love to do work, i.e. the main virtue [here] is when one loves work. Thus, he did not say: "choose work for yourself", but rather "love work".

And in Berachot 8a:
"One who enjoys (nehene) from the work of his hands is greater than a G-d-fearing person. As with regard to a G-d-fearing person, it is merely written: "fortunate is the man who fears the L-ord" (Psalms 112:1), while with regard to one who benefits from the work of his hands, it is written (double expression): 'by the labor of your hands you shall live; fortunate are you and it is good for you' (Psalms 128:2)" end quote.

The explanation is that one who enjoys from the work of his hands is satisfied with what G-d provided for him, and what he has is sufficient for him.

For otherwise, he would not be "enjoying [the work of his hand]". But when he is "enjoying", he is certainly satisfied with what he has and he is not lacking.. Thus it says on him: "fortunate are you..". For such a man, in being a whole creature, in having the trait of histapkut (content with what one has), he is without lacking. Then it is proper for him to have complete Olam Haba and also this world for since he is satisfied with himself and content with his portion, Hash-em helps him to become completely whole, without lacking.

It is known that "existence" is this world and the next. Thus, one who is considered an "existence" (not lacking) is thus worthy of this world and the next which are both existences and which are not lacking. But one who is lacking is close to inexistence, since lacking is the beginning of inexistence. Hence, he who is content with himself is not lacking. For the definition of being satisfied is

Chapter 1 Mishna 11 - Watch Your Words

not lacking. Thus, he is considered an existence and it is proper for him to inherit the existence, namely, this world and the next...

The general principle: when a person is whole with himself, i.e., satisfied with himself, then he has a complete existence without lacking, and it is proper for him to completely have this world and the next, which are [whole] existences...

You should also know that for he who "enjoys from the work of his hand..", it is impossible for him to not also have the trait of love through this. For after he is content and loves the work of his hands, it is also impossible for him to not also love He who bestowed to him all this. For one who receives a gift and the gift is accepted and beloved to him, how could he not love greatly he who gave him the gift?

As we mentioned, each of the pairs came to exhort in some great mussar. According to the greatness of the sage is the greatness of his mussar. Therefore, he came here to exhort one to love work. For it is a great matter and he hangs on this topic a great primary matter (the trait of histapkut-contentment).

But besides the Shlemut (wholeness) one gets from work, more than this, there is also the honor of G-d's Name and it is proper for His Name to be beloved in the world especially through the torah scholars..

For it causes love of G-d when people see the torah scholars conducting themselves properly, when they love work and don't want to benefit from others..

He should hate Rabbanut which distances work to instead have authority over others.

Furthermore every sin and transgression of the public is upon the persons of authority. For they have the ability to admonish them (the sinners).

Avtalyon comes to exhort on the opposite. To not do things which may cause a chilul Hash-em. Thus he said:

"Chachamim (scholars), be careful with your words; lest you be liable for (the punishment of) exile, and are exiled to a place of evil waters, from which the disciples who come after may drink and die, and thus the Name of Heaven will be desecrated"

Thus, Shmaya and Avtalon both taught mussar that G-d's Name be sanctified through the torah scholars..

Chapter 1 Mishna 12 - Love Peace

Hillel and Shammai received from them. Hillel would say: Be of the disciples of Aharon, loving peace, pursuing peace, loving the public and drawing them closer to Torah.

הִלֵּל וְשַׁמַּאי קִבְּלוּ מֵהֶם. הִלֵּל אוֹמֵר, הֱוֵי מִתַּלְמִידָיו שֶׁל אַהֲרֹן, אוֹהֵב שָׁלוֹם וְרוֹדֵף שָׁלוֹם, אוֹהֵב אֶת הַבְּרִיּוֹת וּמְקָרְבָן לַתּוֹרָה:

Q Level 1 — Rashi

Rashi - "be of the disciples of Aharon.." - this is explained in Avot d'Rebbi Natan:

"How would Aharon 'pursue peace'? When he saw two people in dispute, he would go to each one separately without the other's knowledge and say to him: "see how your fellow regrets and hits himself for having wronged you. He asked me to come to you so you would forgive him". Through this, next time they met, they would kiss each other.

How would Aharon "draw them closer to torah"? When he knew about a certain person who had committed a sin, he would befriend him and smile to him. That man would then be embarassed and tell himself: 'if this Tzadik (righteous man) knew my evil deeds, he would keep far away from me'. Due to this, he would repent and return to the good. This is what the prophet testified on him: "he walked with Me in peace and uprightness, and turned many away from iniquity" (Malachi 2:6)

Q Level 2 — Rambam

Rambam - our sages said that when Aharon sensed in a man that his interior is evil or when he was told that the man has sin in his hands, he would befriend him and increase speech with him. That man would become embarrassed of himself and tell himself: "woe to me. If Aharon knew what is hidden in my heart and my evil deeds, he would not permit himself to look at me, all the more so, would he not speak to me. He considers me a kosher person. Therefore, I will make true his words and thoughts by returning to the good.."

Q Level 2

Machzor Vitri - in Avot d'Rebbi natan (ch.12):

If two people were in a quarrel with each other, Aharon would go to each one and sit with him and say: "my son, look at what your fellow is saying to himself. He is wrenching his heart and choking himself and plucking his hair and saying: 'oy to me! how could I lift my eyes and see my friend! I am ashamed of myself for having wronged him!'"

Aharon would sit with him until he extracted all the jealousy (kinna) from his heart. Afterwards, he would go to the other person and say the same thing until both would be embarrased of each other and kiss each other. Likewise, between a man and his wife...

We find in the Midrash (Ber.Rabba) that since the men of the Tower of Bavel loved each other, the Holy One, blessed be He, did not want to eliminate them, so He confounded them instead. But for the men of Sedom who hated each other, He annihilated them from the world, as written: "And the people of Sodom were very evil and sinful against the L-ord" (Gen.13:13), "evil" towards each other and "sinning" with immorality. Furthermore, our sages said "even if the Jewish people worship idols, but there is shalom between them, no nation can rule over them.. and how difficult is dispute (machloket), for even if the Jewish people fulfill the whole torah, but there is dispute among them - they are made hefker (free for all) and vulnerable to damagers (chulin l'mazikin).

Level 4 — Chida

Chida - Zeroa Yamin - "love peace, pursue peace, love the public" - (literal translation: a lover of peace, a pursuer of peace, loving the public..") - he did not say: "love peace and pursue peace" but rather "a lover of peace, a pursuer of peace". This is to teach that one should become so habituated in this that it becomes his name that he is called by, that everyone calls him "lover of peace", "pursuer of peace", and as it is written: "seek peace and pursue it" (Tehilim 34:15).

Level 2 — Ahava b'Taanugim

Rabbi Avraham Azoulai - Ahava b'Taanugim - "love peace" - first, one must himself love Shalom, namely, that Shalom be beloved and good in his eyes, and he loves it for himself. This will lead to making Shalom between others..

"love the public" - i.e. be one who loves the public. This second

trait follows from the first. After one's nature loves shalom, this will lead to love of the public in one's nature. Thus, he did not say "be one who loves the public". For it is as if both are one trait since one leads to the other.

"*love the public*" - (literally: "love the created beings (habriot)") i.e. in their being G-d's creations, blessed be He, one needs to love them. Whether they are Tzadikim (righteous) or otherwise. Through this, you will draw them closer to the torah, even though they are far from it.

Level 2   Tosfot Yom Tov
Tosfot Yom Tov - "love the created beings" - since they are the creations of the Holy One, blessed be He. Therefore it is proper for you to love them and also that the love be due to this aspect, not from a different one, such as from a benefit you may receive from them. The Midrash Shmuel explains along these lines.

Level 2   Ahava b'Taanugim
Rabbi Avraham Azoulai - Ahava b'Taanugim - "drawing them closer to Torah" - we may also infer from "draw them closer to Torah", i.e. that you are primary (ikar) and he is secondary (tafel) and he approaches you. For then he is necessarily secondary (tafel) to you and will learn from you.
(translator: "draw them closer to torah" implies he is approaching you, not the opposite, since you are closer to torah than him instead of drawing him closer to torah.)

But not that he is the primary (ikar) and you approach him and are secondary (tafel) (translator: whereby you would be drawing the torah closer to him).

For then, on the contrary, your words will not avail and there is concern that perhaps you will learn from him, as we mentioned earlier regarding "do not join a wicked man, etc" (Avor 1:7). i.e. when he is primary and you are secondary. Here he exhorted on the opposite case, "drawing them closer to Torah", as we explained. This is a correct inference (dikduk).

Level 2
Vilna Gaon - "love the public" - as written: " 'love your fellow as yourself' (Vayikra 19:18) - this is a great general principle of the torah" (Torat Kohanim parsha Kedoshim).

Level 2

Mili D'Avot - "love peace" - He would very much love that there be Shalom with every person. Therefore, he was very forebearing (savlan meod), and he would not put to heart anything that was said against him. This is the general principle (klal gadol) of the torah. For one who loves Shalom will not steal nor commit adultery nor any other sin between man and his fellow. Love of Shalom also includes love of being in Shalom with Hash-em. Therefore, he will be careful of all sins between himself and Hash-em.. thus in order to love torah, Shalom must be precious in one's eyes, and then there will not be a stumbling of sin. For due to that stumbling block, there will not be Shalom with one's Creator and one's fellow human beings.

Level 3 — Tiferet Yisrael

Tiferet Yisrael - due to his extreme humility, he taught three consecutive Mishnas on humility, the first in speech, the second in deed, and the third in thought..

In this mishna, he exhorts on humility in speech. This includes three matters: speech towards one greater than oneself, one equal, and one less.

Thus regarding one's duty towards one's Rabbi who is greater than oneself, he said a man should learn from Aharon. See how he rejoiced when Moshe Rabeinu was chosen to be the Rav of Israel, how he went out to greet him and called him "my master", despite that Moshe was his younger brother and that he was equal to him (as Rashi on Shmot 26:28). So too, honor your local Rav, even if he is smaller than you.

Regarding one's duty to his equals, he said: "love peace". Not to cause disputes between him and you. And also to "pursue peace", when your peer acts crookedly and causes a dispute between you and him. Nevertheless, pursue and verbally exert yourself after shalom, which ran away from you. Return it to its proper place..

Regarding one's duty towards his students and his flock, he said to "love the created beings" even those who are not even worthy of being called "Adam" (human), due to their weakness of intellect. Rather, they are considered only like other created beings (animals). Nevertheless, benefit them physically and spiritually. When you rebuke them, be concerned for their honor. Not by anger and fury. Rather, by appeasement, favor and kindliness. Like a father who has pity on his sons. For only through this way will you bring them closer to torah. For a man does not listen to the advice of one who hates him but rather only to one who loves him. We likewise find Hillel conducted himself thus towards the convert who came to anger him as brought in the Talmud (Shab.31)...

Level 3 — Ruach Chaim

Ruach Chaim - "be of the disciples.." - as written: "seek peace and pursue it" (Tehilim 34:15). The matter of the double language of "seek" and "pursue" is as follows. When there is a dispute and quarrel between two people and a third person wants to make peace between them, he must appease and go along the spirit of each of the two and say to each one: "yes, true, even though you are right and the other person is wrong, but nevertheless, be a 'pursuer of peace' (rodef shalom)". Because if you tell him that he wronged the other fellow and he is the one that needs to make amends, he will not accept it and won't listen.

It is likely that he will also make a new dispute with the third person who tried to make peace due to this. For "each person's ways are just in his eyes", and he imagines that only his fellow is wrong and must apologize and make amends. This is the meaning of "seek shalom" - i.e. that your will be for peace. Even though you think he wronged you, nevertheless, "pursue it". You chase peace and do not hope/wait until your fellow appeases you.

Another explanation, even though by drawing close to torah, sometimes one can cause a dispute. For example, between a man and his wife. For she imagines that through this, there will be less money (parnassa) and "strife is prevalent in a house on account of food" (Bava Metzia 59a). Nevertheless, draw close to torah. This is "love the public". For this is the true love, and "when a man's ways pleases Hash-em, even his enemies will make peace with him" (Mishlei 16:7), which our sages expounded refers to one's wife, and eventually there will be even greater peace between them.

Level 3 — Maharal

Chapter 1 Mishna 12 - Love Peace

Maharal - *"Hillel and Shamai received from them..."* - they are the fifth pair. They came to teach mussar on a great primary matter. For this world is more prone to dispute (machloket) than anything else in the world. Because this is the matter of this world, it is a world of separation and division (olam hachiluk v'haperud). Therefore, dispute (machloket) is common in the world. You can understand this from that which dispute came to the world on the day the world was created, namely, from Kain and Hevel. From this you will see that this world is prone to dispute due to its being a world of separation and division.

Therefore, he said it is proper for one to support (machzik) the world with the trait of "pursuing peace" between man and his fellow. So that when there is in this world separation and division, his trait will be to join the divisions as will be explained.

There is much to ask on the saying of Hillel who said to be among the disciples of Aharon. Even though it was undoubtedly so that Aharon would love peace and pursue peace, but nevertheless, this was not mentioned explicitly anywhere in the torah.

Only the verse in Malachi hinted at this: "he walked with Me in peace and uprightness, and turned many away from iniquity" (Malachi 2:6).

Hillel did not rely (solely) on this verse when saying: "be of the disciples of Aharon - a lover of peace, a pursuer of peace..", for the verse was [not] well known by everyone.

Furthermore, "loving the public" - it is not mentioned anywhere that he was "loving the public".

Another question: he said to be of the disciples of Aharon. But even if one has these traits, nevertheless, how can we say he is among the disciples of Aharon, for Aharon was the Kohen Gadol (high priest), a holy man of G-d.

Another question: why does he need to say "be of the disciples of Aharon". He should have just said: "be pursuing peace".

Chapter 1 Mishna 12 - Love Peace

Another question, he followed this teaching with: "one who seeks a name, loses his name" (next mishna). What does that have to do with "be of the disciples of Aharon"? Likewise the next teaching: "One who does not increase, ceases". What do these things have to do with each other? They don't seem to have any connection. Likewise for the words of Shammai: "make your torah study fixed.." All these things don't seem to be connected.

The explanation of what he said: "be of the disciples of Aharon.." is as follows. Aharon was the Kohen Gadol (high priest) and the Kohen Gadol is singular in that he unites together (mekasher) the Jewish people until they are one people, with one temple and one altar.

This is the opposite of the nations, as brought in the Midrash (Bamidbar Rabba ch.18): "when Korach disputed the kehuna (priesthood) of Aharon, Moshe Rabeinu said to them: 'it is the way of the nations to have many priests coming to one house, but we have only one G-d, one Torah, one law, one Kohen Gadol, etc.'"..

From this you can see, that through the Kohen Gadol, who is one, the Jewish people become as one people. For Aharon would join and unite the Jewish people until they are one people. Therefore, Aharon would pursue peace between man and his fellow, so that they would not be divided by disputes, but would instead be one people.

So too, Aharon would draw near the Jewish people to "the Place" (haMakom, i.e. G-d) through the temple offerings they served to G-d, blessed be He. Through this, he would draw them nearer to G-d. Thus, Aharon was specially fit (mesugal) to bring the people closer to torah.

If he saw a sinner who sinned, he would draw him to torah. For this is proper for his trait. And just like Aharon would perform the Avodah (temple service) of Israel, bringing good (blessings,etc.) to them through the offerings, and good (blessings) can only come to someone through one who loves him and seeks his good. Therefore, certainly Aharon loved Yisrael.

Chapter 1 Mishna 12 - Love Peace

Furthermore, how could he possibly join and unite the people if he himself was not connected with them and was not "loving the public"?

Therefore, Hillel said: "be of the disciples of Aharon", i.e. since Aharon was singularly and specially fit (meyuchad u'mesugal) for this, more than any other human being, then, if you do thus, you will enter through this to be of the disciples of Aharon. For this thing was the primary essence of the level of Aharon in his being the Kohen Gadol, namely, to bring complete peace to the world.

Thus, there needs to be peace between man and his fellow, and likewise between Yisrael and their Father in Heaven. Through this, all will be at peace. This was through Aharon specifically, more than any other human human being who came to the world. Therefore, if a man enters in these traits, he is considered among the disciples of Aharon. For this matter pertained to Aharon in his being Kohen Gadol and it was the primary level of Aharon.

"a lover of peace, a pursuer of peace" - the explanation is that he "loved" that there not arise dispute (machloket) between people and he "pursued peace". Namely, if dispute came, he pursued to make peace. Since when dispute arises, one needs to pursue until he brings them back to peace. For it is the way of people that when they enter into a dispute, each side distances from the other to the furthest extreme (tachlit harichuk), and that which is distant needs pursuing after.

This that the term "pursuing" is used everywhere regarding "Shalom" will be explained further.

It is also a remarkable (muflag) matter that Hash-em is called "Shalom" and it is forbidden to say "Shalom" in a bathhouse. From this, you will see that the name "Shalom" is a matter of holiness above everything (kadosh al hakol). It is something not of this world (eino mitzad olam haze). And according to this level, it needs to be done with "pursuing" (redifa), not with waiting and delay of time (shehiya v'ikuv zman).

This is so for all [great] things. Due to the loftiness of their level,

Chapter 1 Mishna 12 - Love Peace

it is not proper to do them in [physical] time, as they expounded on the verse:

"you shall guard the matzot" (Shemot 12:17) - "do not read 'matzot' but rather 'mitzvot' - [to teach that] if a mitzva comes to your hand do not sour (delay) it" (Mechilta parsha Bo).

For the mitzvot are divine things (devarim Elokiim). Therefore, they are not performed in waiting and delay of time.

Thus the prohibition to allow the dough to become chametz and the prohibition to delay (le'hachmitz) the mitzva is all one reason. For Yisrael came out of Egypt from the power of the lofty divine level which has no passing of time (ein ba shehiya zman klal), as we explained in its place.

This is the reason it is forbidden to delay (le'hachmitz) the mitzva. For then there is a souring (chimutz) of the mitzva just like for the matza. Since the mitzva is divine, time is not proper to it (ein roy la hazman). For time pertains (zman shayich) to things of this world, the physical world under time.

Thus the matter of "Shalom" whose level is divine such that it is forbidden to utter this name in the bathhouse, until they said: "His (G-d's) Name, blessed be He, is Shalom" (Shab.10b).

This is what they said: "pursue Shalom", completely without any time delay. One should understand this. For it depends (tolei) on the secret (Sod) of Shalom. There is another reason for this which we will clarify in a different place.

"loving the public" - this trait is appropriate for one who is a "pursuer of peace" (rodef shalom), namely, one who joins the public so that the people are one (united). All the more so, that he [himself] loves the public and is united with it, as we said regarding Aharon.

"and drawing them closer to Torah" - for just like he makes Shalom between man and his fellow, so too he should make Shalom and connection between people who distanced from the torah and the mitzvot of Hash-em, blessed be He, thus making

Chapter 1 Mishna 12 - Love Peace

Shalom between Yisrael and their Father in Heaven.

Thus, all these traits Hillel exhorted on is so that man will join everything until all will be united. You will understand through this that all these things mentioned by Hillel, who was the Nassi (Chief Rabbi), are branches of love of G-d. For it is because he loves G-d, blessed be He, that he loves the public, as before. And he said explicitly: "and drawing them closer to Torah", and kiruv (drawing close) to torah and to Hash-em is all because of love of Hash-em, blessed be He. This is clear.

And because one who possesses this trait of "love of Shalom and pursuing Shalom" (ohev shalom v'rodef shalom), his trait is [also] lowliness and humility. For one who pursues peace between man and his fellow must himself go to the person disputing, since the persons disputing will not go after him. And if one is not of humble spirit, he will say: "it is not befitting my honor to lower myself and pursue Shalom between people".

All the more so for "love of the public", where he is mixed (daato keshura) with the public until there will be peace between all of them.

This trait is the opposite of the baal sherara (authority/power seeker). Love of the public does not apply to them, namely, such that they are joined to the public. For on the contrary, they are separated from the public, because the public is not important in their eyes. This is the way of all the baalei sherara (authority seekers). They are out for themselves and are not mixed with the public.

Without a doubt, Hillel exhorted on these things out of his great humility. We find he possessed humility as brought in the talmud (Shab.31a). Therefore, he exhorted on these traits, which are the traits of humility, the opposite of the baalei sherara (authority/power seekers). Therefore, he followed this with "one who seeks a name, loses his name"... (continued next mishna)

Q Level 3 — Chatam Sofer

Chatam Sofer Ki Teitzeh - it is known that man was created only to benefit others. On this, it is written: "you shall cling to Him (G-d)" (Devarim 13:5). For the primary purpose of the creation of the world was in order that the Holy One, blessed be He, benefit another.

Thus, it is written: "you who cling to the L-ord your G-d are all alive today" (Devarim 4:4). Namely, one who wants to be clinging to the Holy One, blessed be He, must see to it that "you are all alive". Namely, "to return many from iniquity" (Malachi 2:6, regarding Aharon), and bring them back to the path of life. But one who labors only to rectify himself and does not benefit others, is not called "clinging to G-d". On this, Hillel said (next mishna): "and when I am for myself, what am I?", that I am not considered as anything when I am only to myself.

Level 3

Meorei Ohr - even though Aharon would say to the arguers what the other party did not say, nevertheless, our sages taught: "One may modify a statement for the sake of peace" (Yevamot 65b)

Level 3 — Chasdei David

Chasdei David - in Avot d'Rebbi Natan (12:3) on the verse: "The torah of truth was in his mouth, and iniquity was not found in his lips he walked with Me in peace and uprightness, and turned many away from iniquity" (Malachi 2:6) - "when Aharon was walking on the way and he encountered a wicked man, he greeted him 'Shalom'. The next day, when the wicked man wanted to sin, he told himself: 'oy to me, how could I raise my eyes afterwards and see Aharon. I am ashamed that he granted me shalom'. Thus, the wicked man refrained from sin."

This needs explanation according to Rashi, who explains that when he saw two people in dispute he would go to each one and tell him the other person sent him, etc. How is it permitted to lie for Shalom?

I saw in the Binyan Yehoshua commentary on Avot d'Rebbi Natan the following. In the Midrash (Ber.Rabba ch.8):

When the Holy One, blessed be He, wanted to create man, the ministering angels were divided into groups. Some said not to create man and others said to create man. This is the meaning of: *"Kindness and truth have met; righteousness and peace have kissed; Truth will sprout from the earth, and righteousness will look down from heaven"* (Tehilim 85:11-12).

Chesed said: "create him for he bestows kindnesses". Truth said: "do not create him for he is all falsehoods". Righteousness said: "create him for he does acts of righteousness". Shalom said: "do not create him for he is all quarrels". What did the Holy One, blessed be He, do? He took Truth and threw it on the ground, as written: "and truth was cast to the earth" (Daniel 8:12) (end of midrash)

He asks there: "why didn't He also throw the trait of Shalom, who also advised not to create man?" He answers: since He cast Truth, it will be permitted to lie for Shalom purposes and the power of Shalom was increased. Thus, Aharon who had the trait of Shalom was granted the powers of Shalom to change words due to disputes (machloket). Therefore, he was a pursuer of Shalom and he would change certain things between man and his felllow as his trait permitted. see also Divrei Yoel (Nasso pg.193) who gave an answer why specifically the trait of Truth was cast on the ground and not the trait of Shalom...

Level 3 — Chatam Sofer

Ketav Sofer haChadash alHatorah, Avot - "pursue (rodef) shalom" - the *Tosfot Yom Tov* already sensed that "rodef shalom", implies he is a rodef to the shalom.
(translator: the term "rodef" by itself refers to one who pursues someone to murder him).

This is a contradiction to "love Shalom". He should have said instead: "pursue after the Shalom" (rodef achar hashalom).

It seems to me to explain according to what our sages said:

"For the death of the wicked benefits themselves and the world, while the death of the righteous, injures themselves and the world. Wine and sleep of the wicked benefits themselves and the world, while the death of the righteous, injures themselves and the world. The scattering of the wicked benefits themselves and the world, while the death of the righteous, injures themselves and the world. The assembling of the wicked injures themselves and the world, while the death of the righteous, injures themselves and the world..." (Sanhedrin 71b)

For in the case of whole and G-d fearing tzadikim, their assembly is l'shem Shamayim (for the sake of Heaven), sharing secrets together to strengthen Judaism. But the joining of the wicked is to turn the pot over on itself, to demolish and uproot Judaism.

By nature, Aharon loved Shalom more than Moshe Rabeinu, peace be unto him, as our sages said. For instance, they said that when two people became enemies, Aharon would go to each one of them and tell each person that the other wants his friendship and is distressed for having wronged him (Avot d'Rebbi Natan 12:3).

It is proper to say that Aharon did thus only between those who love Hash-em and His torah, whereby "their assembly is good for them..". But for the wicked whereby their assembly is evil *(translator: i.e. incorrigibly wicked)*, he did the opposite. He went to each wicked man and told him: "the person who you think is your friend speaks only evil of you all day and curses you behind your back". Likewise for the other until they hated each other. For "scattering is good for the wicked".

Although by nature Aharon was unable to see people's hearts distancing from each other and he tried to unite them together by all means. But for the good of Judaism, he used all means to do the opposite. Despite that this was against his wish and nature, he strengthened and mustered courage in his heart.

This is what they said "pursue (rodef) shalom". Sometimes he would rodef (drive away) Shalom to distance and separate those clinging together and to break the bond of the wicked (kesher reshaim).

He ends off "loving the public", i.e., by nature he loved the public, "and drawing them closer to Torah". For, as before, sometimes he deemed it good to separate people, and that this too would draw them closer to the torah.

Q Level 4 — Chida

Chida - Zeroa Yamin - In the talmud in Gitin (52a):
"There were two men who, being enticed by the Satan, quarreled with one another every Friday afternoon. R. Meir once came to

that place and stopped them from quarreling there Friday afternoons. When he had finally made peace between them, he heard the Satan say: Alas for this man (the Satan) whom R. Meir has driven from his house!".

This is the explanation of "seek Shalom and pursue it" (radfehu implies chase it away, i.e. chase away the evil to make peace).

We may hint that for this Shalom has gematria of Eisav. For when there is Shalom, there is not Eisav, namely, the Sitra Achra. And if ch"v there is not Shalom, Eisav is invited.

We may also explain our mishna, as our sages brought (Ber.Rabba 8:5) on the verse "Kindness and truth have met; righteousness and peace have kissed" (Tehilim 85:11):

"Rabbi Shimon says: when the Holy One, blessed be He, wanted to create man, the Malachim (angels) were [divided] into groups. Some said to create man while others said not to create. Chesed (kindness) said: 'create man, for he does acts of kindness'. Truth said: 'do not create man, for he is all falsehoods'. Righteousness said: 'create man, for he is all full of righteousnesses'. Shalom said: 'do not create him, for he is all quarrel'. What did the Holy One, blessed be He, do? He took Truth and cast it to the ground, as written: "and truth was cast to the earth" (Daniel 8:12), etc." see there.

Thus, Shalom does not want the creation of man, for man is all quarrels. Hence, one should not hold on (le-echoz) to the trait of Shalom directly, but rather only to "love the public (briot)" even though they are quarrelsome.

This is what he said: "love Shalom", that you love Shalom and all your dealings with Shalom. Included in this, see, I have appointed you to be a pursuer (rodef) of Shalom, i.e. a pursuer like an enemy to Shalom.

But how can both love and pursue (rodef) be fulfilled together? To this he explained: that which I told you to pursue (rodef) Shalom, this is because Shalom does not want the continuance of humanity. For Shalom said: "do not create man, for he is all quarrels".

Thus, you must pursue it and become one who "loves the public". Not like the trait of Shalom who hates the public. Towards others you should love Shalom, and draw them to make Shalom between them. Also for torah, to make Shalom between Yisrael and their Father in Heaven. Through this, you wil fulfill both "love Shalom and pursue Shalom".

Level 4 — Ben Ish Chai

Ben Ish Chai - Chasdei Avot - "Hillel.. rodef shalom" - this is difficult. For a "rodef" is the opposite of one who loves (as before, a "rodef" is one pursuing another to murder him). In truth, the mishna used the language of the verse: "seek peace and pursue it" (bakesh shalom v'radfehu) (Tehilim 34:14). But on the verse also it is a wonder. For "redifa" (chasing) implies the opposite of "bakasha" (seek). It seems to me to explain, with G-d's help as follows.

Let us introduce what is written in the Shl"a (Parsha Beshalach) in the name of Rav Galanti in "Kol Bochim". It is written in the Zohar that there are two groups (kitot) in the Sitra Achra (forces of evil). These are the two harlot women (nashim zonot) Machl-at and Li-lit.

Machl-at has 478 warriors (chayalot) as the gematria of Machl-at (Mem-Chet-Lamed-Taf=40+8+30+400=478). Likewise, Li-lit has 480 as the gematria of her name. These (forces of evil) fill the space of the world.

Without a doubt, at the time of the destruction of the temple, there were there great Chachamim (sages) and Tzadikim (righteous men) who were praying exalted prayers to block the decree. But these two women "oppressed Tzion" (anu l'tzion) as written: *"women in Tzion oppressed" (nashim b'tzion anu)* (Eichah 5:11). For their "prosecuting overpowered" (gavar kitrugam), and nothing helped to ascend up the prayers. In our many sins, the verse "my prayer was shut out" (Eichah 3:5) was fulfilled.

These two groups are constantly fighting each other. For they are two opposites. "Machl-at" is from the term "mecholot" and rejoicing. From her is drawn all those letzim (jesters, entertainment seekers, etc.) and party-makers (baalei mishtaot), "slayers of cattle and slaughterers of sheep", joy of futility and foolishness (simcha shel hollelut v'sichlut). All that comes from her.

But Li-lit is the opposite. "Li-lit" is from the word "yelila" (wailing). From her is drawn the "sad/depressed/unhappy people" (baalei mara shechora v'yagon v'anacha), G-d forbid.

Therefore, they are always fighting each other. And due to this, there is great benefit for the prayers of Yisrael. For because they are busy with each other, they are not so involved (einam mashgichim) on the prosecution (kitrug) of Yisrael. And then, it is possible for the prayers to ascend on high. But at the time of the Churban (temple destruction), these enemies made shalom (peace) with each other. This is the meaning of the verse: "her enemies are at ease" (Eichah 1:5), therefore: "prayer was shut out" (Eichah 3:5).

The tikun (rectification) to submit these klipot (evil forces) is from doing the good in those areas.

Namely, submitting "Li-lit" is through afflictions, fasts, broken-heartedness, and tears in prayer (ex. tikun chatzot, the midnight prayer on the temple destruction, or general tears in prayer). Then Li-lit will be submitted.

Submitting "Machl-at" is through joy (simcha) of mitzva, to have joy in doing the mitzvot and to have joy on the Sabbaths and Yom Tovs (and not the opposite), and to bring joy to the poor and the Chatan v'Kalla (groom and bride), and to have joy in knowledge of the Creator, in grasping a bit of His Secrets and knowledge of His Names, blessed be He.

But when Yisrael is not on its land and the temple is destroyed, then all joy has passed in our many sins and no joy is complete. Then it is very difficult to submit the klipa of Machl-at.. But for the Klipa of Li-lit whose submitting is through the gates of tears, she can become submitted through tears. Therefore "all the gates (of prayer) are closed except for the gate of tears" (Berachot 32a).

On these two matters, the verse hints "serve G-d with fear" (Tehilim 2:11), to annul Li-lit and "serve G-d with joy" (Tehilim 100:2), to annul Machl-at. End quote of Shl"A. see there.

According to this, now also when all of Israel wakes up at midnight to recite the Tikun Chatzot, to mourn and cry on the destruction of the temple and the murder of the Tzadikim, and the pain of Moshiach, Machl-at will be roused to fight with Li-lit. For she thinks this crying and lamentations comes from her. And when they sit to learn with joy until the morning and afterwards say songs until the time of prayer, Li-lit will be roused to fight with Machl-at. For she thinks this joy came to Yisrael through her to us. In the meantime, a mighty war will be waged between them, and then automatically the prayers of Yisrael will ascend above. For these will be too busy fighting and not prosecuting....

And likewise on shabbat and Yom Tov, when there is no crying and tears, but rather only joy and machol of mitzva, then Li-lit will think this joy came to Yisrael through Machl-at and she will come to wage war with her. Thus, when distracted with battle, then the prayers of Yisrael will escape and ascend on high without prosecuting (kitrug).

An analogy is to a man who was walking in the forest and he heard the sounds of a lion who was walking towards him nearby. But the lion did not yet see him nor reach him. This man turned around in order to run and escape from the lion. But behold, he saw between the branches of the forest a bear who was coming in his direction. He was caught in the middle. Where should he go? Certainly both will encounter him and rip him to shreds. What did he do? He cunningly climbed a tree of the forest and took a rock in his hands.

When the bear was close to the lion, and its eyes were downwards to eat, he threw the rock on the forehead of the bear. The bear lifted up his head and looked all around to see who struck him. He found no one nearby except the lion who was standing and eating. He thought certainly it was the lion who hit him. He ran to the lion in his rage to fight. The lion also prepared to fight him.

Chapter 1 Mishna 12 - Love Peace

While the two were battling each other, the man descended from the tree and ran away saving himself from them.

So too here, on the Sabbath and Yom Tov when all Yisrael are joyous in the evening meal and sing the Zmirot (songs) through which Li-lit receives submission, she thinks this came from Machl-at who taught them this, and this comes to fight with Machl-at and the war will intensify with them all day. Then the prayers and mitzvot of the day ascend without prosecution and will have a grand escape above...

According to this mentioned earlier, that these two women made Shalom between each other, and there was no longer a free path for the prayers, and they were not spared from the kitrugim (prosecuting) of these klipot, therefore the prayers did not help. The reason was measure for measure (mida keneged mida). For there were some people whose heart was evil. They falsely pretended to be at peace with others and devised stumbling blocks for them, as explained in the words of the prophet Yirmiyahu. Therefore due to that stumbling block that they did while pretending to be with Shalom, these two women made Shalom to harm the Jewish people.

Likewise also (measure for measure) on their leaving the torah, as written regarding the torah: "all its ways are Shalom" (Mishlei 3:17). Therefore, these two women made Shalom to harm them.

For if Yisrael had not left the torah, they would not have had a stumbling (michshol) from the Shalom of them. And as written: "Great shalom have they who love your torah, nothing shall cause them to stumble" (Tehilim 119:165).

From this it is understood the hint in Isaiah (3:12): "As for My people.. women rule over them". For he was prophesying on the temple destruction. And he saw that at the time of the churban these women will make shalom between each other and through this, they will rule over Yisrael with their prosecuting.

This is the meaning of "women rule (mashlu) over them". Mashlu is letters "Shalom", i.e. through these women making Shalom between each other, through this, they ruled with their

Chapter 1 Mishna 12 - Love Peace

prosecuting over my people. Therefore, in his Ruach Hakodesh (holy spirit) Isaiah cursed them to submit them, saying "there is no Shalom for the wicked" (Isaiah 48:22). His intent was on these women.

Likewise, Chizkiyahu saw this with Ruach Hakodesh (holy spirit), and he said: "Behold for Shalom, it is bitter for me, oh it is bitter" (Isaiah 38:17). He was referring to the Shalom of these [women] who did the Churban. Therefore, he toiled to spread torah (l'harbitz torah) which is called "Shalom" to Yisrael in order to destroy the Shalom from these women in the merit of the torah.

Therefore, Yisrael needs to strengthen themselves to be "ohavei shalom" (loving peace), so that the Shalom between these two evil women will be removed, and he should "rodef" (chase it to separate it) between them. Through this, we will understand what our sages said in the Yerushalmi (Peah ch.1):on the verse "seek peace and pursue it" (bakesh shalom v'radfehu) (Tehilim 34:14) - "seek it (bakshehu) in your place, and pursue it (radfehu) in another place."

It appears very difficult to understand. But through our introduction, the words of our sages are clear - "seek it (bakshehu) in your place" - in the sitra d'kedusha (side of holiness, within Yisrael, between each Jew. But "rodfehu" (chase it away) to remove it and drive it away in another place. This is the place of the Sitra Achara, namely, between these evil women, so that there is no Shalom between them.

From this we will understand Hillel's teaching here. "Love Shalom" refers to the Shalom of Yisrael, to strengthen the Shalom between Jews, as written "shalom al yisrael". But for the Sitra Achra - be a "rodef shalom", chase it away and fight to remove it from there, so that there is no shalom for the wicked. How can you do this? Through being careful in this, that you are "loving the public" (ohev et habrios) that you "do not hate your brother in your heart", and that you also "draw them closer to the torah". For "Her ways are ways of pleasantness, and all her paths are shalom" (Mishlei 3:17). Through this you will succeed and be able to "rodef" (drive away) the shalom made in the Sitra Achra to remove it from there, and all the forces of the Sitra

Chapter 1 Mishna 12 - Love Peace

Achara will hate each other and battle each other, and there will be Shalom only on Yisrael.

Level 4 — Chida

Chida - Zeroa Yamin - the humility of Hillel is well known. It is also known that the humble person becomes a chariot (merkava) to the Shechina. Likewise, Hillel is gematria Ado-nai. Another remez (hint): in the talmud: "a talmid chacham may have an eighth of an eighth of pride" (Sotah 5a). This is one part in 64. The gematria of Hillel is 65, hinting that he did not have even one part in 65, and all the more so not one part in 64.

Level 4 — Chida

Chida - Zeroa Yamin - *"be of the disciples of Aharon"* - Hillel was in the semblance (bechina) of Moshe Rabeinu (the paradigm of humility). He exhorted to learn from Aharon. When Hillel died they eulogized him saying: "such a chasid, such a humble person, among the disciples of Ezra" (see Sanhedrin 11b, Sotah 48b). Ezra was a gilgul (reincarnation) of Aharon, and in the book Gilgulei Neshamot (ot 80): "Aharon, Eli, Ezrah, Hillel are all from one Nitzutz (soul branch). With this it is clearer why Hillel said: "be of the disciples of Aharon", and also why the sages eulogized him as "among the disciples of Ezrah" (instead of Aharon)...

Chapter 1 Mishna 13 - Uses The Crown

He would also say: one who seeks a name, loses his name. One who does not increase, ceases. One who does not study incurs death. And one who makes [personal] use of the crown (of Torah) perishes.

הוּא הָיָה אוֹמֵר, נָגֵד שְׁמָא, אָבֵד שְׁמֵהּ. וּדְלֹא מוֹסִיף, יָסֵף. וּדְלֹא יָלֵיף, קְטָלָא חַיָּב. וּדְאִשְׁתַּמֵּשׁ בְּתָגָא, חֲלֵף.

Q Level 1 — Bartenura
Bartenura - "one who seeks a name, loses his name" - one whose name extends out far due to dominion and rulership over others (Sherara and Rabbanut) - his name will be lost swiftly, since "Woe to rulership (rabbanut), for it buries its possessor" (Pesachim 87b).

Q Level 1 — Rabeinu Yonah
Rabeinu Yonah - "one who seeks a name, loses his name" - i.e. a man who prides himself (adam hamitgaei) and his name becomes famous and goes out to the world through his arrogance and aggrandization and he makes a great name for himself, "like the name of the great ones that are in the earth" (Divrei HaYamim I 17:8), then proportionally to his great name which spread out through his arrogance, so too, his name will be lost a great loss and will not be remembered nor mentioned.

Q Level 1 — Sforno
Sforno - "one who seeks a name, loses his name" - one who strives to make his name famous in the world to obtain honor, "loses his name". Honor runs away from him.

Q Level 1 — Rashi
Rashi - "one who seeks a name, loses his name" - every person whose name goes out and he ascends to a high position, his death is near, as they said earlier by Yosef (who died before his brothers)...

Q Level 2 — Translator
Translator - from the commentaries, it seems the reason is because of arrogance and "power corrupts". But Rashi says "every person", and brings the example of Yosef who stayed righteous even after becoming viceroy of Egypt (see Rashi on

Shemot 1:5). Thus, it is not just because of arrogance, etc. "Woe to rulership (rabbanut), for it buries its possessor" applies even to those who stay righteous.

The Chasdei David explains that one in a position of authority receives "ayin hara" (evil eye) from people and as the Talmud says in Bava Metzia 107b:
"Rav went to the graveyard, did what he did and reported that 99 percent of the dead there died from ayin harah (before his time) while only 1 percent died from natural means (at his time)."
Thus, one who attains a position of authority receives lots of ayin hara and dies quickly. see Maharal for another explanation.

Level 1 — Bartenura

Bartenura - "one who does not increase, ceases" - he who does not add on to his [torah] study will cease (yasuf) from his mouth even what he already learned and he will forget his (torah) learning. some have the text "ye'asef", i.e. he wil be gathered to his people and will die before his time.

"he who does not study incurs death" - this is worse than one who does not increase. Therefore he incurs death, i.e. he deserves to be killed, as they said: "it is permitted to rip apart an 'am haaretz' like a fish" (Pesachim 49b).

"uses the crown (of Torah) perishes (chalaf)" - one who uses the crown of torah like a man who uses his tools, passes (chalaf) over the world.. some render: he who uses the Shem Hameforash (kabalistic Name of G-d) passes over and loses his portion in Olam Haba.

Level 1 — Rashi

Rashi - "one who does not study (yalef).." - (yalef also means teach), he who does not teach every asker (melamed lekol shoel) - incurs death.

"uses the crown (of Torah) perishes" - he who uses torah scholars.. dies in half his days because he annulled them from delving in love of torah.

Level 2 — Rambam

Rambam - he who does not study much (marbei b'kria), Hashem will kill him. But for one who does not learn [torah] at all, it is

Chapter 1 Mishna 13 - Uses The Crown

proper to kill him. He who "uses the crown perishes", i.e. he who receives a livelihood from torah or some benefit.. it is not permitted for a talmid chacham to receive service (shimush) from any human being besides his students.

Level 2 — Rabeinu Yonah

Rabeinu Yonah - *"one who does not increase, ceases"* - he who is a chacham (wise man) and does not want to increase wisdom on his wisdom and says to himself: "I have already learned the whole torah and saw its ways and paths. Why should I trouble myself to toil further during my vain days? What should I contemplate further that I do not already know?"

May it be G-d's will that this man die and be gathered to his people. Why should he live further after he has halted from learning further? (translator: since the more he lives, the more he incurs sin for wasting his time).

"One who does not study deserves death" - but he who did not learn altogether is compared to an animal. For why was he created in the world if not to understand and teach torah, "whose ways are ways of pleasantness" (Mishlei 3:17). This person who did not toil in torah all of his days and still holds on to his wickedness, it is not proper for him to live even one day and even one hour. (translator: as before, the more he lives, the more he incurs sin for wasting his time)

Level 2 — Translator

Translator - note that this mishna was written in Aramaic. I read once that this is because it is harsh words and curses.

The Tosfot Yom Tov in chapter 5 brings the Midrash Shmuel in the name of Rabbenu Ephraim saying "that because Torah is something that people greatly need, Ben Bag Bag said his dictum in Aramaic, which everyone knew upon their return from Babylon. Hillel did so as well, in the mishna of 'and he who does not learn' (1:13)"

Level 2 — Sforno

Sforno - *"one who does not increase, ceases"* - for when one does not strive to increase knowledge (daat), it is not proper for him to have "temporary life" (chayei shaah) of this world. For its matters is only for [obtaining] eternal life, as our sages said: "this world is like a corridor before the World to Come" (Avot 4:16).

"one who does not study (yalef).." - (yalef also means teach) one who does not teach knowledge to the people and withholds grain, "deserves death", as written: "He who keeps back grain (torah) - the nation will curse him" (Mishlei 11:26).

"And one who makes [personal] use of the crown of Torah perishes (chalaf)" - one whose purpose in torah is to obtain honor and benefits in "temporary life" [of this world], "chalaf", deserves to die as one who profanes the holy and uses it for the mundane (kimechalel et hakodeh umishtamesh bo bedivrei chol), as written:

"They shall keep My charge and not bear a sin by [eating] it [while unclean] and thereby die through it since they will have profaned it" (Vayikra 22:9).

Rather, the benefit in "temporary life" (chayei shaah) which comes from torah should be aligned towards allowing oneself to strive to obtain eternal life (chayei olam). Similar to: "[And he commanded the inhabitants of Jerusalem to give the portion of the priests and the Levites] in order that they be strengthened in the Torah of the L-ord'" (Divrei Hayamim II 31:4)

Q Level 1 — Tosfot Yom Tov

Tosfot Yom Tov - *"uses the crown (taga) [of Torah] perishes"* - taga refers to the crown of torah. the reason he said "crown" without specifying "of torah", is because a stam (plain) crown refers to the crown of torah. For all crowns besides it are as nothing.

Q Level 2

Mili D'Avot - *"crown" (taga)* - b'taga , i.e. crown. For just like a flesh and blood king places on his head a gold crown full of saphires, rubies, emeralds, diamonds, and other precious stones for honor and glory, so too the Holy One, blessed be He, His crown is the torah. For "it is more precious than pearls, and all your desirable things cannot be compared to it" (Mishlei 3:15).

And just like anyone who uses the crown of a king is immediately sentenced to death, so too one who uses the crown of torah and makes it into a tool for himself incurs death and deserves to be cut off from the world. This is the meaning of "passes (chalaf)", as in "If He passes (yachalif) and confines and assembles, who can hinder Him?" (Iyov 11:10).

Level 2
Toldot Yehoshua - incurs death (katla chayiv)" - the term "katla chayiv" implies death by sword. For "katla" is the targum (translation) of "hereg" (death), and stam hereg is death by sword, and we learned: "a sword comes to the world through perversion of justice, and perversion of torah interpretation..", since he did not learn.

Level 2
Chasid Yaavetz "chalaf" - (another hint) from the term chalipin (exchange), namely, he exchanges what he took in this world with what he should have taken in Olam Haba.

Level 4 — Ben Ish Chai
Ben Ish Chai - Birkat Avot - "one who uses the crown (taga) perishes (chalaf)", i.e. with arrogance, as a tag (crown) which is on the head. Namely, he uses and conducts himself with pride and arrogance. This is "chalaf". As the term "chalipin". For you already know what our teacher, Rav Chaim Vital zt'l said, that arrogance is the *"root that bears bitterness and wormwood"* (Devarim 29:18), the root for all sins of the torah.

Once a person clings to arrogance, he will go out from one evil to another, as explained at length in Shaarei Kedusha. Without a doubt, such a person will eventually stumble in many sins. Then, every mitzvah he has will be exchanged (chalipin) for the sins of his fellow, as our sages said: "if he merits, he will take his portion and his fellow's portion in Gan Eden. But if he is not meritorious, he will take his portion and his fellow's portion in Gehinom.." (Chagigah 15a). This is the meaning of "chalaf", he will exchange his portion of Gan Eden for his fellow's portion in Gehinom.

Level 2
Rabeinu Yitzchak - one who uses the crown of torah to pride himself or to use it as a tool for work - chalaf (passes) and is lost from the world. We find Belshatzar incurred death [by Heaven] for using the vessels of the temple of G-d. All the more so for one who uses the crown of torah (Nedarim 62a).. Another interpretation, one who uses torah scholars, who are the crown

of torah, as written there: "why was Avraham punished that his descendants were slaves in Egypt? Because he made an angaria (armed soldiers) of torah scholars who are the crown of torah (Nedarim 62a). Alternatively, one who uses holy Names..

Level 3 — Tiferet Yisrael

Tiferet Yisrael - he who wants to expand out and aggrandize his name in the world, that his reputation go out and that he rule in his city over everyone, then this is his punishment: "loses his name". For since he wanted honor that was not befitting him, he will lose even the little honor that he had previously, as our sages said: "whoever chases after honor, honor flees away from him" (Eiruvin 13a)..

The general principle: whoever prides himself becomes disappointed. For he thinks that if he runs after honor, people will honor him and if he conducts himself with humility people will debase him.

But it is really the opposite. One who seeks humility will find honor, while one who seeks honor will find shame. For even at his time of power, those before him will pretend [to flatter him] with their tongues but will scorn him in their hearts. Everyone will laugh at him behind his back and call him a fool and an arrogant imbecile. They will fight him and not let him raise his head. Likewise, "From heaven they fought him; the stars from their courses fought.." (Judges 5:20) to lower and debase him. For the Holy One, blessed be He, and the public hate the arrogant person and see him as an abomination. Even if he possesses all beautiful traits, they will only be as extinguished candles when they don't shine with the light of humility from above. For without humility, they will be viewed by everyone as "a gold ring in a pig's snout" (Mishlei 11:22).

The second characteristic of the arrogant person is that he does not want to learn and increase wisdom. Either because he thinks he knows enough. Or because his teachers are lowly in his eyes or because he fears the teacher will see through his deceptive foolishness. On this he said: "he who does not increase" in his learning, his punishment will be that he is gathered in before his time. For the purpose of life is to increase Shelemut (virtue/perfection). And this person who imagines that he already perfected himself sufficiently, why should he have life?

The third characteristic of the arrogant person is that he refuses to teach others what he knows more than them. For he thinks that if he teaches others his knowledge, with what will he have an upper hand over them? Sometimes it is because the student is too lowly in his eyes to bother dealing with him. On this he said: "one who does not study/teach deserves death". As our sages said on the verse: "many has she slayed" (Proverbs 7:26) - this refers to one who reached the level of teaching (torah) but does not. He is like one who removes the nipple from the babies, causing their death. Therefore, his punishment is death.

This is not just for torah. But rather whoever knows something that is beneficial to the world must publicize it unless he needs this (secret) for his livelihood. This is as Rabbi Yochanan who expended much effort to learn refuah tzafidna (special healing), and when he knew it, he immediately taught it to the public (Yomah 84a). Likewise for Ben Kamtzar and his friends who did not want to make their knowledge known, it was said on them: "but the name of the wicked shall rot" (Yomah 38b).

The fourth characteristic of the arrogant person is that all deeds and acts of righteousness and kindness he does are in order to pride himself (lehitgaot) in the eyes of the public. His intent is not to serve Hash-em. But rather to serve himself like idolatry.

Therefore his punishment is "chalaf" (pass over), i.e. one who uses the holy crown to support the bucket of his foul arrogance, will also have his honor profaned. It will chalaf and pass like the shadow of a bird flying overhead and he will not reach the paths to life.

Level 3 — Ruach Chaim

Ruach Chaim - even though at first one is forced to learn even for ulterior motives (shelo lishma). For a man cannot possibly climb up to the highest rungs in the ladder unless he first places his foot on the lowest rung.

Thus, the servant who was commanded by his master to climb the ladder does not transgress by stepping on the lowest rung. But afterwards, if he does not budge from his place and does not strive to climb further up and he just goes up and down, up and down, from the ground to the lowest rung continuously - he is rebelling against his master. This is the meaning of "one who does not increase", to ascend up, "ceases".

Perhaps a man will say: "since it is impossible for the beginning of my learning to be lishma (with proper intent), and learning shelo lishma incurs great punishment, therefore, I will sit idle and won't learn at all".

On this he said: "One who does not study deserves death". One must learn even though it will sometimes be not l'Shem Shamayim (not for the sake of Heaven). Only that he should see that from this he will come afterwards to lishma (properly), as our sages said: "a person should always toil in torah.. even not lishma. For from not lishma, he will come to lishma" (Pesachim 50b), i.e. that one learns even not lishma. However, in the manner and intent (ofen v'kaana) that through this he will come to the level of lishma.

He said "one who does not increase, ceases", i.e. if he does not add on to his learning, he will forget even what he learned already.

We will explain further according to the verse: "to the intelligent person, the path of life is above, in order that he turn away from the Sheol (grave) below" (Mishlei 15:24). For a man tells himself sometimes: "I will not strive for great levels. It is enough for me if I stand guard at my place, holding on to my innocence and fear of G-d. I will not try to increase further".

But in truth it is not so. For it is impossible for a man to stand in one place. If he does not go up, perforce he will fall down. Therefore, it is written: "To the intelligent person, the path of life is above". For if he does not ascend perforce he descends to the Sheol (grave, Gehinom). This is the meaning of "one who does not increase, ceases".

Level 3 — Ahava b'Taanugim

Rabbi Avraham Azoulai - Ahava b'Taanugim - after he said last mishna: "and draws them closer torah", he came to clarify how one's learning should be and one's intent in torah study.

Chapter 1 Mishna 13 - Uses The Crown

There are many types of torah students.

One type learns torah properly and increases to understand (deduce) one thing from another (umosif l'havin davar mitoch davar), but his intent in his learning is in order to make a name for himself in the world.

Corresponding to this, he said: "one who seeks a name, loses his name", i.e. the man who draws out his name, namely, his aspiration (megamato) and goal is for the good name itself, then, not only will he not find the name he seeks to draw out, but even whatever good name he had previously will be lost. This is the meaning of "loses his name", and he will be left bald from here and here (yishaer kerach mikan u'mikan).

Rather, the just way is to only seek to attain wholeness in and of its own good because it is the good (shelemut mitzad atzmo bema shehu tov), and the good name and honor wil come on its own, as written: "a good name is better than good oil" (Kohelet 7:1).

A second type of learner is the opposite of this. He does not at all want to add on what he learned with his Rav and does not want to understand (deduce) one thing from another. This is the meaning of "One who does not increase, ceases".

For one who does not try to increase on what he learned from his Rav "ceases", i.e. he will be cut off quickly from that shelemut (perfection) and learning. For this shows that his goal is not the shelemut itself. Only that the public should think he is a wise man. In hearing that from others, he is satisfied.

A third type does not want to learn at all - "incurs death", he will not succeed.

Another type learns in order to derive benefit from his learning. He makes his learning secondary (tafel) to the [material] benefit he receives to his body, but not to make a name for himself.

This person will be cut off from the world. For the purpose of all [material] good things is to attain the ultimate good, namely, torah study. This person who did the opposite will be cut off from the world, for it would have been better for him had he not been created... (see there for other explanations).

Level 3 — Maharal

Maharal - "one who seeks a name (na'ged shema), loses his name (avad shemei)" - "sherara" (rulership) is called "na'ged" as in "ruler (nagid) over His people" (Shmuel I 13). Thus, he said "na'ged shema" (seeks a name) on "sherara" (rulership), which is a term connoting continuance and permanence. But this name is not befitting to "Sherara". Rather, it should be called by the name "avad" (lost/destruction), as we explained earlier. For it causes destruction to its possessor, as they said: "woe to Rabbanut (dominion) for it buries its possessor" (Pesachim 87b).

Thus he did not use the same term "neged shema aved shema" (shin-mem-aleph both times) or neged shemeih aved shemeih (shin-mem-yud-heh both times, rather he switched terms. First one, then the other).

That is to say: "the name of sherara is "na'ged" (ruler). But this is not the appropriate name that is befitting it completely. Rather it should be called 'aved' (lost/destruction), since the baal sherara is lost through it".

We can also explain this as going on the baal sherara (person of authority) himself: "it is not proper for sherara to be called "na'ged", which connotes permanence. For, the name of the baal sherara (person of authority) is 'aved' (lost/destruction), and since the name of the baal sherara is 'aved' (lost), it is not proper for sherera to be called "na'ged" which connotes permanence...

You should know further, that which Rabanut (dominion) buries its possessor is because man receives life and existence (chiyut v'kiyum) from Hash-em, blessed be He, who is the living G-d and who bestows life and existence to all that is exists.

Thus, whoever lowers himself and makes himself into a receiver, such a person is fit to receive life from Hash-em, blessed be He. But the baal sherera who rules over others and does not make himself into a "receiver", but instead acts and rules (poel u'moshel) over others, he does not receive the continuance and the life (kiyum v'chaim).

For to receive life one needs to be a receiver of the life which Hash-em bestows constantly to man. For man exists only through Him, blessed be He, and the essence of the life itself is the receiving, that one receives the life. Thus, Hash-em is called the "source of life" (mekor haChaim). For a source always bestows. So too, Hash-em bestows life continuously to human beings like this source. Thus, whoever lowers himself receives continuance (kiyum) from Hash-em on Whom everything depends upon. But the Rabanut and Sherera (dominion) does not make itself into a receiver. It only makes itself into a ruler over others. Therefore, it is not fit for the Chiyut (life) as we explained. We will explain further soon.

On what he said "One who does not increase, ceases" - for torah is the opposite of Sherera. Through the torah, man clings to Him, blessed be He, as we explained elsewhere at length. Therefore, on the torah, it is written: "for it is your life and the length of your days" (Devarim 30:20). Due to this, torah is the complete opposite of Sherera. For torah is the essence of life (etzem hachaim). Thus, "one who does not increase, ceases. One who does not study incurs death".

The explanation is that if one does not increase to be toiling in torah, he will "cease", i.e. he will die before his time.

This is as we explained elsewhere that man is called "Adam" due to his being from the ground (adama), which is of physicality (baalat chomer). Therefore man needs to increase in the intellectual torah (torah sichlit) which is the opposite of physicality (chomer) and which is the life (chiyut) of man.

And also though torah, man has clinging (deveikut) with Him, blessed be He, as we explained in several places. For if not for the torah, man who is of physicality (baal chomer) would not have any clinging (deveikut) to Him, blessed be He. Therefore, in the torah is the life. This is the meaning of "he who does not increase, ceases".

Chapter 1 Mishna 13 - Uses The Crown

The explanation of: "one who does not increase" is that he is not exerting and toiling (yaga v'amel) in torah. Even though he learns torah, only that he does not toil in the matter (amal b'davar) and does not strengthen the intellect over the physical on which clings inexistence (eino magbir hasechel al hachomer shedavek bo hahe'eder). Therefore, "ceases".

"but one who does not study" - i.e. he does not learn at all, by justice he incurs death (chayiv b'din katla).

For he distances himself from the torah. Such a man is against (mitnaged) to the torah and brings death on himself, since he distances himself from it.

Likewise they said "why are the words of the Torah compared to a ruler (Nagid)? To tell you: just as a Nagid has power of life and death, so have the words of the Torah [powers] of life and death; [On this Raba said; To those who go to the right hand thereof it is an elixir of life; to those who go to the left hand thereof it is a deadly poison]." (Shab.88b).

The nagid executes through the judicial power. Therefore, he said "incurs death (katla chayiv)", i.e. by justice, because he distanced from the torah.

... through the torah, man clings to G-d, blessed be He. It is as an intermediary between the Holy One, blessed be He, and man, until through the torah man receives the life (hachaim). And when man distances from the torah through which is the clinging to G-d, blessed be He, he shortens his days and years...

"one who makes use of the crown (of Torah) chalaf (passes)" the explanation is that he passes from the world because the torah has divine holiness (kedusha Elokit), just like everything holy whereby the Name of Heaven is upon it (Shem Shamayim chal alav). And one who derives benefit from something which the Name of Heaven is upon it, his judgment is as one who takes benefit from Kodashim (temple offerings), namely, he incurs death.

The reason he incurs death is as follows. A man is a possessor

Chapter 1 Mishna 13 - Uses The Crown

of a body and of physicality (adam hu baal guf v'chomer). And [thus] it is not proper for him to join to something which is holy and separated (nivdal) from man, and which is a portion of Heaven (chelek Shamayim).

As you will find, when man joins with the upper things (elyonim) which do not have a [physical] body, death will come to him. For example: "We shall surely die, because we have seen G-d" (Shoftim 13).

For physical man does not have existence (metziut) with the transcendental (nivdalim). Thus when man joins to derive benefit from that which is a portion of Heaven, he incurs death.

Thus he said: "he who uses the crown (of Torah) passes". For the torah is transcendental intellect and separate (sichlit v'nivdelet) from man, who is of physicality, and who thus has no existence (metziut) with the torah.

Thus he said: "crown (of Torah) passes" for through the crown of majesty (malchut) which is on the king's head, he is separated from the people, as is known regarding a [human] king..

So too for the torah. It is the transcendent intellect (sechel) in man's head. It is the separated intellect (sechel nivdal).

Therefore, torah scholars are called "kings", as written: "Whence do you learn that the Rabbis are called kings? He replied; Because it is written (Mishlei 8:15): 'by me [the torah] kings reign'" (Gitin 62b).

This matter (mentioned above) causes that one who derives benefit from the torah which is the transcendent intellect (sechel nivdal) incurs death.

In tractate Nedarim (60a):
Rebbi Tarfon was found by a man eating [of the figs] when most of the knives had been folded, [whereupon] he threw him into a sack and carried him, to cast him in the river. 'Woe to Tarfon,' he cried out, 'whom this man is about to murder!' When the man heard this, he abandoned him and fled.

Chapter 1 Mishna 13 - Uses The Crown

Rebbi Abbahu said in the name of Rebbi Hananiah ben Gamliel: "All his lifetime that pious man grieved over this, saying. 'Woe is me that I made [profane] use of the crown of the Torah!' For Rabbah b. Bar Hanah said in R. Yohanan's name: "Whoever puts the crown of the Torah to [profane] use, is uprooted from the world".

This follows by logical inference (kal v'chomer): If Belshazzar, who used the holy vessels which had become profaned, as it is written: *"For the robbers shall enter into it, and profane it"* (Yechezkel 7:22) [teaching], since they had broken in, they were profaned; yet he was uprooted from the world, as it is written: *"in that night was Belshazzar slain"* (Daniel 5:30). How much more so he who makes [profane] use of the crown of the Torah, which endures forever!". end quote.

Thus, one who uses for himself that which is transcendent and holy is pushed off (nidche) and uprooted (ne'ekar) from the world. For when two things with no connection come together, the lesser one is pushed off since it has no existence (metziut) with the transcendent (nivdal) one...

He said this here because he said earlier: "one who seeks a name, loses his name". The opposite of this is the torah "One who does not increase, ceases".

He further comes to say that the primary Sherara (rulership) is not one who conducts himself in Rabbanut. Rather, the primary rulership is the crown of torah. This thing (of increasing torah) is called rulership and not any other rulership [is true rulership]. For one who uses for himself the crown of torah "chalaf" (passes) from the world...

After Hillel said these things, he said that a man should not consider himself a possessor of high levels and a possessor of torah (baal maala u'baal torah). Thus, he should strive to acquire torah. For through torah he will be considered a possessor of high levels (baal maala). This is what he continues "If I am not for myself, who will be for me", i.e. if a man does not perfect (mashlim) himself with torah and mitzvot, "who will be for me".

Chapter 1 Mishna 13 - Uses The Crown

For the torah and mitzvot others do are not going to help and perfect him... (continued next mishna)

Level 4 — Ben Ish Chai

Ben Ish Chai - Birkat Avot - (kabalistic) "one who seeks (neged) a name (Shema), loses his name" - this hints to the shin-mem (340) nitzutzot (sparks) that need to be separated out (levarer), and when all of them are separated out the name of the Sitra Achra wil be annulled and only the letters of the holy Name - El (Aleph-Lamed) will remain. Thus, "neged shema", hinting to the Shin-Mem nitzutzot which are gematria Shema (with kolel). And "neged" means to draw out, as in: "A river of fire was flowing and emerging (neged) from before Him" Daniel 7:10. The intent is when the shin-Mem nitzutzot will be drawn out completely, then Aved Shemei (the name will be lost) of the Sitra Achra.

Another interpretation, neged also means separation, as in "Cut down the tree" (gudo ilana)" (Daniel 4:11). The intent is he who blemishes and separates Yud-Heh from Vav-Heh, this is "neged shema", measure for measure, his name wil be lost. For it is known that the letters of a man's name are his life channels (tzinurot hahiyut), as the Rav Arvei Nachal writes on the verse "each living thing, that was its name" (Gen.2:19), see there.

"one who does not increase, ceases" - i.e. a man needs to join and combine (leshalev) the Shem Havaya with the Shem Adnut. This is "one who does not increase (udlo mosif)", namely, if he does not add (holiness), then "yosif" (cease, the word "yosif" can also be rendered as "adds"), i.e. he will at least "add" to the Sitra Achra. Alternatively, if he does not add on the holiness by separating out the nitzutzot of holiness, yasif (he will die).

And if you ask: "but what can he do? He did not learn properly and does not know on the Sod Hash-em, to combine and join (leshalev u'lechaber) the Shem Ha'vaya with the Shem A-donai, and he also does not know how to separate out (levarer) the sparks of holinesss properly and raise them to the holiness?"

On this he said: "one who does not study incurs death". Who told him not to learn? Is not the torah open to all? Let him come and learn. And even one who did not learn in his youth, nevertheless, he can learn afterwards. He should at least learn the seder avodah, as we were taught by the righteous teacher.

Chapter 1 Mishna 14 - What Am I

He would say: If I am not for me, who will be for me? And if I am for myself, what am I? And if not now, when? הוּא הָיָה אוֹמֵר, אִם אֵין אֲנִי לִי, מִי לִי. וּכְשֶׁאֲנִי לְעַצְמִי, מָה אֲנִי. וְאִם לֹא עַכְשָׁיו, אֵימָתָי.

Level 1 — Bartenura

Bartenura - "if I am not for me, who will be for me?" - if I don't merit [torah and mitzvot] for myself, who will merit for me?

"And if I am only for myself, what am I?" - even if I merited for myself, what merit is this and what importance does it have relative to [all] that I am obligated to do?

And if not now, when? - if not in this world, when? For after death it is impossible to merit anything more. Alternatively, if not now during my youth, when? Perhaps in my old age I will not succeed.

Level 1 — Rabeinu Yonah

Rabeinu Yonah - "if I am not for me" - if I don't rebuke and motivate myself in the mitzvot "who will be for me?", to rebuke me and motivate me. For the rousing of others only helps temporarily. But when one rouses himself every day, every hour, he will increasingly think thoughts on doing the work of Hash-em, and will not hide [from his duties] as his heart wishes. This is the just path.

Level 1 — Chida

Chida - Zeroa Yamin - "If I am not for me, who will be for me?" - even if I have a wise and capable son (ben chacham v'yo'il), this may only help to save me from Gehinom, but to complete my tikun (rectification), it will not help much.

Level 1 — Sforno

Sforno - "And if I am only for myself, what am I?" - if I strive only to perfect myself and do not try to teach others to fulfill Hash-em's intent with many (b'rov am), what importance am I that through me alone the will of my Master be fulfilled. This fits well with my explanation (previous mishna) of "one who does not teach (yalef) incurs death" (delo yalef katala chayiv) - he who does not teach (yalef) incurs death, since he did not care to elevate the honor of his Maker with what he was able to do, as happened to Moshe with the rock...

Level 1 — Rambam
Rambam - and if not now, when? - for the acquired (habits) and character traits strengthen and settle in..

Level 1 — Rabeinu Yonah
Rabeinu Yonah - Included also in this phrase is if not now in the days of youth, when? If he leaves it for the days of old age, he will not be able to do it. On this David said: "for our sons are like saplings, grown up in their youth" (Tehilim 144:12). For when a tree is a small sapling, a man can adjust it to grow straight instead of crooked. But after it grows, it is extremely difficult to straighten it. So too for man. When he is young it is easy for him to grow in the good path and turn from evil. But after he grew old in wickedness, will it be easy for him to leave it?!.. Furthermore, teshuva (repentance) in old age is not full teshuva. For then, the yetzer is not strong and lusts increasingly weaken and are not pleasing to the nefesh (soul), and he has no desire or pleasure in sins...

Level 2
Rabeinu Yosef ben Sasson: "if not now when?", i.e. if I will not toil in torah now, namely, this second that I stand inside, when will another second come in the future which will be more proper to toil than this one, or equal to it? For if I abandon this second, it will require more effort to toil in a future second, for habit rules over everything.

Another explanation, if I don't toil now in this second I stand in, and I waste it and lose it, when will I find this lost object? For there is no second of my time that I am free to waste. This reason causes the intelligent man to not waste his time for even a second and to not be lax in this time to rely on a future time.

Level 2 — Rabeinu Yonah
Rabeinu Yonah - "And if I am only for myself, what am I?" - even if others rebuke me and I rebuke myself, I still can't accomplish even a thousandth of what I am obligated. The sages gave an analogy: "a king gave a field to his servants and fixed with them to produce 30 measures per year. They worked hard but produced only 5 measures. The king said to them: "but you

pledged 30 measures". They replied: "the land you gave us is weak (ziborit) we worked hard but were unable to produce more than 5 measures from it."

So too we tell the Holy One, blessed be He: "the yetzer hara You placed in us is evil from youth, as written: 'for the imagination of man's heart is evil from his youth' (Ber.8:21) For even if a man works hard to do what is just in Hash-em's eyes, nevertheless, he will attain only a little bit of what was proper to do..

For without the yetzer hara which rules much over people, one would perform the mitzvot even without toiling and without going after them, like a fertile field (idit), which produces even without much work. But now that one knows that even if he works a lot, he will only attain a little due to the yetzer in the heart of man who corrupts his body, all the more so if he does not toil at all will his soul be empty of mitzvot, like a non-fertile field...

Thus "if I am for me, what am I?", if I don't rouse myself to go after the mitzvot, I will remain empty of them, and even if I am for myself and toil in the mitzvot, I will only attain a small fraction of my portion. Thus, what will I attain if I don't toil at all?

"And if not now, when?" - if one says: "today I will do my work and tomorrow I will be free to rectify myself". Perhaps you will not be free and even if you will be free, all of your life, you will never be able to pay back that day which has passed by idly without the work of Heaven. For one is obligated to rectify his body and toil in mitzvot all the days of his life on the earth, and he does not have permission to be idle from his work for even one hour.

Q Level 2   Ahava b'Taanugim

Rabbi Avraham Azoulai - Ahava b'Taanugim - "If I am not to me, who will be for me?" - the intent is that a man should not become proud because of his money or sons. It is a kal v'chomer (logical inference): "if I, namely, my body, does not belong to me, for every moment and every second, I am destined to die, if so, what can I call mine? My money is not mine, my sons are not mine. For if my body and self is not mine, all the more so for things external to me. If so, how could I pride myself in them?

And if I am for myself, what am I? - If I think: I am still a young man and according to nature, my time [to die] has not come, for I am still for myself since I am young. But what am I really worth? As in "what are we?" (Shemot 16:7). For young men are destined to die just like old men. If so, when I am a young, I am futility and emptiness (hevel v'rik).

And if not now, when? - if so, if I don't serve my Maker now, when will I serve Him? For if we say: "tomorrow I will pay back what I owe", but tomorrow I need to serve what I am obligated in for tomorrow and Halevai (would that it were) that I will pay what I owe for tomorrow...

Ben Ish Chai
Level 2

Ben Ish Chai - Zechut Avot - this hints on the trait of humility. It is known that one who holds onto the trait of humility gains that he will have no enemies and accusers. Rather, he will be beloved above and cherished below. Thus, "if I am not for me", i.e. I think myself as nothing, "who will be for me?", who will fight me and be jealous of me? "And if I am only for myself", but when I make myself appear full of wisdom and wealth, "what am I" (people will question what is he really?).

Tiferet Yisrael
Level 3

Tiferet Yisrael - here Hillel is speaking about humility in thought. There are three reasons in thought for the arrogant person to feel arrogance.

One, he thinks he possesses some quality (maala), such as wealth, beauty, wisdom, or the like. On this he answers: "if I am not for me", i.e. if I and my arrogant thoughts do not belong to me to conquer [them], who and with what can I pride myself in that does belong to me? (translator: i.e. the only quality that truly belongs to me is the quality of conquering my arrogant thoughts). Or, on who can I rule over if I am unable to rule over myself?

Two, that he thinks and prides himself on every little thing he does as if he did grand things and wonders in the world. He tells himself in his heart: "indeed, by my own efforts, I have accomplished all these things. How could my heart not become proud?"

On this he answers:
"And if I am only for myself, what am I?", i.e. I know that I did not

Chapter 1 Mishna 14 - What Am I

do the good because it is good, nor did I do it because this is the will of the Creator. Rather, I did it for myself, to pride myself, and all my deeds are tainted with arrogance. What importance can such a deed have?

Alternatively, when I sit in solitude with myself and examine myself well, I find many personal flaws. Although they are concealed from all other people, it is enough for me that they are known to He who knows hidden things and to myself. How could my heart not be broken inside?..

Three, he thinks humility is only befitting and noble to someone who has reached great levels and honor. Then, when such a person stoops down from his high throne to speak and deal with the small people, a "thread of kindness will be drawn from him", and humility will be befitting him.

But as long as one's honor has not taken root, he thinks humility and submission will damage him. For people will consider him a simpleton and will scorn him. On this he answered *"And if not now, when?"*, if you don't employ the trait of humility now while you are still truly small and lowly, and while it befits your standing, "when" will you employ it? For when your feathers (honor) grow a bit, you will consider yourself like an eagle in the sky and say "I am, and there is none else besides me (ani vafsi od)" (Isaiah 47:8).

Level 3 — Maharal

Maharal - in the Midrash (Vayikra Rabba ch.4): "all a man's labor is for his mouth [and also the nefesh (soul) will not be satiated]" (Kohelet 6:7), R. Shmuel bar Yitchak says: "all that a man labors in mitzvot and good deeds is only for his mouth and not for the mouth of his son or daughter".

The Midrash continues:
R. Levi says: "and also the soul will not be satiated". Since the soul knows that all that it toils in is for itself, therefore it is not satiated with mitzvot and good deeds.

R. Levi says: this is analogous to a peasant farmer who married a princess. Even if he brings her his choicest goods.. he does not fulfill his duty (lo yotzei yedei chovato). Why? Because she is a princess. So too, for all that a man labors on his soul, he does not discharge his duty. Why? Because the soul is from on high (milemaala, i.e. higher worlds). end quote.

Through this Midrash, they clarified that however much a man perfects (mashlim) himself, this perfection is only for himself and does not go to anyone else, not even his son or daughter; only to him.

R. Levi said on this verse: "also the nefesh (soul) will not be satiated", this adds so that one does not say: "it is possible for one's soul to be satiated with mitzvot and good deeds, just like when a man eats and drinks much he will certainly fill his stomach [and be satiated]". On this he answered: "also the nefesh (soul) will not be satiated". For the soul always wants to perfect (mashlim) itself more and more.

R. Levi then brings an analogy to a peasant farmer who married a princess whereby he cannot possibly fulfill his duty towards the princess.

So too for the neshama who is from on high; she is married to a man possessing a physical body, and even if the man does mitzvot and good deeds and they are perfection to the soul, but nevertheless, the soul will not be filled, namely that it be whole with complete perfection (sheleimut gamur). For it itself is from Hash-em, blessed be He, according to what is proper to it.

Due to this, it is not satiated from the torah, mitzvot, and good deeds man does with his body. For according to the exaltedness of the soul, who is from above, while man possessing a physical body, is from below. Thus the soul is not satisfied from this completely as is befitting the soul who is from Heaven.

On these things, Hillel said: "If I am not for me, who will be for me?". For man needs to perfect (mashlim) himself, and the perfection (sheleimut) will not come to him from someone else.

"And if I am for myself, what am I?" - i.e. [even if] man does mitzvot with his body and as we explained in the introduction on the verse: "a mitzvah is a candle, and the Torah is light" (Mishlei

6:23), this does not bring complete hashlama (perfection) to the soul. Thus, he said "what am I?", for I am but a man. (translator: i.e. even if I do my best, nevertheless, I cannot perfect my soul completely)

He added a third statement: "if not now, when?" For man's days are few. Thus it is incumbent on man to wake up from his sleep and do mitzvot and good deeds. Since he cannot rely on others and even if he does all that is incumbent on him, he should not think that he can complete and satiate his soul. For even if he is for himself, what is he? He is unable to satiate his soul with mitzvot and good deeds. All the more so, if not now, when? For his days are few and he will be taken away suddenly and be no more (in this world).

All of Hillel's words are of humility as was his trait. Thus he said them together. Shammai likewise gave mussar according to his trait.. (continued next mishna).

Translator

Translator - "And if I am for myself, what am I?" - the arrogant Haman said: "all this is worth nothing to me" (kol ze eineno shavei li). Although the whole world bowed down to him and he was the richest man, he felt totally empty because he didn't have everything and everyone bowing to him.

Both the righteous and the wicked are never satiated. But the righteous feeds his soul real food while the wicked feeds himself imaginary food. The righteous man feels real joy and his soul thirsts for more joy, while the wicked man feels emptiness and sadness. But instead of giving up his toys, he tries to fill himself with more toys which only increase his emptiness and sadness. And as the Vilna Gaon wrote: "The world is like one who drinks salty water: he thinks it quenches his thirst, but it only makes him thirstier" (Iggeret HaGra).

Ruach Chaim

Ruach Chaim - if I am not for me.. - for the yetzer hara (evil inclination) blinds a man's eyes by telling him always: "how can you possibly learn torah? You are forced to toil in your livelihood to provide for your wife and small children. And how much more so in our times when the yoke of earning a livelihood has grown heavy.

But in truth it is only the counsel of the blinding yetzer. For our sages taught: "before the formation of the fetus, it was decreed on the drop whether he will be rich or poor" (Nidah 16b). This is in a general way for all of one's lifetime. And in particular, each and every year it is said: "a person's sustenance is fixed for him from Rosh Hashana".

Thus, despite all his toil, he will not attain even a tiny bit more than what was fixed for him, and he could have attained this same amount even with little toil. But for torah, everything is according to the toil. The more he exerts himself, the more he will increase knowledge (daat). This is what Hillel said regarding toil in torah: *"if I am not for me who will be for me?"* For everything depends on me. But regarding matters of this world: *"And if I am only for myself, what am I?"*, for this depends on Hash-em (what He fixed on Rosh Hashana).

Furthermore, in three ways toil in torah and yirah is different from toil in one's livelihood.

One, toil in torah and yira is incumbent on man and Hash-em asks this from him, unlike one's livelihood. For there, although we were commanded to "benefit from the work of our hands", but salvation comes from Hash-em and extra toil will not avail nor succeed. So why would a man toil much for that which Hash-em can provide without any toil (livelihood) while leaving aside that which is in his ability and incumbent on him (torah).

Two, for matters of this world, he will not add anything to what was fixed for him by toiling more. But in torah, "he who comes to purify himself is helped", and even so, he will be paid full reward, as written in Sukkah...

Three, for matters of this world, if one skips a day, he can make it up the next day. But for service of Hash-em, one cannot fulfill today the obligations of another day. Would that it were (halevai) that one could fulfill each day's obligations. If one discharged his obligations for today, fortunate is he.

another explanation:

Chapter 1 Mishna 14 - What Am I

"If I am not for me, who will be for me? And if I am only for myself, what am I? And if not now, when?"

(1) *"if I am not for me"*, for matters of Heaven, *"who will be for me?"*, for it is in my hands only, not in the hands of Heaven.

(2) *"And if I am only for myself"*, i.e. without help from my Creator, *"what am I?"* For "every day the yetzer of a man strengthens itself seeking to slay him, without Hash-m's help, man could not prevail" (Kiddushin 30b).

One should not say: "if so, I will wait until I am granted help from Heaven".

For the beginning needs to come from man himself, and according to the magnitude of the preparation and strengthening, will be the corresponding increase in divine help from Heaven, as our sages said: "one who comes to purify himself is helped", i.e. only if he comes first, as before. This is what he said: "if I am not for me", if I am not the one who begins, "who will be for me?", "And if I am only for myself", without help from Hash-em, "what am I", "and if not now, when?", for tomorrow cannot pay the debt of now.

Furthermore later in chapter 2: "repent one day before your death". But here he says even at all times, every second, one needs to repent. For a man is not assured of what will be for even one second. This is the meaning of "if not now, when?"...

For the yetzer hara comes to entice a man on three fronts.

One, a man imagines to himself that he is a tzadik (righteous).

Two, or he tells him: "repent in your old age".

Three, wait until you repent out of love.. corresponding to these David said: *"I am poor, and close to sudden death; I have borne Your fear.."* (Tehilim 89:16). Corresponding to the first: "I am poor", i.e. I am poor in good deeds.

Corresponding to the second "close to sudden death", I don't know the day of my death and every day I think maybe it is today and I need to repent before death.

Corresponding to the third: "I have borne Your fear..", and halevai that I repent out of fear.

Level 1 — Chida

Chida - Roshei Avot - in their wisdom, the language of the Tannaim (sages of the mishna) includes many different things simultaneously. For the Ruach Hash-em (Spirit of G-d) spoke through them...

Translator - we will now see many more amazing facets of this mishna...

Level 3 — Chasdei David

In the Talmud (Yomah 35b):
"It was reported about Hillel the Elder that every day he used to chop wood and earn one tropaik, half of which he would give to the guard at the Beit Midrash (House of Learning), the other half he spent for his food and for that of his family. One day he found nothing to earn and the guard at the Beit Midrash would not permit him to enter. He climbed up the roof and sat upon the window, to hear the words of the living G-d from the mouths of Shemayah and Avtalion - That day was the eve of Sabbath in the winter solstice and snow fell down upon him from the sky.

When the dawn rose, Shemayah said to Avtalion: Avtalion, my brother, on every day there is light in this house and today it is dark, is it perhaps a cloudy day? They looked up and saw the figure of a man in the window. They went up and found him covered by three cubits of snow. They removed him, bathed and anointed him and placed him opposite the fire and they said: This man deserves that the Sabbath be profaned on his behalf..." end quote.

Chasdei David - "If I am not for me, who will be for me?" - if I did not go up on the roof [who will be for me?], for they did not allow me to enter the Beit Midrash.

If you say: "you should have learned torah at home", "And if I am for myself, what am I?". I needed to hear the words of the living G-d from the mouths of Shemaya and Avtalyon..

And if you say: "you should have waited until you earned enough money to be able to enter". On this, he answered: "And if not now, when?", if I don't hear now the words of torah from the mouths of Shemaya and Avtalyon, when will I hear?

And as taught later: "do not say: 'When I am free, I will study'"; perhaps you will never be free'"..., and in the talmud: "Rav said: 'a man should not absent himself from the Beit Midrash even one hour" (Beitzah 24b).

Level 2 — Chatam Sofer

Chatam Sofer end of Vayikra - "If I am not for me, who will be for me?" - one can be a good speaker, but if he does not practice what he preaches, if the Rav does not "appear like an angel of G-d" (Chagigah 15b), then also his students won't succeed.

"And if I am for myself" - if I am completely righteous (tzadik gamur) but don't raise up students *"what am I?"* And if one says: "while I am young, I will work on myself, and later on when I am old, I will raise up some students. This, way I will succeed in both areas". On this he answered: *"if not now, when?"*

Level 2 — Chatam Sofer

Chatam Sofer Drashot vol.3 24:1 - it is known to every intelligent person that our intent in these days (high holidays) is not to pray for the livelihood and sustenance of this dark physical body, whose good will not benefit us, who obstructs the intellect (sechel) and brings up powerfuls fumes and fogs to darken one's eye, to extinguish its light, the candle of G-d, the soul of man.

Rather, our intent and purpose is to rectify our souls, to raise the eternal lamp towards the path which ascends to the House of G-d. But since this is impossible without the assistance of the body, for a man cannot serve G-d while he is hungry, thirsty and tired, worn out and without desire. Therefore, we put our heart to pray on this hotel-keeper, to provide his sustenance and benefit from his folly.

Perhaps on this Hillel had intent when telling himself:
"If I am not for me, who will be for me?" - for in this body there is no help and no avail. Perhaps you will say: "if so, for what purpose were we placed in physical bodies?".

"And if I am for myself", without a body, *"what am I?* For I would be on a spiritual plane (without free will) and without reward and punishment.

"And if not now", before I separate from the body, *"when?"* For death is waiting.

Level 3 — Chasdei David

Chasdei David - in the book Magen Avot (Maharshak) the words of Hillel are explained as going on tefila (prayer). Here is a summary of his words.

Prayer is a positive mitzvah (commandment) from the torah, to pray before Hash-em, blessed be He. Even though one should trust in G-d, but nevertheless, one is obligated to pray for his needs. And if he does not pray, it will not be given to him from Heaven.

The manner of prayer needs to be according to our sages: "whoever associates (meshatef) the Name of Heaven with his suffering, will have his livelihood doubled" (Berachot 63a).

According to this, here is the explanation of the Mishna:
"If I am not for me" - if I don't pray for myself, to ask for my needs, *"who will be for me?"*. No creature will care at all for me. Rather, I need to beseech Him, blessed be He, for my livelihood.

Nevertheless, *"if I am for myself"*, if I don't associate (meshatef) the Name of Heaven in my suffering (tzaari), that I have intent only for myself, *"what am I?"*, that I be worthy of having my prayer accepted and what will I attain for myself alone?

But if I have intent to associate (leshatef) Him, blessed be He, then I will receive much. For then "his livelihood is doubled". And he said: *"and if not now, when?"*. For our sages said: "one should always pray before troubles come" (Sanhedrin 44b). Namely, during troubles, it is a time of wrath (charon af) and it is difficult for one's prayer to be accepted. But if one prays not during troubles, then it is a favorable time (eit ratzon). Therefore, it will be easier for the prayer to be accepted.

Level 2 — Chatam Sofer

Ketav Sofer, Derashot, Derash Shabbat HaGadol - Hillel was the Nassi of Israel (leader of the generation). Although he was extremely humble, nevertheless, he would conduct his position in an elevated manner, not associating excessively with everyone. He said: *"if am not for me"*, to conduct myself in an elevated manner, *"who will be for me?"*.

No one will listen to my words. Therefore, he adorned himself (hithader) before the people. But he did not become proud in his heart due to this. Because when he was by himself, he would consider in his heart that he has nothing to be proud of. Thus, "when I am for myself?", when I am by myself in solitude and separated from the people, I know that *"what am I?"*, there is nothing in me, as before.

Q Level 2 — Ben Ish Chai
Ben Ish Chai - Zechut Avot - this hints on the trait of humility. It is known that one who holds onto the trait of humility gains that he will have no enemies and accusers. Rather, he will be beloved above and cherished below. Thus, "if I am not for me", i.e. I think myself as nothing, "who will be for me?", who will fight me and be jealous of me? "And if I am only for myself", but when I make myself appear full of wisdom and wealth, "what am I" (people will question what is he really?).

Q Level 4 — Ben Ish Chai
Ben Ish Chai - Zechut Avot - "if I am not for me.." (kabalistic) - it is known that Moshe Rabeinu is of the "Mi", which is the Sod of Bina.. it is known that Hillel was extremely humble. And in order to not attribute good to himself, he said: "if I am not for me who is for me (Mi li)", i.e. if you see that it appears that I don't consider myself as anything, this is not due to me. Rather, it is from the power of "Mi Li", "Mi" to me, i.e., a hint to Moshe Rabeinu who merited Binah which is called "Mi". For I was a nitzutz (spark) of him. Due to this I merited humility.

Q Level 4 — Ben Ish Chai
Ben Ish Chai - Chasdei Avot - "if I (ani) am not (ain) to me (li), who (mi) is for me?" (kabalistic) - it is known that the Keter is called "ain" (aleph-yud-nun), and the Malchut which is the tenth (sefira) is called "ani". It is also known that Bina, which is the Sod (secret) of Olam Haba (the world to come), is called "mi", and the tzadik who is called a "ben olam haba" elevates the mayim

nukvim to Bina above from the Malchut who is called "ani", for the small lower ones (people), elevate only in Malchut specifically.

This is the meaning of *"if I am not for me (im ain ani li mi li)"*, i.e. I miyached all the ten sefirot from the Keter which is called "ain" until the Malchut which is called "ani", that through this I draw down shefa from the Keter to the Malchut, then "mi li", I will merit to be called a "ben Olam Haba", and I will have the power to elevate the mayim nukvim to Binah who is called "mi". But when I am for myself, i.e. the malchut which is called "I am only for myself" (ani hi levada l'atzmi), for all that I elevate above only goes to the Malchut and not higher, then *"what am I?"*, i.e. what can such a small man be considered compared to other great tzadikim who are Benei Olam Haba?

Level 4 — Ben Ish Chai

Ben Ish Chai - Birkat Avot - (kabalistic) - it is known that during the Galut (exile), we need to scream (in prayer) before the Holy One, blessed be He, to bring the Geulah (redemption). This needs to be for the honor of the Shechinah, so to speak, who is with us in exile and not for our own honor. For what are we worth? Where is our torah and our mitzvot to protect us? On this, he said:

"if I (ani) am not for me", i.e. if the Shechinah who is called "Ani" is not for me, to help me when I scream to the Holy One, blessed be He, "who is for me?", i.e. who will help me? For where is our torah and our mitzvot to protect us.

"And if I am for myself", i.e. if I ask for the Geulah for myself only, *"what am I"*, that I be worthy of screaming for myself?...

Level 4 — Ben Ish Chai

Ben Ish Chai - Birkat Avot - (kabalistic) - *"And if I am for myself, what am I?"* - Rabeinu Chaim Vital wrote in his commentary on pirkei avot as follows:

"Know that G-d and His torah are one, and likewise on Yisrael, His people, it is written: 'who is like Your people Israel, one people..' (Shmuel II 7:23). And He said: 'all that is called by My Name, and whom I created for My glory, I formed him and I made him' (Isaiah 43:7)".

Chapter 1 Mishna 14 - What Am I

The matter (inyan) is as follows. You already know that the soul has five names: Nefesh, Ruach, Neshama, Chaya, Yechida. These correspond to the five worlds. For Nefesh is from the world of Asiyah, Ruach from the world of Yetzira, Neshama from Beriah, and Neshama of Neshama is from Atzilut. In this way too is man's body. The skin corresponds to the world of Asiyah, the flesh corresponds to Yetzira, the Gidim (sinews) to Briah, and the bones to Atzilut...". end quote. see there his holy words.

Thus, we learned that the bones correspond to Atzilut. And behold all of our aspirations in our good deeds are in order to elevate the fruit of our deeds to the world of Atzilut, which is called the "world of machshava (thought)", for there is the absolute rectification (tachlit hatikun).

For "through wisdom all is purified" (b'chachma itbarir kula). Behold man is called by several names: "Enosh", "Gever", "Ish", and "Adam". But the choicest of them is the title (to'ar) "Adam". For thus our sages, of blessed memory, said: "you are called Adam but the nations are not called Adam".

For Adam is gematria 45. This equals the Name Havaya with Milui Alephin as brought in the petichat Eliyahu.. see there. With this we understand:
"if I am for myself (l'atzmi)", i.e. I strive to ascend the tikun l'atzmi (to my bones), a hint to Atzilut, which is on the level of bones, in this, I will merit to be called Adam. This is *"what am I"* (ma ani), I am "ma", which is gematria 45, as the Name Havaya with Milui Alephin, which corresponds to Atzilut.. (see there for more)

Q Level 4 — Chida

Chida - Zeroa Yamin - *"And when I am for myself"*, namely, I did all my righteous acts, I must still know *"what am I?"*, what did I become obligated in from past Gilgulim (lives).. and if you say: since I know that I am a tzadik (righteous man) now, what do I care about the past? On this he answered: *"if not now, when"* will I rectify? For I will need to come back in a different Gilgul, and who knows if I will be ready to rectify like this day.

Q Level 4 — Chida

Chida - Chasdei Avot - (kabalistic) if a man sinned a great sin whereby there is no teshuva (repentance) for him due to the

Chapter 1 Mishna 14 - What Am I

enormity of his sin, this is only if he did a medium (beinonit) teshuva. But if he does a great teshuva in the level (bechina) of Binah, then his teshuva is accepted.

They also said that a man needs to [always] increase his deeds and to ascend higher levels.

At first, he willl merit to the Nefesh which is the level (Bechina) of Malchut.

Afterwards, if he merits further, he will merit the Ruach, the level (Bechina) of Ze'er Anpin (Yesod) and so on.

"If I am not for me, who will be for me? And if I am for myself, what am I? And if not now, when?"

We may say this is a hint here:
"if I (ani) am not for me", i.e. if I sinned to the extent that the Malchut does not accept me with Teshuva beinonit, for "ani" hints to Malchut. Thus, *"if I (ani) am not"*, of the bechina of Malchut, since my sins were great, nevertheless, there is still hope, "who is for me? (mi li?)". *"Mi"* hints to Binah which has 50 gates, as the gematria of "Mi" (mem-yud). If I strengthen in teshuva to the level of Binah, "mi li" (Binah is to me)..

"And if I am for myself", i.e. one who merited to the level of Nefesh, the level of Malchut, which is *"Ani"*, he must nevertheless strive to acquire the Ruach, Ze'er Anpin, "what am I? (ma ani)", the level of the "Ma" (Mem- Heh), which is Ze'er Anpin. This is the meaning of "ma ani?" - "mem-heh ani", that I merit to the level of "mem-heh ani". "And if not now, when", for "there is neither deed nor reckoning, neither knowledge nor wisdom in the grave, where you are going" (Kohelet 9:10).

Chapter 1 Mishna 15 - Torah Fixed

Shammai would say: Make your Torah fixed, say little and do much, and receive every person with a pleasant countenance.

שַׁמַּאי אוֹמֵר, עֲשֵׂה תוֹרָתְךָ קֶבַע. אֱמֹר מְעַט וַעֲשֵׂה הַרְבֵּה, וֶהֱוֵי מְקַבֵּל אֶת כָּל הָאָדָם בְּסֵבֶר פָּנִים יָפוֹת.

Level 1 — Bartenura

Bartenura - "make your Torah fixed" - let your primary occupation day and night be in torah. And when you are tired from torah study, do work.

But not that your primary occupation is in work and when you are free from work, you toil in torah.

Level 1 — Rambam

Rambam - "make your Torah fixed" - the root and primary [occupation], and all your other occupations follow after it. If there comes (nizdamen) [work], there comes. If not, not. No damage when lacking.

Level 2 — Rabeinu Yonah

Rabeinu Yonah - "make your Torah fixed" - as written in Avot d'Rebbi Natan (28:10) "whoever makes his torah primary and his work secondary is made primary in Olam Haba (the World to Come). But he who makes his work primary and his torah secondary is made secondary in Olam Haba" - that is to say, if he did not commit any sins but nevertheless did not make torah primary, then even if he merits to be in Gan Eden, he will be secondary there.

"receive every person with a pleasant countenance" - show others a joyous, pleasant face in order that the public benefit from you, i.e. distance from the trait of anger. For it is a very evil trait, and conduct yourself with the trait of contentment (ratzon), in such a way that people will be pleased with you..

On this the mussar masters said: "do you wish to want (that others like you)? - want what you don't want". For a man cannot attain that others want (like) him, without overriding his own wishes for their wishes, i.e. to annul one's own wish for theirs.

Chapter 1 Mishna 15 - Torah Fixed

Through this, he will have many friends and guard himself from their damages. For one who shows others a sullen face (panim zoafot), they will hate him and distance from him and seek to harm him.

Level 2 — Chida

Chida - Chasdei Avot - in the Sefer Chareidim page 68: "make your torah fixed" - such number of chapters every day, such number of halachot per day, like the fixed workload (chok) of a servant.

Level 2 — Tiferet Yisrael

Tiferet Yisrael - "Shammai..." - he also said three things corresponding to the three thing said by Shimon HaTzadik.

Corresponding to torah, he said *"make your Torah fixed"*. Corresponding to Avodah, he said: "say little and do much", i.e. in your service of G-d promise little..

Corresponding to acts of kindness, he said *"receive every person with a pleasant countenance"*. This is the first act of kindness to do to the guest and also to other people. Through this, love between others will increase. One will also gain that he will have many friends..

Level 1 — Bartenura

Bartenura - "receive every person with a pleasant countenance" - when you bring guests in your house, don't give to them while your face is facing the ground. For whoever gives while his face is facing the ground, even if he gives all the gifts of the world, it is as if he gave nothing...

Level 3 — Ben Ish Chai

Ben Ish Chai - Zechut Avot - even though I told you to exert yourself greatly in torah, do not think that if a guest comes to you, push him away and don't "receive him with a pleasant countenance", lest he disturb you from your learning for some time. Rather remember what they said: "derech eretz (decency) preceded torah".

Level 3 — Chatam Sofer

Ketav Sofer, Derashot, Peticha l'Bnei Yeshivot - "make your Torah fixed" - that your toil in torah be fixed, i.e. fixed day and night without letup (b'keviut yomam v'layla m'ein hafugot).

"say little and do much" - i.e. that one learns alot of torah. But in one's own eyes, he should diminish himself (yaktin atzmo) and say that it is only little. Through this, he will add on always and not be quiet day and night, abandoning his nefesh (i.e. lust for bodily comfort).

But in order to increase and amass torah and mitzot, he will be disgusted by worldly matters and may abandon honor of the public (kavod habriot). This is what the Tanna exhorts and warns greatly to he who says little and does much - even so, *"receive every person with a pleasant countenance"*.

In truth, this is among the difficulties and tests, may Hash-em teach us and help us...

Level 3 — Alei Shur

Alei Shur II 6:3 - "receive every person with a pleasant countenance" - when G-d created man in His image, not only did He bestow of His glory granting man the crown of intellect and virtuous traits, but also in this He created man in His image - that He granted man the power of heerat panim (shining [spiritual] light through his facial countenance)...

The holy Rav Avraham Grodzinsky toiled two years on this. All those who met him tell stories just how much this trait was [deeply] acquired in his soul. Even during the most difficult years in the ghetto, his sorrow was concealed in his heart but the illumination did not leave his face (Toras Avraham pg.11).

If such a great man toiled two years in this, we can toil in this at least two months!

Another point in this, one should not be choosy to who he shines countenance of the face to. Certainly, it is easier and more pleasant to do this to friends and acquaintances. One may not even consider that it is possible to do this to the shopkeeper, the bank teller or the driver - but they also have an image of G-d.

However, specifically through this will the Shem Shamayim (Name of Heaven) become beloved through us - when we show a pleasant countenance to the simple people!

A certain baal teshuva (non observant Jew who became observant) was asked who roused him to return to Judaism? He answered:

"I was born in a secular city. I lived in a neighborhood where there was only one religious Jew there. The Jews in the area were not used to saying "shalom" to each other. Only this religious Jew did.

Every morning when I went to school, I saw him and he greeted me with a warm shalom. I began to think to myself: 'how could it be that of all the neighbors, only this religious Jew gives me Shalom, and with such warmth - it seems the torah is true! Then I drew closer to being observant".

This story should be enough to strengthen us in this area!

Chatam Sofer
Shevet Sofer - Chelek Aleph, Lech Lecha - "say little and do much" - in truth, one who thinks he has already fulfilled his duty will step back and fall from level to level. For he becomes lazy in the service of Hash-em, and through this, his hands slack off.. but if one tell himself always: "what I did is only a little bit", and on the contrary he is still on the same level and is always afraid for his soul, and "fortunate is the man who is always afraid" (Mishlei 28:14), in fear of G-d. Through this, he will go forth and grow, with G-d's help..

Ben Ish Chai
Ben Ish Chai - Zechut Avot - "say little and do much" - this hints to what our sages said: "a person should look at the whole world as if equally balanced between merit and sin. If a single person performs one sin, or one good deed, he tips his own scales, and that of the entire world.." This is: "say little and do much". For sometimes a few words of torah are considered that you did much. For you tipped the scales of the whole world to the side of merit.

Ruach Chaim
Ruach Chaim - "your torah fixed" - for all wealth that a man attains is for the needs of others, and as written: *"they will leave their wealth to others"* (Tehilim 49:11) and as Moonbaz said: "my

Chapter 1 Mishna 15 - Torah Fixed

fathers amassed for others..." (Bava Batra 11a). But that which one attains in torah is only for himself. Thus he said: "make **your** torah primary", since it is yours (i.e. only it is yours, not material possessions). Thus it is proper to make it primary... "and in his torah he contemplates.." (Tehilim 1:2) For the torah itself is the reward, as known.. *Ruach Chaim* - *"your torah fixed"* - for all wealth that a man attains is for the needs of others, and as written: *"they will leave their wealth to others"* (Tehilim 49:11) and as Moonbaz said: "my fathers amassed for others..." (Bava Batra 11a). But that which one attains in torah is only for himself. Thus he said: "make **your** torah primary", since it is yours (i.e. only it is yours, not material possessions). Thus it is proper to make it primary... "and in his torah he contemplates.." (Tehilim 1:2) For the torah itself is the reward, as known..

Level 3 — Chasdei David

Chasdei David - *"make your torah fixed* - I saw fit to explain according to an analogy I read in the name of the holy Rav Nachman of Breslov:

There was a city with two wealthy leaders. One was a great miser while the other was very generous and very hospitable. A poor man came to the city and behold "poverty follows the poor" (Bava Kama 92a) - by accident, he arrived at the home of the miser. He begged to the miser for some food, for he ate nothing since morning. The miser told him: "we will need to heat the stove. If you go run and chop some wood, we will have enough to heat it till the morning".

The poor man toiled to chop wood and when morning came, he asked the miser if there is what to eat.

"certainly there is", replied the miser, "just enter the house next door and there you will be given".

The poor man went to the other house (which belonged to the second leader), and the rich man opened the door "with a pleasant countenance", greeted him Shalom and gave him food to eat. He sat next to him to honor him and in the middle of the meal, the poor man sighed.

The rich man asked him why he sighed. He replied: "the meal is truly good and nice, but I worked extremely hard for it".

The rich man asked him to explain. He answered that he chopped wood since midnight.

The rich man understood what the other man did to him and told the poor man: "you worked for free and ate for free"!

The understanding person will understand. (that money comes from G-d not the work)

Level 3 — Chida

Chida - Zeroa Yamin - "your torah fixed" - we may explain as the talmud (Kidushin 32b, see Rashi there): "at first the torah is called on the Name of the Holy One, blessed be He, as written *'his desire is in the torah of G-d'* (Tehilim 1:2). Afterwards, it is called on his own name, as written: *'and in his torah he contemplates [day and night]'"* (Kidushin 32b, see Rashi there)

And in Sotah 21b: "When, however, he reaches the cross-roads, he is saved from everything... what is meant by cross-roads? [Answer:] It refers to a talmid chacham (torah scholar) whose words are accepted to be the halachah".

Tosfot writes there: "since he has arrived at Horaah (ability to rule on halacha), he always thinks in the torah".

The commentators explained that which the torah is called on the Name of the Holy One, blessed be He, that refers to the beginning of one's study. But afterwards, when he reaches "Horaah" and becomes an important man (gavra raba), the torah is called on his own name.

One might think that since he reached the level in torah that it is called on his own name, he no longer needs to learn it diligently always. For he is already crowned with the crown of torah everywhere in torah. But this is not true. On the contrary, then it says *"and in his torah he contemplates day and night"* (Tehilim 1:2). For even when he walks on the road, he thinks [in torah], as Tosfot writes. And through this he is saved from sin (as in Sotah: "when he reaches the cross-roads, he is saved from everything").

Chapter 1 Mishna 15 - Torah Fixed

This is the meaning of "make your torah [fixed]" - even though you merited that it be called "your torah", don't think that now you no longer need to toil in it always. Rather, "make your torah", even though it is called "yours" - fixed.

And since you think in torah always, you are assured that the yetzer hara (evil inclination) will not attack you (yitgare) and you will be meritorious. For "a mitzvah brings another mitzvah" (Avot 4:2).

"say little and do much" - for torah drives away the yetzer harah.

"receive every person with a pleasant countenance" - for *"if a Rabbi pardons his honor, it is not pardoned"* (Kidushin 32a). All the more so then that he needs to show a nice facial expression to everyone.

Level 3 — Ben Ish Chai

Ben Ish Chai - Chasdei Avot - one who learns torah lishma will have his torah fixed for all generations. For such a person merits to arrive at the truth and according to the Halacha. The Halacha wil be like him everywhere. Thus, the torah he will mechadesh (derive) in Halacha will not be forgotten and leave the mouth of the sages for all generations. Since the Halacha is like him.. and even if he says things in Agadah, Hash-em will make it fixed in the mouths of the wise for several generations. On this he said: "make your torah fixed", i.e. learn lishma. For then "your torah", namely, the chidush (novel idea), you derive in torah in halacha or Agadah will be fixed in the mouths of the sages.

Thus, in this you said little. For your words were said in a short time and it became a teaching for many times, since the Halacha is like you. Thus whenever the topic is studied, your teaching is mentioned and people walk in your light and it is as if you are alive again and saying this teaching again.

How do you merit to learn lishma through which your torah wil be fixed? Through "greeting every person with a pleasant countenance", namely, even for a student who has a hard time understanding, like the student of Rav Freida who did not understand a teaching until his Rebbi repeated it to him 400 times.

So too, do not become disgusted (lo takutz) by him when he comes to learn torah from you. Rather, "greet him with a pleasant countenance" to teach him torah. In the merit of this trait, you will merit to learn torah lishma and through this your torah wil be fixed.

Level 3 — Chasdei David

Chasdei David - "receive every person with a pleasant countenance" - there is to ask here that Shammai speaks nicely here but in the Talmud (Shab.31a) it seems from several stories that he did not act like this...

We may answer that these three were different in that they appeared to be denying the torah. One denied the oral law, one wanted to be the high priest thus denying that Moshe Rabeinu appointed Aharon and his descendants to be priests by G-d's command, while the third who wanted to learn the whole torah on one foot held the torah had much unnecessary material.

Thus Shammai pushed them away and did not receive them with a pleasant countenance. But for other people, yes one should receive them with a pleasant countenance, even a non-jew.

In the talmud (Chulin 5a) on the verse "When a man from [among] you brings a sacrifice.. (adam ki yakriv mikem)" - Vayikra 1:2. "among you" implies some of you but not all of you. This excludes a mumar (apostate Jew). "among the animals" this includes people who are like animals. From here they learn that one may accept an offering from sinners so they repent, but not from a mumar... (hence a mumar is different).

However Hillel the elder had a different trait (and learned differently). In the talmud there, they expound the previous verse "adam ki yakriv mikem" - in you I made a distinction but not in the nations.

i.e. the distinction between kosher Jews and mumerim is only for you, but not for the nations. Rather, every gentile is permitted to offer a sacrifice.. Shamai held that although we accept sacrifices from the [mumar of the] nations, but we don't accept them for conversion.

Hillel the elder saw that it was possible to accept them, and the reason they denied the torah was due to ignorance.. the end result demonstrated his view. For all three became righteous converts.

Level 3 — Tiferet Yisrael

Tiferet Yisrael - make your torah fixed - he included 5 general principles for success in learning and remembering, namely to not learn in a non-fixed way (derech aray).

This includes:
1. In body: learning in a non-fixed or lazy manner such as lying down or sitting prakdon (placing one's hand on his forehead leads to sleep - Pesachim 112a). Or to put one's hand in a plate during winter, "[any Torah scholar who feasts excessively everywhere degrades himself and brings suffering upon himself. He will ultimately destroy his house, widow his wife, orphan his children, and his studies will be forgotten...] his son is called the son of one who fires up ovens (to eat gluttonously)" (Pesachim 49a).

These things cause one's thoughts to sleep and not understand the matter properly.

All the more so, should one not eat or do work while learning.

2. In thoughts: to think on other things when learning. For there is nothing which rattles and ruins grasping of the intellect and of memory than dispersion of thoughts.

For this, they enacted to learn verbally. Through this, other thoughts will disperse away. Furthermore, learning verbally makes a greater imprint in the soul and is better remembered...

Even more damaging to memory is thoughts of worry as our sages said in Sanhedrin 26a.. Rashi explains there: "worry causes one to forget his learning".

Likewise in Menachot 102b and in Eiruvin 65a..

This is not only for thoughts of worry, but even for thoughts of excessive joy. They also damage the intellect and memory in what he is learning then as in the talmud Beitza 21a

However, joy in the thing itself that he is learning - this strengthens the intellect and memory, as written: "I delight in your Law, I will not forget Your word" (Tehilim 119:16), i.e. when the learning is a delight, then "I will not forget your word".

On all this Shammai said: "make your torah fixed", and not unfixed.

3. The word "fixed (keva)" also connotes the matter of tranquility, i.e. tranquility of spirit (menuchat hanefesh). To not learn in a place of commotion, where many people are talking (non-torah) or there are banging noises or other loud noises. All these ruin one's understanding, grasp, and remembrance. Rather, one should have a quiet solitary (undistracted) place for his studies. This helps much in understanding and remembering, be'H.

Thus, it is good to learn in a nice spacious room with many windows and also using a nice, well printed book. For all these things bring tranquility and joy to the soul, broaden his mind, and relieve him of his sadness. Through this, the things [he learns] will firmly take root in his heart.

4. The word "fixed (keva)" also connotes "continuation (hemshech)". Namely, that his learning not be full of interruptions, to learn a little then interrupt, to learn a little more then interrupt. For such interruptions cause one to forget his learning.

For this reason, one's daily learning schedule should not contain too many different matters. Rather, he shoud be fixed (kavua) in no more than three subjects, as our sages said in Eiruvin 54. For by skipping around much in different areas, he will not be free for what he is learning and the matter will not firmly take hold in his heart. For each thought pushes away the other and both are ruined.

And even within one matter, one should not change from one

Chapter 1 Mishna 15 - Torah Fixed

print edition to another, or one room to another, or even from one place in the room to another, even if this is just sometimes. Rather, one should be habituated to fix a fixed time for this learning and a different one for another learning. For a firm schedule will strengthen one's memory, while a changing one weakens it.

5. The word fixed (kavua) also connotes strength and clarity. Namely, that you strengthen your learning and not move from the matter until you feel it is fixed firmly in you like a nail, and clear before you without any darkness or confusion. Then review it quickly by heart until it is fluent in your mouth without needing to look in the book..

After one or two weeks test yourself again whether you remember everything or part of it. When you need to, look again a bit in the book and review it by heart. For experience testifies that habit rules over memory also. This habituating oneself helps most in one's youth. Thus, it is good to habituate a child to review what he learned by heart.

All the more so if one wants to expound publicly or the like, he should review the matter in-depth well a few times at night just before he goes to sleep. Then the matter will not be interrupted by other thoughts afterwards. When one rises in the morning, let him immediately review it again a few times and then it will be like written on a new parchment which does not easily become erased. All this and maybe (he will succeed). For siyata d'shmaya (divine help) is needed to remember the teachings (Megilah 6b)...

Level 3 — Maharal

Maharal - like Hillel, Shamai also gave mussar according to his trait. We have already clarified that the second of the pair always exhorts on fear, on not doing [something].

"make your torah fixed", to not transgress one's fixed [times of] torah (keviut hatorah).

"say little and do much", for if you say much, perhaps you will not fulfill [your word] and will transgress.

Likewise, *"receive every person with a pleasant countenance"*. For otherwise, it will be as if you are dishonoring (mevaze) your fellow.

All this is a branch of fear of G-d, to not dishonor a man who was created in the divine image.

That which Hillel said: "love peace, pursue peace", certainly one whose trait is thus does not "stand on his trait" (omed al midotav, i.e. such a person tends to overlook wrongs done to him). For if he would "stand on his traits" (and not overlook his honor), how could he "pursue peace"?

For the whole matter of one who "pursues peace" is that he tells his fellow to overlook (mevater) what the other did to him and to not "stand on his trait".

This was certainly the trait of Hillel who was not a kapdan (unforgiving) and whose trait was to overlook.

Thus, Shamai came and said "true, this trait to not 'stand on one's traits' (overlook) is good and this applies to worldly matters . But to lean completely in this way and run everything in this manner is not good.

For in matters of Heaven, it is proper for one's torah to be fixed. If all a person's trait was to not stand on his matters, his conduct in matters of Heaven would also become like this and his torah would not be fixed.

That would not be proper. But for worldly matters, it would be proper for a man to overlook and not stand on his traits. For in his being a human being, he is a changing being and of physicality. He changes and does not stand on one matter. Thus, it is proper for man to not 'stand on his traits' (but rather to overlook).

This is proper only for worldly matters. For in worldly matters, man is physical. Therefore, he should conduct himself in like manner.

Chapter 1 Mishna 15 - Torah Fixed

But for matters of Heaven such as mitzvot and the torah which is intellect (sichlit), and which does not depend on the body who is physical and subject to change, there it is proper for his torah to be fixed and that he not overlook (mevater) at all. He should not transgress his fixing, but rather 'stand on his trait' and not change except when it is proper according to one's intellect...

Likewise on *"say little and do much"*. For if one says (he will learn) but does not do, this is not proper in torah. For there is no changing in things of intellect (sichli), rather only in things of physicality. Thus, just like in torah itself there is no change, so too it is not proper for there to be any change at all in the study of torah...

"receive every person with a pleasant countenance" - here too Shammai follows his trait. For according to Hillel, whose trait is for one not to stand on his trait and to not be upset (kepeda) on anything, there should be no claims for not "receiving a person with a pleasant countenance" (by the recipient).

For it is not proper to be upset (makpid) on this. Nevertheless, from the side of the person doing, it is proper for him to be meticulous (makpid) in this to the utmost extent until he receives "every person with a pleasant countenance".

He should not tell himself: "there is no kepeda (claim) on this and that man will not be makpid (upset) in this if he is not received with a pleasant countenance.

Through this, Shammai compliments (mashlim) his mussar and the mussar of Hillel, such that both together are certainly good. For between man and his fellow, one should not have any claims (kepeda).

But for matters of Heaven, he should have claims (kepeda), even though from the side of the receiver, he will (should) certainly not be upset (makpid) if his fellow does not "receive him with a pleasant countenance". But the person doing should be meticulous (makpid)...

Thus the mussar of Shammai and Hillel was regarding that there not be separation (peirud) between people, rather only friendship.

If you ask: "but Yehoshua ben Perachya of the third pair already said: "judge every person favorably"?

Answer: that is not the same as here. For there he was only saying that the public should not be evil in your eyes, as he said "make yourself a Rav and acquire a friend", and do not say they are not proper for you. Thus, he was not referring to joining people together such that there is no separation (peirud, ill-feeling) between them (like Hillel and Shammai).

Furthermore, there it was not the primary mussar [of his teaching]. It was only mentioned as a side point. In this the mussar of the fifth pair is complete...

Level 4 — Maharal

Maharal - (summary of the five pairs) - We have clarified that all five pairs, and also Antignos who was first, were always adding on the previous teaching...

Antignos began with man himself, how he should conduct himself..

Afterwards, the first pair rectified man's conduct with the members of his household who are close to him but are not the man himself.

Afterwards, the second pair rectified his Rav, friends and neighbors who are further away but are nevertheless close to him.

Afterwards the third pair rectified the conduct of those who are judges and leaders. This is further still.

Afterwards the fourth pair speaks of the conduct of the Baal Sherara (person of authority) who is even further in his being a Baal Sherara, separate from them. But nevertheless there is some connection in that he is their Baal Sherara.

Afterwards, the fifth pair rectified every person, so that the connection of peace not be severed. There is no further rectification in the order of the world (everything was included).

All of them rectified man in love and fear. From here on, the receivers were not singular (meyuchadim) in that they did not fully receive from their Rav (lo shimshu Rabam kol tzarkam) (i.e. they were unable to receive all the torah of their Rav due to the diminishing of the generations [in wisdom]).

You will see that the number of pairs was five. This number corresponds to the five earlier receivers (Moshe, Yehoshua, Elders, Prophets, Men of the Great Assembly).

For Shimon Hatzadik, who was of the remnants of the "Men of the Great Assembly" is considered by himself, as we explained earlier. Likewise Antignos of Socho was a single individual and is not counted with the pairs.

For the pairs, one was Nassi (chief leader), while the second was Av Beit Din (chief judge). The five pairs correspond to the five earlier receivers and Antignos was only to separate between the early receivers and the later receivers.

He was like the early receivers in that he did not have a pair. For Moshe, Yehoshua, the Elders, the Prophets, and the "Men of the Great Assembly" also did not have a pair, since they all had one name.. (each individual received the whole torah unlike the pairs where the torah was received by both together as before).

Thus Antignos would separate between the two sets of receivers. For it is not proper for the pairs to receive from the Men of the great assembly, who don't have pairs. For the pairs who are two individuals are not worth (great in torah) like the men of the great assembly.

But Antignos was similar to the early ones in that the Tradition did not have division and he was like the later ones in being an individual (without equal), as we explained. In this, way the receivers are connected together.

That which the receivers were always five is not a coincidence..

Chapter 1 Mishna 15 - Torah Fixed

You will likewise find that when the torah was given to the Jewish people, it was given through five "voices" (kolot). Through these five voices it spread to the whole world, as they said in a Midrash on the verse: "in the beginning I did not speak in secret, from the time it was" (Isaiah 48:16) That there were five voices, the voice would go out to all 4 directions and the fifth one in the middle. Therefore, the torah was given in five voices (kolot). Through them the torah spread out to the whole world.

Because of this, the receivers through which the torah spread to the whole world were five early ones and five later ones. For it was not proper for the torah to spread to the whole world through a single individual. Rather, through five as it did originally..

From here on, the torah diminishes. But until the five, the torah did not diminish. Each had a pair to help him in the receiving of the torah. But before the pairs, the receiving of the torah was not in pairs. For that which the prophets received from Yehoshua, each individual received [the whole torah] without a helper as was with the pairs.

Therefore at first, before the Second Temple, the torah had the power to spread until five [receivers]. And likewise for the pairs whereby there was a new matter of a helper, the torah also had power to spread until five... you must understand this well.

Now it is clear that the whole matter of the receiving of the torah was very orderly.. The first five before the second temple whereby torah was more in the world and five pairs during the second temple when wisdom began to diminish from people. Thus the receivers were pairs.

Athough Shimon Hatzadik was in the beginning of the Second Temple, he was also before the Second Temple. For he was of the "Men of the Great Assembly"...

It is also proper that there be pairs, one Nassi and one Av Beit Din, during the second temple era. This is known to the men of understanding. For it is written on the second Temple: "The glory of this last House shall be greater than the first one" (Chagai 2:9).

The reason is known to the men of understanding. For the Temple was built with two hands.. as brought in the talmud (Ketuvot 5a).

Due to this, it included two aspects, the right hand and the left hand, which are the powers of the Nassi and Av Beit Din.

Thus, there were pairs specifically during the second temple, and there was then more love and fear.

Hence, Antignos exhorted on the foundation, namely, love and fear. Afterwards, the pairs came. For each pair, one exhorted on love and the other on fear. This is as the level of the second Temple which included love and fear.

You shoud understand these things very very well, for they are clear.

Level 4 — Ben Ish Chai

Ben Ish Chai - Chasdei Avot - (kabalistic) - it is known that the torah is called "emuna" (faith). For emuna has gematria "kav" (kuf-beit=102), to hint that the torah has four parts - pshat, remez, drosh, sod. Thus it is called "kav" whose gematria is emuna. For a "kav" has four lugin, corresponding to the four parts of torah - pshat, remez, drosh, sod. It is also known that the torah has 70 facets (panim). Namely, for these four parts hinted in "kav", each part has 70 facets. On this he said: "make your torah fixed (kevah)", ie "kav-ayin", that in each part of "kav" derive chidushim in 70 facets.

"say little (mem-ayin-tet)" - our sages said that Moshe Rabeinu received 49 reasons (taamim) on everything.. our sages said this is independent of the 70 facets (panim). For facets (panim) means ways (ofanim). Namely, each verse in the torah can be explained in 70 ways.

But taamim means that in every Halacha, there are 49 reasons (taamim), whether on it being permitted or forbidden. Thus the words of torah have 49 reasons (taamim) and 70 (facets). The sage hinted to this in the letters "little" (mem-ayin-tet), which are "mem-tet" (49) "ayin" (70).

The intent is: "strive and toil to arrive at the 49 reasons and 70 facets". This is the meaning of "say little (mem-ayin-tet)", and "do much" (aseh harbe), make many students and do not be weary of their great multitude. Rather, "receive every person" who comes to learn from you, "with a pleasant countenance".

Chapter 1 Mishna 16 - Remove Doubt

Rabban Gamliel would say: make for yourself a Rav, and remove yourself from doubt, and do not frequently Maaser (tithe) by estimation.

רַבָּן גַּמְלִיאֵל הָיָה אוֹמֵר, עֲשֵׂה לְךָ רַב, וְהִסְתַּלֵּק מִן הַסָּפֵק, וְאַל תַּרְבֶּה לְעַשֵּׂר אֲמָדוֹת:

Level 1 — Bartenura

Bartenura - *"make for yourself a Rav"* - he is now speaking on horaah (halachic rulings). If a din (halachic question) comes before you and you are in doubt on it, make for yourself a Rav.

"and remove yourself from doubt" - and do not rule on it by yourself..

"do not frequently Maaser (tithe) by estimation" - for one who separates maaser (tithe) by estimate is not saved from mishap. If he separates less than a tenth, his maaser is rectified, but his fruit are bungled (mixed with tevel). Likewise, if he separates more than a tenth for maaser, his fruit are rectified but his maaser is bungled (mixed with tevel).

Level 1 — Rashi

Rashi - *"Rabban Gamliel would say"* - this is Rabban Gamliel the son of Rebbi Shimon the son of Hillel.

"make yourself a Rav" - I explained this earlier in Mishna 6.

"remove yourself from doubt" - if you learn by yourself, you will have many doubts. Alternatively, do not decide *Halacha* for yourself and stand confidently [by your ruling]. Rather, since it (the *Halacha*) is not explicitly stated, one needs to go to his Rav, as explained in Yevamot 109b, see there.

"remove yourself from doubt" - that you not have a doubt in your heart regarding the foundation of the foundations (yesod haesodot) or the knowledge of the secrets (yediat hasodot). Rather, it should be with certainty and confirmed in the eye of the heart. For this is the primary thing.

"do not frequently Maaser (tithe) by estimation" - do not maaser (tithe) by estimating for sometimes it will not be well estimated, like a person who does not learn from the Received Tradition (oral law from a Rav).

Level 2 — Rabeinu Yonah

Rabeinu Yonah - "do not frequently Maaser (tithe) by estimation" - to not maaser by estimate.. for one who maasers by estimate, his fruit are rectified, but his maaser is bungled (mekulkal). For example: let's say he separated maaser generously, the extra amount over a tenth which he separated is tevel, not maasered, until he maasers that extra amount. Thus, if he does not notice to do so, his maaser has a bungle (kilkul).

This matter is an analogy for a logical argument (svara). A man should not do it approximately. Rather, the primary way is to plumb to the full depth of the knowledge (yered le sof hadaat). For not all logical arguments are equal. Some have two sides. Even though one wise man's logic (svara) leans to one side, but he understands and recognizes that a different wise man can also say a different argument in this, only that this way appears more right in his eyes. Sometimes a wise man conceives a logical argument of his own and thinks it is irrefutable by sound reason and there is no other way to see it and no other wise man who could possibly argue with him. The understanding person will understand. This is why he brought this analogy after "make for yourself a Rav and remove yourself from doubt", which are also regarding rational argument (svara).

Level 2

Likutim - why did it not say right away: "Rabban Yochanan ben Zakai received from Hillel..." (but instead mentions it later in Avot 2:8)? [answer:] It was for the honor of Hillel and his seed. For after Hillel, Rabban Yochanan ben Zakai was the Nassi (head leader) for forty years. After that, the title of Nassi returned to the royal seed. Thus, Rebbi (who wrote the mishna) did not want to interrupt the order of his yichus (ancestry) with Rabban Yochanan ben Zakai. Although he was humble, he was careful (makpid) for the honor of the Nessiot, as we find written: "who are these people? They are people who seek to uproot your honor and the honor of your father's house.." (Horayot 14a)

Level 2 — Rambam

Rambam - Mishne Torah Sanhedrin 20:8 - any judge who begins comparing a judgment that is brought before him to a judgment that was already rendered with which he was familiar is considered as wicked and haughty when rendering judgment if there is a scholar in his city who is wiser than him and he fails to consult him. Our Sages comment: "May evil upon evil befall him." For these and similar concepts stem from haughtiness which leads to the perversion of justice.

Chida
Chida - Chasdei Avot - the Rambam (Sanhedrin 20:8) and Tur (Choshen Mishpat s.62) wrote that it is not only one's own Rav. Rather, if there is a talmid chacham in the city, you must ask him. Likewise, the Maharshal writes in the Yam Shel Shlomo there and in teshuva siman 35. Rabeinu Yerucham writes in the Sefer Mesharim (Netiv 1, chelek 2): "if there is a talmid chacham in the city, a judge is not allowed to judge a doubtful matter before asking him. [Namely,] comparing one thing to another, unless it is clear to him as the morning [light]." end quote.

This implies, if it is clear to him, there is no shayla (question).

Perhaps this is the meaning of "make for yourself a Rav and remove yourself from doubt", i.e., this is when you have a doubt - then make for yourself a Rav. But if the matter is clear to you, then you may judge using your own judgment and you don't need to ask a Chacham, as Rabeinu Yerucham.

Ahava b'Taanugim
Rabbi Avraham Azoulai - Ahava b'Taanugim - earlier in mishna 6, he exhorted "make for yourself a Rav" regarding learning, namely, that one's [Torah] wisdom be received from those earlier than him. But here, he exhorts on the matter of halachic rulings (hora'ah). Namely, that if one learns from many sages, his rulings are not reliable. This is as our sages said on Rav Yehuda: "one shoud not rely on his hora'ah because he learned from everyone".

Alternatively, some explain that if a hora'ah comes to you that is not clear from the talmud and you need to decide by logic (svara), make for yourself a Rav, in order to clarify the matter, and "remove yourself from doubt" and do not be embarrased to ask. And even if you dont find anyone as big as yourself to ask,

ask even one smaller than yourself.

Perhaps it will be clear to him through some teaching he heard. And even if it is not clear to anyone and you are forced to rule by svara (reason), "make yourself a rav" so that the entire punishment of the doubt not be on you alone. Rather, join in others and make him a Rav on you even if they are not so. In order that each one receive only a small portion of the punishment. (see Sanhedrin 7b).

"do not frequently Maaser by estimation" - do not habitually rule in that which is not clear from the talmud using your own estimation and logic (omed v'svara).

Rather, investigate the books of Halachot until you find help and support to your words.

Level 3 — Chasdei David

Chasdei David - "make for yourself a Rav" - it is the way of the world that when there is a doubt on issur v'heter (ex. mixtures of meat and milk), one immediately goes to ask a Rav, even though most of the time it is only a distant concern (chashash rachok) and it does not really even enter into the category of a "question" (Shayla). For example, "noten taam lepagam" or "kli sheni". The concern is at most a Rabbinical doubt (safek d'rabanan).

But for matters between man and his fellow such as "words that hurt" (onaat devarim) which have a biblical prohibition as written: "you shall not wrong, one man his fellow" (Vayikra 25:17), which the talmud expounds: "this refers to 'words that hurt' (onaat devarim)" (Bava Metzia 58b). The talmud explains there:

"What is the case of 'words that hurt' (onaat devarim)? If he were a baal teshuva (penitent), do not tell him: 'remember your previous deeds', or if he were a convert coming to learn Torah, do not tell him: 'the mouth who ate unkosher meat should now learn Torah??'" end quote.

Likewise for onnat mamon (monetary oppression) or embarassing one's fellow - no one opens their mouth to ask! This is *"make for yourself a Rav"*, that you ask a Rav for matters people are lax in, namely, matters between man and his fellow,

Chapter 1 Mishna 16 - Remove Doubt

and "remove yourself from doubt", i.e. refrain from things which have a trace of doubt.

Level 3 — Maharal

Maharal - it is proper to ask: what do these three things have to do with each other?

Another question: "make for yourself a Rav" was already said earlier by Yehoshua ben Perachya (Mishna 6).

Know that Rabban Gamliel came to give mussar to a man that all his matters be clear till there is no doubt in them. For when one's actions contain doubt, he is not called a baal sechel (possessor of intellect). For regarding the sechel (intellect), all its matters are clear, without doubt.

On the fool it is written: "the fool walks in darkness" (Kohelet 2:14). But for a man who wants to be a baal sechel, his matters will be clear. And if a man goes out of this trait, it is as if he goes out of the boundary of a human, who is a baal sechel (possessor of intellect).

Doubt can occur to man in three areas.

One, in his sechel (intellect), when the matter is not clear, and he has sides (panim) to here and to here.

Two, for all matters where one is in doubt due to lack of knowledge and which do not depend at all on intellect.

Three, doubts a man has regarding the performance of mitzvot, [namely] when the performance of the mitzah is not clear.

We will further explain these three later on.

Corresponding to the first, he said "make for yourself a Rav", so that what one acquires of wisdom is something clear, without doubt.

"remove yourself from doubt" - i.e. from every thing which one is in doubt.

Chapter 1 Mishna 16 - Remove Doubt

Regarding forbidden things (issur), it is certainly superfluous to say. For "safek issur l'chumra" (a doubtful prohibition is treated stringently).

Rather the intent is that for everything which may possibly lead to damage (hezek), one should not at all enter in the doubt. For this is not proper for a baal sechel (possessor of intellect) to enter in a doubt.

Corresponding to the third, he said to not frequently "Maaser (tithe) by estimation", ie to not rely on estimates in the performance of mitzvot.

And even though the Torah permitted this, as brought in Bechorot (58b): "just as Terumah Gedolah may be set apart by estimating so too Terumah Maaser..."

Thus, even though Terumat Maaser has a fixed amount of a tenth, one may separate it by estimate, and all the more so for Maaser. But nevertheless, do not frequently Maaser by estimate, in a habitual manner. Only when it is necessary and one does not have time, then it is permitted.

And even if the estimate is close to exact, nevertheless, remove yourself even from this. For it is only proper for a man that all his deeds be clear, removed from doubt.

Because thus is proper for a possessor of intellect (baal sechel) to not walk in darkness.

And certainly when he conducts himself in this trait, it is a great perfection (shlemut) for him. For many, many lackings follow when a man's deeds are not clear.

Furthermore, this trait is proper for a possessor of intellect (baal sechel), that his deeds stem from a clear intellect..

Level 3 — Maharal

Some explanations on the order of the Mishna in this chapter
Maharal - Why did the mishna not say "Rabban Gamliel received..." (but instead just "Rabban Gamliel would say")?

Chapter 1 Mishna 16 - Remove Doubt

He did not say here [Rabban Gamliel] "received". For the Tradition (kabala) continued (intact) only until Hillel and Shammai, as written in the Talmud "when the disciples of Shammai and Hillel, who had insufficiently studied, increased [in number], disputes multiplied in Israel, and the Torah became as two Torahs" (Sanhedrin 88b). Therefore, he did not say "received" (kabala) after Hillel and Shammai.

(Translator: Some important background info. According to Rambam's introduction to Mishneh Torah, here is the order of transmission after Hillel and Shammai:
1. Rabban Yochanan ben Zakkai and Rabban Shimon the son of Hillel received from Hillel and Shammai.
2. Afterwards, Rabban Gamliel HaZaken ben Rabban Shimon
3. Afterwards, Rabban Shimon (son of 2.)
4. Afterwards, Rabban Gamliel II (son of 3.)
5. Afterwards, Rabban Shimon ben Gamliel (son of 4.)
6. Afterwards, Rebbi Yehuda HaNassi (son of 5., this is Rabeinu HaKadosh compiler of the mishna)
7. Afterwards, Rabban Gamliel III (son of 6., brought next chapter)
back to Maharal...)

The mishna here also did not mention Rabban Shimon, the son of Hillel, and instead skipped to Rabban Shimon's son - Rabban Gamliel (grandson of Hillel).

Likewise, later it does not mention Rabban Gamliel (#4, the grandson of Rabban Gamliel HaZaken #2) who was the father of Rabban Shimon ben Gamliel (#5) in the last mishna who said "on three things the world stands..".

All of them were Nesiim (chief leaders), as brought in the talmud "Hillel, Shimon, Gamliel, and Shimon assumed their Nassi position for 100 years during the temple" (Shab.15a).

It seems the reason the Mishna did not mention Rabban Shimon (#1), the son of Hillel, is because during his time, Rabban Yochanan ben Zakai was also a leader and as great as him. For everywhere it says: "when the temple was destroyed Rabban Yochanan ben Zakkai decreed.."

Rabban Yochanan ben Zakkai was a disciple of Hillel. Thus he was also a leader and Nassi, and it is not possible to mention both of them. For they were not of the pairs whereby one was Nassi and the other was Av Beit Din. Therefore, he mentioned neither. For which one should he mention?

Likewise in the time of Rabban Gamliel (#4) father of Rabban Shimon ben Gamliel (#5), there was Elazar ben Azarya who was also Nassi, as brought in Berachot (28a) (therefore he was also not mentioned in this chapter)...
(Translator: the Maharal will give another reason for this in Mishna 18. see there)

Q Level 4 — Ben Ish Chai

Ben Ish Chai - Chasdei Avot - "make for yourself a Rav" - it is known why the sages (Chachamim) are called "Talmidei Chachamim" (disciples of sages) everywhere, and as they said: "Talmidei Chachamim bring Shalom to the world", and likewise in hundreds of places, whether when referring to single individuals or many [sages].

The reason for this is in order to teach that even if a man toiled in Torah for 80+ years, nevertheless, it is proper for him to conduct himself as a disciple. Namely, that he learns from his colleagues and even from his students. And even if he learned from many Rabbis, he should not be satisfied with this. Rather, whenever he can find a wise man (chacham) to learn from, he should do so. He should not have the trait of Histapkut (being satisfied with little) in this.

Thus, *"make for yourself a Rav"*, always, all your days, seek a Rav to teach you. For it is not possible that you will not find a new Chidush (insight) that you did not know and you will learn it from him. And as Ben Zoma said: "who is wise? he who learns from every person" (Avot 4:1).

In this matter of study which I commanded you to learn from every person and make a new Rav always - "remove yourself from doubt (Safek)" - from the word "Histapkut" (contentment), ie do not have Histapkut (contentment) in this matter saying: "I already learned from several Rabbis and received from them many kabalot (teachings). It is enough for me these sages I learned and received from. Rather consider yourself that all you learned is not enough for you and you are still in the category of "disciple" (talmid) who needs to learn from others.

Chapter 1 Mishna 17 - Silence

Shimon his son said: All my days I have grown up among the Sages and I have not found anything as good for the body as silence. And not study but practice is the primary thing. And whoever multiplies words brings sin. שִׁמְעוֹן בְּנוֹ אוֹמֵר, כָּל יָמַי גָּדַלְתִּי בֵּין הַחֲכָמִים, וְלֹא מָצָאתִי לַגּוּף טוֹב אֶלָּא שְׁתִיקָה. וְלֹא הַמִּדְרָשׁ הוּא הָעִקָּר, אֶלָּא הַמַּעֲשֶׂה. וְכָל הַמַּרְבֶּה דְבָרִים, מֵבִיא חֵטְא:

Rashi
Rashi - "silence" - for even a silent fool will be considered a wise man. So too for the opposite. If one speaks much with people, and for everything he advances himself in to answer (makdim atzmo lehashiv), then even if he is a wise man, people will consider him a fool. Therefore, there is nothing as good as silence until one can see.

"not study but practice is the primary thing" - for one who does the mitzva is greater than one who learns but does not do.

Bartenura
Bartenura - "silence" - he who hears insults and remains quiet.

"not study but practice is the primary thing" - know that silence is good, for even learning studying and expounding Torah of which nothing is greater, nevertheless, the primary reward therein is only for deed (fulfilling what one learns). And one who preaches but does not fulfill (doresh v'eino mekayem), it would have been better for him had he remained silent and not preached.

"whoever multiplies words brings sin" - as we find by Chava. She increased speech and said: "but G-d said, 'you shall not eat of it, and you shall not touch it, lest you die.'" (Gen.3:3)

She added "touching", which was not forbidden to her. The serpent pushed her till she touched it and then said: "just like there is no death in touching it, so too there is no death in eating from it". Due to this, she came to sin, eating from the tree. This is what Shlomo said: "Do not add to His words, lest He prove to you, and you be found a liar" (Mishlei 30).

Chapter 1 Mishna 17 - Silence

Ruach Chaim

Ruach Chaim - i.e. regarding matters of the body, silence is a good trait. But in Torah, one needs to specifically speak fully (davka b'peh maleh), as our sages said on the verse "for they are life for those who find (motzehem) them" (Mishlei 4:22) - "for those who utter them (motziem b'pe)" (Eiruvin 64a).

But even so, do not think that "study is the primary thing".

"whoever multiplies words brings sin" - in Avot d'Rebbi Natan (1:5), they brought a proof to this from Adam HaRishon. In order to fence (protect) the matter, he added words on his own and told Chava (Eve) that even touching the tree is forbidden. This made things worse (for Chava touched the tree and nothing happened, thus leading her to eat from it). And that which was said earlier: "make a fence for the Torah" (Avot 1:1), this refers to when one informs the people what is the main law (ikar hadin) and what is the fence.

For then, even if ch'v they transgress the fence, at least they will not transgress the main law. But Adam HaRishon told Chava that G-d commanded even on touching. Thus he came to make things worse.

Ahava b'Taanugim

Rabbi Avraham Azoulai - Ahava b'Taanugim - "Shimon his son said" - some say this is Rabban Shimon ben Gamliel mentioned next mishna. But this was said in his youth before he received smicha (as Nassi).

"All my days I have grown up among the Sages" - i.e. it is proper for you to rely on me in this. For I checked it and tested it much and found it to be true... this comes to exhort the students who grow among the sages, as he in his youth was silent before his Rabbis. But this exhortation is not for the sages when they teach the students. The Rav does not need to be silent. But rather, to teach the student in concise manner. Perhaps this is what he said afterwards *"whoever multiplies words brings sin"*.

Some explain: I did not find mussar which avails more than silence (mussar yoter mo'il min hashtika). If you ask: "but one needs to speak with people so they will like him and draw him close and benefit him?" On this he said: *"And not study but practice is the primary thing"*, for the drawing close or distancing of him will be according to his deeds.

Ben Ish Chai
Level 2

Ben Ish Chai - Chasdei Avot - "all my days I have grown up among the Sages and I have not found anything as good for the body as silence" - the sages' occupation is in speech, as written: "it is life for those who utter them (motziem b'pe)" (Eiruvin 64a), and "a certain student (of her husband) was learning Torah quietly, she kicked him...", as brought in Eiruvin.

Thus, I am used to speaking much. But nevertheless, "I have not found anything as good for the body as silence", i.e., in matters of the body. Despite that I am a talker in divrei Torah and am used to speaking and not keeping quiet.

Ben Ish Chai
Level 2

Ben Ish Chai - Birkat Avot - "whoever multiplies words brings sin" - it is known that one who speaks evil speech (lashon hara) on his fellow, through this, he takes all his fellow's sins. It is also known that one who increases to talk useless speech (marbe l'daber devarim beteilim) will perforce come to speak lashon hara also.

For this is the way of excessive speech. It goes from one evil to another until he stumbles in the sin of lashon hara or the like. Through this it is understood: "whoever multiplies words brings sin", in the end, he will bring sin to himself from others.

Namely, he will stumble in the sin of lashon hara, and through this he takes sins from other people which he spoke lashon hara against and brings them to himself. This is the meaning of "brings sin". He brings them from others.

It is known that just like it is a mitzva to say something that will be listened to, so too, it is a mitzva to not say something that will not be listened to. On this he said: "And not study but practice is the primary thing".

Thus one who expounds to the public needs to expound on something that will be listened to in order that action will result from this. For "the drash (sermon) is not primary rather

Chapter 1 Mishna 17 - Silence

"practise", which the people will do through the power of the drosh".

Thus, "whoever multiplies words brings sin", i.e., that he says something that will not be listened to and nothing but words without action will come out from this - in this he brings sin. For on the contrary, better to not say it..

Level 2 — Chida

Chida - Chasdei Avot - i.e. those who expound to the public (doresh b'rabim), they try to expound wondrous matters and complex expositions in sugyot of tosfot and poskim.

But they don't expound to rebuke the people, to inform them of the large or small sins they stumble in.

For this is the whole fruit of the exposition (drosh) - to bring the people to repentance (teshuva).

This is: "And not study but practice is the primary thing" - to not make primary to expound and present sayings and teachings to demonstrate wisdom. Rather "practice is the primary thing" - to rebuke the people..

Level 3 — Rambam

Rambam - the wise man already said: "in the multitude of words there lacks not sin" (Mishlei 10:19)..

The reason for this is increasing of words is considered "superfluous of permitted" and sin. (explained shortly)

For when one increases speech he will inevitably come to transgression, since it is impossible that in his words there will not be [at least] one word which is not proper to say.

Among the signs of the wise is few words while among the signs of the fool is many words, as written: "and the voice of the fool with many words" (Kohelet 5:2). And our sages said that speaking few words is a mark of the [inherited] virtue of the forefathers and indicates one's genealogy from them. Thus they said: "silence in Babylon is the mark of genealogy" (Kidushin 71b).

Chapter 1 Mishna 17 - Silence

It is written in the book of Middot (see Orchot Tzadikim shaar hashtika) that one of the sages appeared to be very silent. He would not utter a word that was not proper to say and only spoke a little bit. He was asked on this and he replied:

I examined all words and found that they fall into four categories.

The first: these are entirely harmful, without any benefit, such as cursing people, obscene words, or the like, where speaking them is a complete foolishness.

The second category: these are harmful from one side and beneficial from another. For example, praising a person in order to receive some benefit whereby this praise will anger his enemy and harm the person praised. Due to this reason (of harm), one needs to refrain from this category also.

The third category: these are neither beneficial nor harmful such as most words of the masses. "How was that wall built?", "How was that palace built", talking over about "how beautiful is such and such's house", "the many towers in such and such a country", or the like of permitted things. These things are also superfluous. There is no benefit in them.

The fourth category: these are entirely beneficial, such as words of wisdom and virtue (chochmot u'maalot). Likewise for speaking in things which his life depends on and which will prolong his existence (his livelihood). For these one needs to speak.

Thus, whenever I hear things, I examine them. If I find they belong to this fourth category, I speak in them. But if I find they belong to the other categories, I keep silent from them. end quote.

The men of virtue (baalei middot) said (regarding this silent man): "examine this man and his wisdom. For he lacks three fourths of the words (of most people). This is a wisdom which one needs to study".

(Rambam continues:) I say that according to the obligations of the Torah, speech falls into five categories:

One, speech which is a mitzva.
Two, speech which is forbidden and we are warned against.
Three, speech which is repulsive (nimas).
Four, speech which is beloved (ne'ehav).
Five, speech which is permitted (mutar).

One, speech which is a mitzva: this refers to reading and study of the Torah and reading its talmud (explanations). This is a positive obligatory mitzvah, as written: "you shall speak in them" (Devarim 6:7). And this mitzvah weighs like all the other mitzvot [combined]. We have already elaborated more on this elsewhere.

Two, speech which is forbidden: such as false testimony, lies, slander, obscene talk, and curses. The Torah teaches on this division.

Three, repulsive speech: this kind has no benefit. But it is not sin nor rebelling, such as most speech of the masses on what happened and what was, what are the conducts of king so and so in his palace, what caused the death of so and so, how so and so became rich, etc.

The sages called these "idle speech" (Sicha beteila). The Chasidim strove to abstain from this category of speech. It was said on Rav, the disciple of Rebbi Chiya that he never spoke idle talk all of his life.

Included in this category is to scorn a virtue or praise an evil, whether in traits or in intellect (wisdom).

Four, speech which is beloved: this refers to speech in praising virtues of intellect or good traits, and likewise in scorning the disgraceful of both types (intellect or bad traits).

For example, to rouse the soul to the virtues through stories and songs, and to praise the virtuous people and commend their virtues in order to esteem them in the eyes of people and inspire them to walk in their ways.

This category also includes scorning the disgracefulness of the evil people in order to belittle their ways and remembrance in the

Chapter 1 Mishna 17 - Silence

eyes of people so that they will distance from them and their evil ways and will not act like them.

This category, namely, study of the virtuous traits and distancing from the reprehensible ones is called "derech eretz" (lit. the way of the land).

The fifth category is permitted speech. This refers to speech regarding people's business trade, livelihood, food, drink, clothing, and other needs. It is "permitted", not having of the "beloved" nor of the "repulsive" [content]. But [it is optional], if he wants, he may speak in this, and if he does not want, he may refrain from speaking.

In this category, a man is praiseworthy when he minimizes speaking therein. The men of mussar exhorted to not increase speech in this.

But the "forbidden" and "repulsive" do not need exhorting nor command (to minimize in them). For it is proper to be completely silent from these.

But for the type which is "mitzva" or "beloved", if a man could speak in them all his days, it would be good. But one needs to be careful of two things:

One, that one's words are consistent with one's deeds, as they said: "the words are pleasing when uttered by those who practice them" (Tosefta Yevamot ch.8).

This is the intent of *"And not study but practice is the primary thing"*.

The sages told the tzadik to learn the virtues, as they said: "expound! it is becoming of you to expound (derosh ulecha na'eh lidrosh)" (Bava Batra 75a), and the prophet said: "sing praises to the L-ord, O you righteous: for praise is befitting for the upright" (Tehilim 33:1).

The second matter is conciseness (kitzur), to strive to include much in few words, and not the opposite.

Chapter 1 Mishna 17 - Silence

This is what they said: "one should always teach his student in concise terms" (Pesachim 3b)...

Since we mentioned slander (lashon hara) in the category of forbidden speech, I saw proper to discuss a bit on this. For people are greatly blind to this, and it is always the greatest sin of people. All the more so in light of what our sages said that a man is not saved from the "dust of slander" every day (Bava Batra 164b). And would that it were (halevai), that we were saved from slander itself... (see there for more)

Q Level 3 — Sforno

Sforno - "I have not found anything as good for the body as silence" - many think the power of speech in man is his most noble power. Some even say that this is what distinguishes man from the other living creatures and a man is greater than his fellow in proportion to his greater wisdom of speech (chachmat hadibur).

But this sage states that despite all its qualities, speech does not avail the body at all. As we find that other living things (animals) live long and attain their sustenance painlessly without employing any speech at all.

Rather the benefit obtained from speech is in its use by the practical intellect (sechel hamaasi) for secular matters and in the in-depth intellect (sechel iyuni) for teaching others.

But even with all this benefit, "not study" and speech "is primary", and the intended purpose. Rather, the intended purpose is "practice is the primary thing" that follows from it, whether in secular matters or in the study of intellectual matters. And even in these, minimal speech is good as is learning in a concise manner.

"whoever multiplies words brings sin" - for more doubts, errors, and forgetting will befall the (many) words.

From all this, it follows that speech itself is not sheleimut (perfection). Without a doubt, it is merely a tool to attain the intended purpose in secular matters and in wisdom. Namely, to communicate the thoughts of one's heart to another. This should be done in as few words as possible. This is unlike all things which are in and of themselves perfection (shelemut), whereby the more the better.

Level 3 — Maharal

Maharal - This sage came to exhort on rectifying man's body. After seeing his father (Rabban Gamliel) giving mussar that man's deeds should be proper in his being a possessor of intellect (baal sechel), namely, that he not walk in darkness (doubt), as explained, this sage now came to give mussar on rectifying a man in his being a possessor of body (baal guf).

It is proper to ask:
1. why does he need to say: "all my days I have grown up among the Sages, etc".

2. what does this have to do with "And not study but practice is the primary thing".

3. likewise, he starts with "silence" and afterwards moves to "And not study but practice is the primary thing" and then returns back to the original matter "whoever multiplies words brings sin"?

4. the choice of language "I have not found anything as good for the body as silence", he should have said "I have not found anything as good for a man as silence".

5. he said "whoever multiplies words brings sin" - this is already stated explicitly in scripture - "in the multitude of words there lacks not sin" (Mishlei 10:19).

Rashi explains that even by the sages (Chachamim), I found that silence is good (yafeh) for them. For thus they would conduct themselves in silence. And all the more so for people who are not sages (Chachamim), silence is good (yafeh) for them.

The explanation of "I have not found anything as good for the body as silence" is that in man being possessor of a body (baal guf), silence is good for him (yafe lo). This is because speech is from the "nefesh hamedaberet" (speaking soul), which is a power of the body (koach gufani) and not entirely intellect (eino sichli l'gamrei).

Therefore, silence is proper for him, so he does not come to error and confusion (ta'ut v'shibush).

Because when he activates (poel) the power of speech, he annuls (bitel) the power of intellect, as we will explain shortly.

Therefore, he should keep silent and activate the power of intellect which is not bodily like the power of speech. For the latter inevitably comes to err.

It is proper to know that the intellect and the body are opposites to each other. Therefore, he said: "I have not found anything as good for the body as silence", instead of "it is not good (yafeh) for the body to speak". For the lacking is not from the side of speech itself. Only that silence is good for a person so that he can activate the power of the intellect.

This comes to teach that when a man is silent, then the intellect can activate its work. For it is impossible for two opposites to operate simultaneously in man - the intellect and the body. Therefore, if the power of the body operates, namely, the intellect of speech (sechel hadavri), then the intellect of in-depth thought (sechel iyuni) cannot operate and he will come to error.

Thus, it is proper for him to be silent and not activate the power of speech and then the intellect can activate its working (az hasechel yifal peulato).

This is the meaning of "the only good for the body is silence (ein tov laguf rak shetika)". For certainly it is good and proper for the body to keep quiet and give room for the intellect to activate its working.

Thus the body will be annulled (subordinate) to the intellect and become a "tail to a lion". But if he increases speech, then the intellect is annulled to the body and becomes a "tail to a fox", and then there is no intellect at all.

Therefore, he said "I have not found anything as good for the body as silence" due to the reason we mentioned.

Thus every fool increases speech. For the intellect and the body are two opposites. But the Chacham (wise man) will operate always with his intellect and not with the bodily speech...

"not study but action is the primary thing" - so that you should not say: "since silence, which is absence of acting, is best for man because he needs to operate with the intellect, if so, the midrash (study) is primary, not the action. For action is of the body, while midrash (study) is of the intellect".

Even though midrash is very great indeed, but nevertheless, the primary thing is action. Only that the midrash which is the intellect is a lofty quality. But nevertheless action is the foundation (yesod), and one needs to have a prepared foundation first before he can acquire the virtues of intellect (maalot hasechel). After the foundation is ready, he can build up and up. This is clear to anyone whose (good) deeds are many..

"whoever multiplies words brings sin" - i.e. certainly silence is good for the body as we explained, since it allows the intellect to operate its work and this is a virtue (maala).

But it is not proper to say that he sins if he increases speech. For the power of speech is a power by itself. If he wishes to operate this power and not grant all his power to the intellect, it is not relevant to call this sin.

However, when one increases speech, he nevertheless brings sin. For according to what we explained, silence is proper so that the intellect be primary and the power of speech be annulled to it.

Granted, if he does not choose to be silent, there is no sin here also. But nevertheless to increase speech and make the power of speech primary [he will thus] annul the power of the intellect. Since as before, all the time the power of speech operates, it is impossible for the intellect to activate its work properly. For they are two opposites. And certainly, this is a lacking for a man - to be drawn after the power of speech completely, a power which is

Chapter 1 Mishna 17 - Silence

not completely intellect (eino sichli legamrei).

Therefore, it is considered a lacking when he is drawn after it. And a lacking draws another lacking after it. For every lacking pulls in another lacking.

This is the meaning of "brings sin". For sin is lacking. Because the term "sin" (chet) means everywhere "lacking". For example: "I and my son Shlomo will be found lacking (chataim)" (Melachim I 1:1), or "I [bore] the loss (echatena)" (Bereishit 31).

Therefore, one who increases speech will come to sin and lacking. This is especially so when the lacking is from something stemming from the powers of the body. Such a lacking will draw more lackings after it.

Furthermore, there is another very deep matter in this. The power of speech is unlike the power of intellect. The power of intellect has no limit.

The power of speech is like a tzura (form), For the tzura (form/definition) of man is a "speaking creature" (chai medaber). And as known regarding the tzura, it has no superfluousness at all (ein bo tosefet klal). Therefore, whoever increases speech comes out of the proper and coming out of the proper in something like this brings sin. Understand this.

If you ask: but this teaching was already explicitly stated in scripture: "in the multitude of words there lacks not sin" (Mishlei 10)?

[answer]: that verse is not referring to "coming to sin" (like here). Rather, it is only saying that due to speaking many words, it is impossible to not sin and utter words of foolishness and vanity. But here he says "brings sin", i.e. draws sin after himself. This is a different matter.

This is the explanation of the mishna when you understand..

Q Level 4

Birkat Shmuel - "for the body (guf) as silence" - a hint to the Geula, as written "[Moshiach] Ben David won't arrive until all the

souls are depleted from the body (Guf)" (Yevamot 63b).
(Translator: i.e. best to keep quiet and not make predictions as the Rambam wrote: "man will not know how they will occur until they occur.." (Hilchot Melachim 12:2)

Ben Ish Chai - Chasdei Avot - since Moshiach will come with *Hesech Daat* (momentarily forgetting). Thus, it is best to keep quiet to hasten the Redemption.

Level 4 — Chasdei David

Chasdei David - "not study but practice is the primary thing" - in the talmud when Rabbi Yochanan implies Torah study is greater than action, the talmud asks (Bava Kamma 17a): "but did not the master say that Torah study is great in that it brings to action?" (Rashi-which implies action is greater than Torah study). The talmud answers:

"it is not difficult. One refers to study of Torah, and the other refers to teaching of Torah".

Rashi there explains: "to learn for yourself, action is greater. But teaching others is greater than action"..

According to Rashi's explanation, there are three levels. The lowest is to learn for oneself. Middle level is to fulfill, for this is the purpose of learning. The highest of all is teaching others. For "the merit of the masses depends on him" (Avot 5:21)..

Tosfot says there that learning is greater than action.. as the talmud says: "learning is greater since it brings to action" (Kidushin 40b)..

Thus that which we say learning is greater, this refers to one who did not learn yet and comes to ask what he should do. Should he learn first or toil in action? We tell him to learn first. For "an ignorant man cannot be pious" (Avot 2:6). But for one who is already a Chacham (scholar), action is better than learning.

Thus here he says: "All my days I have grown up among the Sages". For specifically for a Chacham who already learned "action is better than learning".

Chapter 1 Mishna 17 - Silence

In the Talmud: "three people I hate, a sar hanargan..." (Niddah 16b).

Rashi explains "sar hanargan" refers to a Torah scholar who speaks much. According to this, on the contrary, a Torah scholar is worse than other people.

Level 4 — Chida

Chida - Chasdei Avot - "And not study but practice is the primary thing" - perhaps because action (maase) is to rectify [the world] of Asiyah while speech in Torah is to rectify [the world] of Yetzira, and how is it possible to rectify Yetzira before Asiyah? Therefore "action is primary" for it rectifies Asiyah. And after he rectifies Asiyah, his torah study avails to rectify Yetzira.

Level 4 — Chida

Chida - Chasdei Avot - "whoever multiplies words brings sin" - perhaps this is as brought in the Reishit Chachma that our sages said that one who increases evil speech (marbe lashon hara) causes the Samech-Mem to enter among the holy Tzadikim elyonim above, etc. and this is an extremely severe sin (avon plili). He is a cause of damage (shehu garma b'nezikin). For he caused to grant the Samech-Mem permission to enter in a holy place... (see there at length). This is the hint: "whoever increases speech (kol hamarbe devarim)" - he will nevertheless come to say forbidden words. This causes that he "brings sin" (mevi chet), a hint to the Samech-Mem who is himself a sin (chet), and he brings him to the holy place..

Level 4 — Chida

Chida - Roshei Avot - "all my days I have grown up among the Sages and I have not found anything as good for the body as silence" - we may explain according to what our sages said in the Midrash Shocher Tov: "when a man speaks devarim betalim (useless chatter), correspondingly words of Torah come out. This is analogous to a barrel full of honey.. [when one adds things a corresponding volume of honey comes out of the barrel].."

Likewise the kabbalists wrote that due to sin, some or all of one's holiness departs, and then, immediately, the Sitra Achra comes.

When a man fulfills a positive commandment, he rectifies the nefesh (lower soul), and when he learns Torah, he rectifies the ruach (higher soul). If so, the body has nothing. But we find that the body does have a quality, namely, it is a temple (mishkan) to the Torah. Thus holiness rests in his innards and the body is a temple (mishkan) of holiness (kedusha).

However, if he speaks useless speech (devarim betalim), words of Torah come out and the sitra achra enters. This is the meaning of: "All my days I have grown up among the Sages", already in my youth I received Torah (gamirna girsa) from one Rav and afterwards I contemplated it (lemisbar) among many sages. For to contemplate it, many Rabbis is better, as written in Avodah Zara 19a.

"and I have not found anything as good for the body as silence" - for then, the Torah is guarded inside and the body becomes a mishkan for Torah and kedusha, and this is good for it. For "one saves the cover of a sefer Torah with the sefer Torah".

"whoever multiplies words brings sin" - besides that he takes out Torah and holiness from inside himself, furthermore, he stumbles in bringing the Sitra Achra in place of the holiness, may Hash-em save us.

Chapter 1 Mishna 18 - World Stands

Rabban Shimon ben Gamliel said: "on three things the world stands (endures), on judgment, on truth, and on peace, as written:'judge truth and the justice of peace in your gates'(Zachariah 8:16)"

רַבָּן שִׁמְעוֹן בֶּן גַּמְלִיאֵל אוֹמֵר, עַל שְׁלשָׁה דְבָרִים הָעוֹלָם עוֹמֵד, עַל הַדִּין וְעַל הָאֱמֶת וְעַל הַשָּׁלוֹם, שֶׁנֶּאֱמַר (זכריה ח) אֱמֶת וּמִשְׁפַּט שָׁלוֹם שִׁפְטוּ בְּשַׁעֲרֵיכֶם:

Q Level 1   Bartenura

Bartenura - "the world stands" - human society endures.
"on judgment" - to merit the meritorious and obligate the guilty.
"on truth" - to not lie to your fellow
"on shalom" - between nations and between people.

Q Level 1   Rambam

Rambam - "on judgment" - governing the country justly
"on truth" - virtues of intellect
"on shalom" - virtues of middot (character traits).

when these three are found, the existence will undoubtedly be as whole as possible. (yiheyu hametziut b'shelemut sh'efshar lo blo safek).

Q Level 1   Rabeinu Yonah

Rabeinu Yonah - "on truth" - that one goes in the way of G-d, who is Truth, whose Torah is Truth, and who walks in the ways of truth. So too a man should walk in this path, as written: "you shall walk in His ways" (Devarim 28:9)...

"on shalom" - this includes all good in the world. There is no limit to its benefit.

Q Level 2

Beit Yosef (beginning of Tur Choshen Mishpat): if you ask: "if the three things the world was created for [as brought by Shimon HaTzadik in mishna 2) were enough to create it, all the more so they should be enough to maintain its existence?" Answer: Shimon HaTzadik spoke according to his time when the Temple stood. While Rabban Shimon ben Gamliel lived at the time of the destruction. Thus he came to say that even though the temple is not standing and we don't have Avodah and also we cannot toil in Torah and acts of kindness properly due to the yoke of the exile, but nevertheless, the world is maintained by three other similar things...

Maharal
Level 3

Maharal - this mishna needs explanation. Why did he say on these three things the world stands. Furthermore, in the beginning of this chapter it already says "on three things the world stands.." - and they are not the same three things brought here.

It is proper to explain as follows.

G-d created man as a being containing different parts.

One, the Intellect (Sechel) which is an acquisition (kinyan) of man, as our sages said: "an elder is only one who has acquired wisdom" (Kidushin 32b).

Two, the second acquisition is the man himself. Namely, the "speaking creature" (chai medaber).

Three, his money, which is considered his acquisition.

These three things belong (shayich) to man. One of them is man himself (speaking creature) and the other two are his acquisitions.

Thus, sometimes one finds a man who lacks the acquisition of intellect or who lacks the acquisition of money (possessions).

The [mishna is] teaching on these things as will be explained. Thus, he said: "on three things the world stands.." These pillars are needed to support the three parts of man to prevent their collapse.

"on truth" - for when falsehood intensifies in the world, it annuls the intellect completely till it no longer exists.

For G-d granted intellect to the world (humanity), and it is one of the three parts of the world. When a man chases after truth, the intellect emerges into the world properly.

"on judgment (din)" - the second part which is an acquisition of man is his money. G-d granted every person an acquisition suitable to him. And it is not proper for man to touch what is designated for his fellow. Rather, each creature according to what G-d granted it only.

Thus, if there is no din (judgment), there will come an annulment in this area. The acquisition of what belongs to one man will go to another, and this is not proper.. But when there is din in the world, each person merits properly and according to how G-d created the world and granted each person an acquisition suited to him. Through din, each person stands on what is his.

The sages said: "every judge who judges truthfully even for one hour, it is as if he becomes a partner with G-d, blessed be He, in the creation of the world" (Shab.10a).

For G-d created the world and granted to each person what is proper to him then. And if the judge judges truthfully then each person keeps what is proper to him, as G-d created the world and granted an acquisition of money (possessions) suitable to each person...

"on peace (shalom)" - this is regarding man himself. For in creating human beings in this world, they entered into dispute (machloket). For each person wants to be everything.

Thus, human beings are in conflict when together. For each one annuls the other.
On this, they said the world stands on shalom, namely, that disputes not come between a man and his fellow. This is not referring to monetary [disputes], but rather to those from the aspect of human beings themselves.

To summarize, these three things are the pillars of the world corresponding to the three parts of the world.

Namely, (1) the intellect. It is not the man himself. For the intellect comes to a man when he grows up and he acquires the intellect. (2) the man himself and (3) man's material possessions which are his money.

These three things depend on Din, truth, and Shalom, so the world does not collapse.

According to all this, it is not difficult that Shimon Hatzadik counted three different things.

For those were the reasons why G-d, who is the reason and Cause of the world, upholds (maamid) the world, as we explained there at length.

While the three things here are so that loss and annulment not befall the world from its own aspect.

Thus, Shimon Hatzadik began with those three things, for through them G-d upholds the world. If they cease to exist, the beginning (root) of the world is annulled. While Rabban Shimon ben Gamliel, who was later, says the three things which are the causes for the world standing on its proper standing and not changing due its own aspect.

These three things maintain the world so it does not incur annulment from its own aspect.

THREE WORLDS
There is more one should know regarding these three things mentioned by Rabban Shimon ben Gamliel.

It is known that the sages said there are three worlds: this lower world (olam hashafel) which is until the olam hagalgalim (world of spheres). This world is one of being and loss (change. ex. conception, growth, and death). This phenomena (of changing) applies only to this lower world.

Every coming into being is through something else (a cause) which brings it into being. For a coming into being does not occur by itself. Rather something else acts to bring it into being.

Next, there is the middle world. It has no (new) being after its

Chapter 1 Mishna 18 - World Stands

creation. For this (middle) world has no lacking which would cause it to need (new) being. Rather everything is perfect (b'shlemut).

Due to this, this middle world is called "the world of Shalom". For due to the perfection (shlemut) there, they have Shalom... (skipping forward)

In this middle world, everything is in Shalom. For there they are not susceptible to being and change after their creation from nothing.

And since they are not susceptible to change, this is the Shalom found there. For one who changes has no Shalom.

Thus, since they remain in their (perfect) state without changing. Therefore, they have Shalom.

But if they did not have the bond of Shalom between them, they would not be considered themselves whole (shleimim b'atzman).

For since each is itself a separate (independent) part, then if this middle world did not have Shalom, namely, connection and joining together each one with the other till all are connected together, then there would not be wholeness (shelemut) there. Each (part) would be by itself, and a part is already not whole (shalem)...

Furthermore, the middle world is the world of Shalom because Shalom is when each one stands without entering in the domain of the other, as it is in this middle world, whereby each one stands on his place (mishmarto). This is Shalom. Thus, the middle world is singular in [the quality of] Shalom and there is complete Shalom. Thus, the sages said: "He who makes Shalom on high..." (ose shalom bimeromav.. in the amidah prayer) From this you can see that it is singular in Shalom.

Next, is the upper world, the world of intellect (Sechel), which is attainment of truth. It is called the world of pure intellects (sechalim nifradim).. It is a world which has no falsehood, only truth.. it is called - the world of truth.

Chapter 1 Mishna 18 - World Stands

Thus, in these three worlds, each one is singular in one area. The upper world is singular in truth. The middle is singular in perfection of Shalom. While, the lower world, is the world of being, and this being does not occur by itself. Rather, it receives this being from agents (which cause it to come to being).

It is known that there are agents (poalim) in this lower world. This is as written: "the great luminary [to rule the day]" (Gen.1:16). These agents decree laws on those below..

(translator: perhaps he means the energy of the sun's rays causes drives things to happen down here via the laws of physics.)

This is complete Din. Due to this the Name "Elokim" is used throughout the account of creation. The term "Elokim" means "judge". For G-d decreed being on the world, like a judge which decrees on its subject through the power of din.

From this, you will see that (coming into) "being" is Din itself, when being is decreed according to the law that is befitting it. Thus, they said: "every judge who judges a case to its ultimate truth, even for a short time, the Torah considers him G-d's partner in creation" (Shab.10a)... (skipping forward. see there...)

This is the meaning of: "on three things the world stands". For man was created to include all the three worlds... until he ties together all three worlds.

Thus if he lacks truth, he annuls (batel) the world. For it is proper for him to have truth, since truth is from the upper world and he needs to join together all three worlds. And when this connection is lacking, it is an annulment of the world. Therefore, the world stands on din, truth and shalom....
(see there for a deeper kabalistic explanation)

ORDER OF TEACHINGS
Regarding the order of the mussar of Rabban Gamliel, Rabban Shimon, and Rabban Shimon ben Gamliel. All the mussar of the early sages (rishonim) was in order to perfect (mashlim) a man in

Chapter 1 Mishna 18 - World Stands

love and fear. But these mussars of the later sages (acharonim) was only to perfect (mashlim) a man with himself.

Therefore, when he completed the mussar of the pairs which completed a man in proper love and fear of G-d, the Tanna turned to man himself, to give him mussar through which he will be whole with himself.

This is what he wrote (Mishna 16): "[Rabban Gamliel would say:] 'make for yourself a Rav and remove yourself from doubt'". We already explained that the primary mussar there was that man be on the level of intellect (madrega hasichlit). This is proper for a man in his being a "possessor of intellect" (baal sechel).

Thus, it is proper that his deeds be of intellect (sichliim), namely, clear (not in doubt). For the intellect is clear, as we wrote earlier. On this he brought that general mussar.

Afterwards, his son Rabban Shimon gave mussar to a man in his being a possessor of body (baal guf). Namely, that he conduct himself properly. Therefore, he said: "all my days I have grown up among the Sages and I have not found anything as good for the body as silence". This matter is a virtue (maala) for man...

Afterwards, Rabban Shimon ben Gamliel said : "on three things the world stands.."

The world precedes man from the aspect of it being first (Rosh) as we explained. Therefore, Shimon Hatzadik mentioned the world first and afterwards the receivers brought mussar on the perfection of man (in love and fear of G-d).

For when man is perfected, he is before the world in level, and the world is lower than him. For man is higher than world (since the world was created for man). Therefore, he brought the words of Rabban Shimon ben Gamliel last saying: "on three things the world endures.."...

(see there for more deep teachings. he ends there:) These things are exceedingly deep and we cannot explain further. Only that you must understand very much the words of the sages.

Chapter 1 Mishna 18 - World Stands

According to all this, it seems the reason he skipped Rabban Shimon ben Hillel is because he came to separate between the mussar of the early sages (rishonim) and that of the later sages (acharonim). For all the mussar of the rishonim is one matter (love and fear of G-d) while these latter three are other things..

Likewise, he skipped between Rabban Shimon the son of Rabban Gamliel (senior) and Rabban Shimon ben Gamliel (junior), since the mussar of the latter is on the world.

Thus to separate them it is proper to make a separation, and therefore he skipped Rabban Gamliel (junior).

All the words of the sages are ordered with very very great wisdom to he who understands words of wisdom.

Know and understand that from the words of Shimon Hatzadik who began to speak on the world until the end of the chapter, there are ten subjects of mussar. This number corresponds to the ten sayings through which the world was created. And in the end there was rest of Shalom and tranquility (Sabbath). Thus, he ended his words here too with Shalom..

Due to this reason also he needed to skip from the generations. For he only came to bring ten teachings corresponding to the ten sayings of creation, and he wanted to make the words of Rebbi head of chapter two, since Rebbi was head of all Yisrael. For by him there was Torah and Gedulah (majesty) in one place...

Likewise for the words of Rebbi which start next chapter. It was not for nothing that he did not put them with the words of his fathers (in chapter 1). For the mussar of Rebbi applies to [all] man's actions generally.

This is not like the words of Rabban Gamliel and Rabban Shimon which are on perfecting man himself from his own aspect.

Rather, Rebbi's words encompass [all of] man's actions generally..

Man's deeds are called his offsprings (toldot). As our sages said that the deeds of the righteous are called "fruits", as written: "praise the righteous man for he is good, for the fruit of their deeds they shall eat" (Isaiah 3:10).

They are his fruit and offsprings. This matter is expressed by the sages, as Rashi explains on Gen.6:1 - "the main offsprings of the righteous are good deeds".

Therefore, Rebbi's words are: "Which is the right path for man to choose for himself" (Avot 2:1), and likewise afterwards: "Be as careful with a minor mitzvah as with a major one" (Avot 2:1) - all things which encompass all of man's deeds which are his offsprings.

It is known that after the account of creation, it is written: "these are the generations of the heavens and the earth when they were created" (Gen.2:4)

Corresponding to this, the mussar of Rebbi came that man's offsprings (acts) be good and just and not evil and strange (zar).

Therefore, he placed Rebbi's words at the head of the next chapter. For they correspond not to the ten sayings (of creation), but to "these are the generations of heaven and earth" (Gen.2:4). Namely, man's acts. For it is proper for man to produce whole deeds (maasim shelemim) and this is a separate matter.. Thus, it is proper for his words to be at the head of the chapter.

Afterwards the words of Rabban Gamliel his son who said: "beautiful is the study of Torah with the way of the world (Derech Eretz, i.e. work)". For work is also man's acts. Only that it is below Torah and mitzvot. For it is only man's acts regarding his conduct in this world.

This teaching corresponds to what occurred after Adam sinned and was expelled from Gan Eden. Then he acquired a new matter which he did not at all have previously, namely, derech eretz. For he did not need it before. Thus it says: "And the L-ord G-d sent him out of the Garden of Eden, to till the soil, whence he had been taken" (Gen.3:23)...

This explanation is very clear when you reflect and understand words of wisdom and realize how the words of the sages contain such deep wisdom. This is sufficient. We have explained these things in truth if you delve deeply in them.

The correct wording of the text of the mishna is: "on three things the world endures".

Earlier Shimon Hatzadik said: "on three things the world stands".

But here the explanation is so that the world stand and endure and not be destroyed (translator - from within itself). Thus, the three things here are from the aspect of the completion of the world and its maintenance (gemar haolam v'kiyumo).

Level 4 — Ben Ish Chai

Ben Ish Chai - Chasdei Avot - "on three things the world stands (endures), on judgment...

"on judgment (din)" - let us first introduce with a (true) story (maase). A thief was caught and the king sentenced him to death by being hanged on a tree. For death by hanging was the standard punishment in previous times.

On the appointed day, the king's officers marched the thief to the place prepared for the hanging, i.e. on a platform in the king's courtyard. The thief's mother came and sat under the tree weeping bitterly. A big crowd formed to watch the execution, as is their way.

The thief requested from the executioner permission to approach his mother to tell her some final words. The executioner granted permission and the thief approached his mother who sat weeping heavily under the tree. He brought his lips to her ear to whisper to her. But he did not say a word. Instead he bit her ear and ripped it off completely!

His mother screamed bitterly and fainted. The king's courtyard had been full of men and women who came to watch the execution, as is the way of the masses to crowd together at executions, and especially public hangings of thieves. All those standing there were astonished at the great evil this thief just did to his mother. She was crying for him and now, before his hanging, he bit her ear off!

They all said to themselves that this must be the most wicked man on the earth. In his final moments of life in this world, he adds on sin and commits such a horrible act to bite off his mother's ear, and while she is weeping on his coming to be hanged! If we could only kill him twice! Certainly he deserves to be hanged just for that alone!

When the thief heard the commotion and outrage of all those standing there, he called out in a loud voice: "please allow me to speak and do not be angry with me on this. For I did not do this out of wickedness but rather for the rectification of my soul. Perhaps through this I will receive atonement for the sin of theft I commited."

They asked him: how will your sin be rectified by an even greater sin?!

He answered: know that this mother was the cause of my evil way of stealing which is now the cause of my death. For when I was young, I lusted greatly to eat sweets. And since the sweets cost money which I did not have, I was forced to steal a few childrens' books from school. I would then bring them to my mother so she could sell them and give me money to buy sweets to eat.

I was also forced to go stealthily in shops to steal from them whatever I could, and bring the goods to mother so she could sell them and give me some money.

Not only did she not rebuke me on my deeds and did not teach me mussar (ethics) on my evil way, but on the contrary, she rejoiced in my deeds and said "smart boy! my son is smart".

Due to my mother's reaction, I would strengthen more in my evil ways of stealing until I habituated in this.

Even after I grew up and was successful in business, my hands were still habituated in this. Although I did not need the money and was intelligent and knew that the end of a thief is the gallows, but nevertheless, I was unable to rule over my hands and prevent them from stealing. I had become unable to change my nature and habit in this area. And as people say: "many wise men toiled to try to straighten the natural crookedness in the tail of the dog but they all failed". so too, I tried to change my nature and failed. For this habit had become second nature..

I saw many people standing here now. Therefore I did this astonishing thing before everyone here so that afterwards I can tell you all the reason and all who hear my words will recognize and know how much evil a father and mother cause to their children when they don't rebuke them and discipline them in their youth while their children are still under their hands, eating under their shadow, and listening to their words. And how much good comes to a father, mother, and child through rebuking mussar and teaching of derech eretz. Then, certainly, every person who hears this will strive to be careful in this and through this the evil of the wicked will diminish and there will be less wicked people in the world. Thus, I thought this thing I did will avail for the rectification of my soul.

The people standing there said to him:

"What you say is good. For certainly all of us here received big mussar from your words and they have roused our hearts greatly that each man and woman must put their eyes and hearts on their children to discipline them and guide them in the proper path from their youth, to benefit them in their final end.

But please tell us why you cut off her ear and not her nose or some other flesh on her face?"

He answered: "this too I did with thought and wisdom, to make known that in my youth, I was not wild and rebellious. I lent my ear to listen to mussar and rebuke. On the contrary, I listened to my mother's words and lent ear to what she uttered to fulfill her words and commands. Thus, she did not need to punish me and force me with a rod. Rather, with her words only it would have sufficed to refrain me from all abominations.

But she did not do so, and since she kept her mouth shut from me and did not utter any words into my ears, therefore, now I opened my mouth against her and bit off her ear".

All those standing there who heard his words found favor in his words. The mother also heard even though she had fainted when he ripped off her ear. She opened her mouth and said: "he is right in his words and did not testify any falsehood on me".

When the king who was sitting in his palace was told what happened. It pleased him and he immediately hit his bell and announced to the executioner to exempt him from being hanged.

For the king saw that his words bore fruit of rebuke and mussar in the hearts of all the listeners.

Therefore, king Shlomo, peace be unto him, said: "He who holds back his rod hates his son, but he who loves him disciplines him early" (Mishlei 13:24), and "educate a child according to his way; even when he grows old, he will not turn away from it" (Mishlei 22:6), and "Foolishness is bound in a child's heart; the rod of discipline will drive it far from him" (Mishlei 22:15), and likewise he wrote: "Do not withhold discipline from a child; when you strike him with a rod, he will not die; You shall strike him with a rod, and you will save his soul from the grave" (Mishlei 23:13-14).

All these verses Shlomo said tell that the primary guarding and good of a person is through the judgment and accounting his father and mother did on him in the days of his youth. And this was the strong foundation building for his body and soul all the days he lives on the face of the earth.

Know please, that the courthouses (batei dinim) and judges sit only on mondays and thursdays to judge. And even in places where they are open daily, nevertheless, they don't sit all day. Rather, they sit only fixed hours of the day.

But the beit din of the child, namely, his father and mother, this beit din needs to sit each and every hour of the day, and not only the day but also at night. It needs to sit in judgment on him and rebuke him, and investigate and interrogate, asking him: what did you do? where did you go? from which place did you come and with who did you speak? What did they speak to you about? what do you do with child such and such and what did you speak to each other? Where did you two sit and where did you go? What did you do with the money you took? what did you buy? and other similar questions of chakira and drisha (examination), on his whereabouts, words and times, day and night. Those who conduct thus are assured that afterwards the child will grow up with good and just middot which will benefit him in this world and the next.

Furthermore, after a man grows up and is independent from his father and mother, he needs to bring himself to judgment on himself. To be on himself both judge and defendant.

Namely, if he stumbled in some sin whatever it is, he should not tell himself: "who knows what I did? who will judge and prosecute me? what's done is done!"

Rather, he needs to be a judge over himself to make a judgment and accounting on himself and he knows what he committed.

Let him go to a Chacham and ask him a way to rectify the sin through afflictions, fasts and tzedaka (charity) as proper for each and every sin by itself. The Chacham will inform him of the severity of each sin and just how far its destruction goes.

Then even if the Chacham does not instruct him and inform him on the number of fasts for each sin and where its destruction reaches above and the Chacham instead makes for him a compromise according to his capacity to bear, whether in torah study or tzedaka.

Then, in Heaven, the Heavenly Beit Din (court) will exempt him through the partial obligation he has been obligated in (by the Chacham). For since Din was done below, there is no Din above. This is as brought in a Midrash regarding the zealousness of Pinchas who saved all of the Jewish people through the little Din he did below. And as written there an analogy:

"a king was traveling on the road with his servants behind him. A group of young men came against the king and began to mock and laugh at him. The king's servant saw that the king became full of anger. He feared lest his wrath boil over and he decrees their death and then there will be no way to save them. What did he do? Before the king spoke, he took his staff, ran after them, and struck them on the head a mighty blow.

According to the king's honor, certainly these strikes are not enough of a punishment. But they helped to cool down the king's wrath in seeing his servant run to exact justice on his own to them. Then the king did not decree anything on them.

So too here. If a man initiates din on himself below, then the attribute of Din will be sweetened and will not exact the din above that he deserves.

Thus, according to all that we said, it is understood that through the Din that a father and mother do to their sons every day at all times, until they leave their domain, and also through the Din a man makes on himself after he grew up and separated from his parents - through this Din there will be a continuance and standing of man, who is a miniature universe in this world.

On this it is written: "on three things the world stands...", one of which is Din, namely, the Din done to a person, who is a miniature world, by his father and mother and afterwards by himself when he grows up.

on truth - since if one is a liar, people will catch on and eventually his words will not be believed by anyone, even when he is telling the truth.. sometimes this will cause him great damage or worse, as the story of the boy who cried thieves (wolf)...

The third matter is Shalom. One who holds on to the trait of Shalom, all his days are calm, tranquil, peaceful, and secure. He eats and drinks calmly and sleeps peacefully and securely. He leaves home peacefully and enters peacefully. Everyone loves him. He is happy to see them and they are happy to see him. He is surrounded with tranquility. There is no Satan and no evil mishap. Thus, the letters of Shalom are "Shelo-Mem", i.e. "to him is Menucha" (tranquility).

But for the person of disputes and arguments, all his days are pains. When he goes out to the marketplace, he finds dispute. When he enters his home, he finds dispute. When he eats and drinks, the whole meal is arguments and bickerings. When he sleeps on his bed, all his dreams are of arguments and bickerings, such that he has no tranquility.

Thus, the three things which uphold the body who is the miniature world is Din, Truth, and Shalom...

Printed in Great Britain
by Amazon